BALANCE OF POWER

Chandler Publications in
POLITICAL SCIENCE
VICTOR JONES, *Editor*

International Relations Series
PAUL SEABURY, *Editor*

Balance of Power

Edited by

PAUL SEABURY

University of California

CHANDLER PUBLISHING COMPANY

124 Spear Street, San Francisco, California, 94105

Contents

Acknowledgments

The editor wishes to acknowledge, with thanks, the essay by Professor Glenn Snyder, of the State University of New York at Buffalo, entitled "The Balance of Power and the Balance of Terror," which is published here for the first time. He also wishes to acknowledge his gratitude to Mr. Arthur Benvenuto, for his invaluable help in gathering this collection together and preparing introductions to the various sections throughout.

BALANCE OF POWER

Introduction

In nature and art, as in politics and economics, the idea of equilibrium or balance has provided insights into the relationships of things to things, forces to forces, men to men, and men to nature. The same idea has served also to suggest ways in which such relationships might be consciously reordered or improved. In nature as in politics, the idea of equilibrium means a state of balance between opposing forces or actions—a relationship which may be either static or dynamic, stable or unstable. A body may be in stable equilibrium, for instance, if when slightly displaced it tends to return to its former position; unstable, if such displacement prompts it to move further from its original position. In thermodynamics, a condition of static equilibrium is said to exist when, in the case of a system, no spontaneous change can take place since temperature and pressure are the same throughout. So also, within such a system, a condition of dynamic equilibrium might be said to exist if temperature and pressure were uniformly increased.

In both art and music, as also in some utopian schools of political thought, the idea of equilibrium suggests harmony—a pleasing consonance of tones, colors or shapes in any work which comprises a connected whole. Such an idea of harmony suggests the possibility of peaceful relationships among things or men; disharmony suggests relationships of friction, discord and imbalance. In his *Civilization of the Renaissance in Italy,* the historian Jacob Burckhardt spoke of the emergent Renaissance

1

city-state as "the outcome of reflection and calculation, the State as work of art." Perhaps what he meant to suggest by this was that the equilibrium and harmony of the State can be obtained by reason and artifice.

When the idea of balance is applied to human affairs, Society and the State in particular, it may be said to have two general kinds of meanings. The first of these focuses principally on the effect of energy and force on constitutional form through time. It is concerned with matters of conservation and change within a social system, or between that system and others. The second focuses principally on the relationships among specific elements within a given system, or on specific systems in their relation to each other. Today some would say that in modern political systems it is desirable to have an equilibrium between the conserving and the innovating forces within society—a balance between those forces making for perpetual change and those seeking to maintain "things as they are."

In Western politics, since the French Revolution, a balance of this sort has been said to obtain when there is equilibrium between forces of movement and forces of order, between Left and Right. In this sense, political forces are primarily judged with reference to their innovating or their conserving characteristics. Whereas the extreme Right might proffer an ideal social system in perpetual *stasis,* the extreme Left would offer perpetual movement and change at the expense of order. Between such polar extremes, centrist forces are said to exist, maintaining equilibrium by adapting and incorporating innovations into an existing system. The politics of moderation thus are said to act through time as an equilibrating device.

If the first of these two meanings of equilibrium stresses energy and motion, the second stresses matter and form. Any given political system may be said to contain a "mix" of elements, whether this mixture be one of sociological components (classes, for instance), "interests" or "factions" (as Madison saw them in eighteenth-century America), or institutions (as Montesquieu saw them in the seventeenth-century British constitution). Two perennial questions for political theorists since the time of Plato and Aristotle have been these: what balance of classes, factions or institutions might be most desirable for society? What balance might prove to be most stable through time? The idea of political equilibrium thus might be said to have both an ethical and a scientific dimension; that which proved to be the most stable arrangement of forces in society might not be "best"; that which was best might not be stable. An equilibrium among social forces could be a balance among scoundrels, or a balance among angels; so also, a just distribution of power in society might be ideally imagined, yet it still might not work.

Regardless of this difficulty, the idea of equilibrium applied to political institutions—whether seen as an ethical or a scientific proposition—is antithetic to the notion of tyranny and absolute centralized power. There are obvious difficulties with Lord Acton's famous maxim, that "absolute power corrupts absolutely." (Does absolute impotence, its opposite, "absolutely purify"?) Yet a fear of tyranny and the absolute power which it commands is a perennial concern of men; Western political thought since the time of the Greeks has been concerned to establish means of controlling, regularizing, and distributing power in society. The absence of tyranny is hardly the sufficient condition for human freedom, however this may be defined; yet the presence of tyranny certainly makes human freedom impossible.

The idea of equilibrium, in its political sense, may be said to apply to two quite distinct theaters: a domestic, and an international one. It may apply to the internal relationship among the political or social forces of a society or a state; it may also apply to the relationships among whole societies or whole states in international politics. This volume of writings chiefly is concerned with this latter meaning of political equilibrium.

When we deal with international equilibrium, we usually employ the concept of the Balance of Power. This concept should be distinguished from equilibrium theory within a state or society since it lays far greater stress upon the idea of power, than does domestic equilibrium theory. In the relationships among social forces within a given political order, such relationships need not necessarily depend exclusively or chiefly on the actual power of each element in relation to others. In the American political system, for instance, the Constitution and many other political conventions set checks and limits on the exercise of political power. The Constitution in fact was devised to check and to distribute power rationally. It might be said to serve as a regulatory device, since it provides rules of the game which Americans generally take for granted. So it is with the constitutional systems of most stable polities. The rule of law within a system of political order serves to limit and direct power into proper and accepted channels.

In international politics however, there is no such constitutional order. Custom, international law, and treaties among states provide considerable regularity in relations among states; yet what equilibrium there may be at any moment in time may be said to arise chiefly from the relative power of states. At certain points in time (as at the Congress of Vienna in 1815) statesmen of individual sovereign states may attempt to fashion a rational equilibrium in which political power is distributed in such a manner that stability and durability ensue. But such international acts of "constitution-making" are rare; at other times, power relationships among states shift, unregulated by any overarching constitutional system. The history of world politics in the past two centuries has seen among states massive rearrangements of power relationships which were not the result of constitutive acts but rather of wars, and of secular changes in the power and influence possessed by such states.

The selections contained in this volume are chosen not to present a comprehensive collection of classical writings about the *Balance of Power,* but rather to present the reader with a spectrum of important views about the nature of that balance, and about how, at various times, it has been seen to work or not to work.

I

The Idea of Balance in Classical Thought

Political order, harmony and peace are perennial aspirations of men; but they are also ideas used to describe real relationships among men and nations. They are aspirations in the sense that a vision of perpetual peace among men and nations seems at all times to contradict political reality and to affront common sense; for the life of men and nations is dynamic and always changing, and political change entails conflict of some sort. Yet just as life without change seems a contradiction in terms, and certainly not worth living, so also life without order and regularity would be impossible and intolerable. One may commence the study of politics taking as one's a priori assumption the notion that man's natural state is one of conflict, or that it is fundamentally orderly and peaceable. But as "hell hath its own laws," so even heaven may have its own lawbreakers. The modern social sciences—which search for regularities and laws of human behavior—are heavily indebted to realists who, like Marx, thought of historical societies in terms of conflict, not of peace and harmony.

Among students of politics in ancient times, as now, the idea of balance of power and equilibrium has suggested this ironic tension between order and conflict in human affairs. On the

5

one hand, its realistic stress upon tensions and conflict among groups, classes, nations and states as a permanent political condition would seem to deny the possibility of harmony and fraternity among men; while its rational stress upon regularity, symmetry, and equilibrium in politics either as natural condition or artifice would seem to unrealistically ignore or underrate the random, often chaotic and unpredictable qualities of political life.

The political concept of equilibrium is today often regarded as of quite recent origin within Western society; yet this is not the case. Newtonian physics, and the peculiarly eighteenth-century notion of the universe as a great machine governed by mechanical laws, only seemed to scientifically confirm ideas which actually had been developed long before.

As the following selections show, the idea of equilibrium can be discerned both in early Graeco-Roman thought, and even among non-Western political thinkers. The Hindu writer, Kautilya, in the fourth century B.C., *in his advice to princes, employed the notion of balancing, in foreign affairs; the survival of principalities depended upon alliances so fashioned as to create combinations of power greater than those of threatening neighbor states. In the West, Aristotle, employing the notion of equilibrium to the domestic affairs of city-states, argued that the best polity was that in which a balance of power existed among classes, with the middle class acting as balancer between the extremes of wealth and poverty, and between classes which were either unable, or unwilling, to obey or to rule. Demosthenes, in his* Oration for the Megalopolitans, *appealed to them for support to Athens in her struggle against Sparta, arguing that an Athenian defeat would upset the equilibrium of power among the Greek city-states, and result in Spartan tyranny over them all.*

1. ARTHASASTRA *

By the fourth century B.C. *the Hindu literature of Arthasastra (science of politics) had grown into a maze of contradicting and divergent views. Kautilya, of whom little is known except that he lived between 321 and 300* B.C., *abstracted and ordered this earlier political literature. However, his* Arthasastra *is much more than a summary, for it involves a close analysis and synthesis of the basic writings which resulted in the reconstruction of the Indian science of politics.*

Kautilya's Arthasastra, *which in many ways can be compared to Machiavelli's* The Prince, *is concerned with the survival and aggrandizement of the state. Government exists, argues Kautilya, because of the innate wickedness of men; the Monarch's function, as absolute ruler, is to prevent anarchy, to insure survival, and to increase the power and glory of the state. Toward these ends the arts of government and diplomacy, war and treachery are worked out in pedantic detail.*

In foreign relations the basic principle is that neighboring states are enemies and alternate ones allies. In dealing with his enemies and allies the Arthasastra *clearly instructs the King in the principles of a balance of power system. In order to prevent his state's defeat and to insure its eventual victory, the King must follow a judicious policy of continual combination and recombination with other states against his enemies. Thus the concept of a balance of power between states received an early and totally non-Western statement.*

KAUTILYA

Concerning Peace and Exertion

Deterioration, stagnation, and progress are the three aspects of position.

Those causes of human make which affect position are policy and impolicy (naya and apanaya); fortune and misfortune (aya

---

* Ed. and tr. by R. Shamasastry. 4th ed., 1951, pp. 289–299; 344–348. Footnotes omitted.

and anaya) are providential causes. Causes, both human and providential, govern the world and its affairs.

What is unforeseen is providential; here, the attainment of that desired end which seemed almost lost is (termed) fortune.

What is anticipated is human; and the attainment of a desired end as anticipated is (due to policy).

What produces unfavourable results is impolicy. This can be foreseen; but misfortune due to providence cannot be known.

The king who, being possessed of good character and bestfitted elements of sovereignty, is the fountain of policy, is termed the conqueror.

The king who is situated anywhere immediately on the circumference of the conqueror's territory is termed the enemy.

The king who is likewise situated close to the enemy, but separated from the conqueror only by the enemy, is termed the friend (of the conqueror).

A neighbouring foe of considerable power is styled an enemy; and when he is involved in calamities or has taken himself to evil ways, he becomes assailable; and when he has little or no help, he becomes destructible; otherwise (*i.e.* when he is provided with some help), he deserves to be harassed or reduced. Such are the aspects of an enemy.

In front of the conqueror and close to his enemy, there happen to be situated kings such as the conqueror's friend, next to him the enemy's friend, and next to the last, the conqueror's friend, and next, the enemy's friend's friend.

In the rear of the conqueror, there happen to be situated a rearward enemy (pārshnigrāha), a rearward friend (ākranda), an ally of the rearward enemy (pārshnigrāhāsāra), and an ally of the rearward friend (ākrandāsāra).

That foe who is equally of high birth and occupies a territory close to that of the conqueror is a natural enemy; while he who is merely antagonistic and creates enemies to the conqueror is a factitious enemy.

He whose friendship is derived from father and grandfather, and who is situated close to the territory of the immediate enemy of the conqueror is a natural friend; while he whose friendship is courted for self-maintenance is an acquired friend.

The king who occupies a territory close to both the conqueror and his immediate enemy in front and who is capable of helping both the kings, whether united or disunited, or of resisting either of them individually is termed a Madhyama (mediatory) king.

He who is situated beyond the territory of any of the above kings, and who is very powerful and capable of the helping the enemy, the conqueror, and the Madhyama king, together or individually, or of resisting any of them individually, is a neutral king (udāsīna)—these are the (twelve) primary kings.

The conqueror, his friend, and his friend's friend are the three primary kings constituting a circle of states. As each of these three kings possesses the five elements of sovereignty, such as the minister, the country, the fort, the treasury, and the army, a circle of states consists of eighteen elements. Thus, it needs no commentary to understand that the (three) Circles of States having the enemy (of the conqueror), the Madhyama king, or the neutral king at the centre of each of the three circles, are different from that of the conqueror. Thus there are four primary Circles of States, twelve kings, sixty elements of sovereignty, and seventy-two elements of states.

Each of the twelve primary kings shall have their elements of sovereignty, power and end. *Strength is power, and happiness is the end.*

Strength is of three kinds: power of deliberation is intellectual strength; the possession of a prosperous treasury and a strong army is the strength of sovereignty; and martial power is physical strength.

The end is also of three kinds: that which is attainable by deliberation is the end of deliberation; that which is attainable by the strength of sovereignty is the end of sovereignty; and that which is to be secured by perseverance is the end of martial power.

The possession of power and happiness in a greater degree makes a king superior to another; in a less degree, inferior, and in equal degree, equal. Hence a king shall always endeavour to augment his power and elevate his happiness.

A king who is equal to his enemy in the matter of his sovereign

elements shall, in virtue of his own righteous conduct or with the
help of those who are hostile or conspiring against his enemy,
endeavour to throw his enemy's power into the shade. . . .

Throwing the circumference of the Circle of States beyond his
friends' territory, and making the kings of those states as the
spokes of that circle, the conqueror shall make himself as the
nave of that circle. . . .

THE SIX-FOLD POLICY

Kautilya holds that, as their respective conditions differ, the
forms of policy are six.

Of these, agreement with pledges is peace; offensive operation
is war; indifference is neutrality; making preparations is marching; seeking the protection of another is alliance; and making
peace with one and waging war with another, is termed a double
policy (dvaidhībhāva). These are the six forms.

Whoever is inferior to another shall make peace with him;
whoever is superior in power shall wage war; whoever thinks,
"No enemy can hurt me, nor am I strong enough to destroy my
enemy," shall observe neutrality; whoever is possessed of necessary means shall march against his enemy; whoever is devoid of
necessary strength to defend himself shall seek the protection of
another; whoever thinks that help is necessary to work out an
end shall make peace with one and wage war with another.
Such is the aspect of the six forms of policy.

Of these, a wise king shall observe that form of policy which,
in his opinion, enables him to build forts, to construct buildings
and commercial roads, to open new plantations and villages, to
exploit mines and timber and elephant forests and at the same
time to harass similar works of his enemy.

Whoever thinks himself to be growing in power more rapidly
both in quality and quantity (than his enemy), and the reverse
of his enemy, may neglect his enemy's progress for the time.

If any two kings, hostile to each other, find the time of
achieving the results of their respective works to be equal, they
shall make peace with each other.

No king shall keep that form of policy, which causes him the
loss of profit from his own works, but which entails no such
loss on the enemy; for it is deterioration.

Whoever thinks that in the course of time his loss will be less than his acquisition as contrasted with that of his enemy, may neglect his temporary deterioration.

If any two kings, hostile to each other, and deteriorating, expect to acquire equal amount of wealth in equal time, they shall make peace with each other.

That position in which neither progress nor retrogression is seen is stagnation.

Whoever thinks his stagnancy to be of a shorter duration and his prosperity in the long run to be greater than his enemy's may neglect his temporary stagnation.

. . . [If] any two kings, who are hostile to each other, and are in a stationary condition, expect to acquire equal amount of wealth and power in equal time, they shall make peace with each other. . . .

Or if a king thinks:

"That keeping the agreement of peace, I can undertake productive works of considerable importance and destroy at the same time those of my enemy; or apart from enjoying the results of my own works, I shall also enjoy those of my enemy in virtue of the agreement of peace; or I can destroy the works of my enemy by employing spies and other secret means; or by holding out such inducements as a happy dwelling, rewards, remission of taxes, little work and large profits and wages, I can empty my enemy's country of its population, with which he has been able to carry his own works; or being allied with a king of considerable power, my enemy will have his own works destroyed; or I can prolong my enemy's hostility with another king whose threats have driven my enemy to seek my protection; or being allied with me, my enemy can harass the country of another king who hates me; or oppressed by another king, the subjects of my enemy will immigrate into my country, and I can, therefore, achieve the results of my own works very easily; or being in a precarious condition due to the destruction of his works, my enemy will not be so powerful as to attack me; or by exploiting my own resources in alliance with any two (friendly) kings, I can augment my resources; or if a Circle of States is formed by my enemy as one of its members, I can divide them and combine with the others; or by threats or favour,

I can catch hold of my enemy and when he desires to be a member of my own Circle of States, I can make him incur the displeasure of the other members and fall a victim to their own fury"—if a king thinks thus, then he may increase his resources by keeping peace. . . .

Or if a king thinks:

"That neither is my enemy strong enough to destroy my works, nor am I his; or if he comes to fight with me like a dog with a boar, I can increase his afflictions without incurring any loss in my own works," then he may observe neutrality and augment his own resources.

Or if a king thinks:

"That by marching my troops it is possible to destroy the works of my enemy; and as for myself, I have made proper arrangements to safeguard my own works," then he may increase his resources by marching.

Or if a king thinks:

"That I am strong enough neither to harass my enemy's works nor to defend my own against my enemy's attack," then he shall seek protection from a king of superior power, and endeavour . . . to pass from the stage of deterioration to that of stagnancy and from the latter to that of progress.

Or if a king thinks:

"That by making peace with one, I can work out my own resources, and by waging war with another, I can destroy the works of my enemy," then he may adopt that double policy and improve his resources.

Thus, a king in the circle of sovereign states shall, by adopting the six-fold policy, endeavour to pass from the state of deterioration to that of stagnation, and from the latter to that of progress. . . .

THE NATURE OF ALLIANCE

When the advantages derivable from peace and war are of equal character, one should prefer peace; for disadvantages, such as the loss of power and wealth, sojourning, and sin, are ever attending upon war.

The same holds good in the case of neutrality and war.

Of the two (forms of policy), double policy and alliance, double policy (*i.e.* making peace with one and waging war with another) is preferable; for whoever adopts the double policy enriches himself, being ever attentive to his own works, whereas an allied king has to help his ally at his own expense.

One shall make an alliance with a king who is stronger than one's neighbouring enemy; in the absence of such a king, one should ingratiate oneself with one's neighbouring enemy, either by supplying money or army or by ceding a part of one's territory and by keeping oneself aloof; for there can be no greater evil to kings than alliance with a king of considerable power, unless one is actually attacked by one's enemy.

A powerless king should behave as a conquered king (towards his immediate enemy); but when he finds that the time of his own ascendancy is at hand, due to a fatal disease, internal troubles, increase of enemies, or a friend's calamities that are vexing his enemy, then under the pretence of performing some expiatory rites to avert the danger of his enemy, he may get out (of the enemy's court); or if he is in his own territory, he should not go to see his suffering enemy; or if he is near to his enemy, he may murder the enemy when opportunity affords itself.

A king who is situated between two powerful kings shall seek protection from the stronger of the two; or from one of them on whom he can rely; or he may make peace with both of them on equal terms. Then he may begin to set one of them against the other by telling each that the other is a tyrant causing utter ruin to himself, and thus cause dissension between them. When they are divided, he may put down each separately by secret or covert means. Or, throwing himself under the protection of any two immediate kings of considerable power, he may defend himself against an immediate enemy. Or, having made an alliance with a chief in a stronghold, he may adopt the double policy (*i.e.* make peace with one of the two kings and wage war with another.) Or, he may adapt himself to circumstances, depending upon the causes of peace and war in order. Or, he may make friendship with traitors, enemies, and wild chiefs who are conspiring against both the kings. Or, pretending to be a close friend of one of them, he may strike the other at the latter's weak point by employing enemies and wild tribes. Or, having made friendship with both, he may form a Circle of States. Or, he may make an alliance with the Madhyama or the neutral king; and with this help he may put down one of them or both. Or when hurt by both, he may seek protection from a king of righteous character among the Madhyama king, the neutral king, and their friends or equals, or from any other king whose subjects are so disposed as to increase his happiness and peace, with whose help he may be able to recover his last position, with whom his ancestors were in close intimacy or blood relationship, and in whose kingdom he can find a number of powerful friends.

Of two powerful kings who are on amicable terms with each other, a king shall make alliance with one of them who likes him and whom he likes; this is the best way of making alliance. . . .

EQUAL, INFERIOR AND SUPERIOR KINGS

A king desirous of expanding his own power shall make use of the six-fold policy.

Agreements of peace shall be made with equal and superior kings: and an inferior king shall be attacked.

Whoever goes to wage war with a superior king will be reduced to the same condition as that of a foot-soldier opposing an elephant.

Just as the collision of an unbaked mud-vessel with a similar vessel is destructive to both, so war with an equal king brings ruin to both.

Like a stone striking an earthen pot, a superior king attains decisive victory over an inferior king.

If a superior king discards the proposal of an inferior king for peace, the latter should take the attitude of a conquered king, or play the part of an inferior king towards a superior.

When a king of equal power does not like peace, then the same amount of vexation as his opponent has received at his hands should be given to him in return; for it is power that brings about peace between any two kings: no peace of iron that is not made red-hot will combine with another piece of iron.

When an inferior king is all submissive, peace should be made with him; for when provoked by causing him troubles and anger, an inferior king, like a wild fire, will attack his enemy and will be also favoured by (his) Circle of States.

When a king in peace with another finds that greedy, impoverished, and oppressed as are the subjects of his ally, they do not yet immigrate into his own territory lest they might be called back by their master, then he should, though of inferior power, proclaim war against his ally.

When a king at war with another finds that greedy, impoverished, and oppressed as are the subjects of his enemy, still they do not come to his side in consequence of the troubles of war, then he should, though of superior power, make peace with his enemy or remove the troubles of war as far as possible.

When one of the two kings at war with each other and equally involved in trouble finds his own troubles to be greater than his enemy's, and thinks that by getting rid of his (enemy's) trouble his enemy can successfully wage war with him, then he should, though possessing greater resources, sue for peace.

When, either in peace or war, a king finds neither loss to his enemy nor gain to himself, he should, though superior, observe neutrality.

When a king finds the troubles of his enemy irremediable, he should, though of inferior power, march against the enemy.

When a king finds himself threatened by imminent danger or troubles, he should, though superior, seek the protection of another.

When a king is sure to achieve his desired ends by making peace with one and waging war with another, he should, though superior, adopt the double policy.

Thus it is that the six forms of policy are applied together.

The Conduct of a Madhyama King, a Neutral King, and of a Circle of States

The third and the fifth states from a Madhyama king are states friendly to him; while the second, the fourth, and the sixth are unfriendly. If the Madhyama king shows favour to both of these states, the conqueror should be friendly with him; if he does not favour them, the conqueror should be friendly with those states. . . .

If the neutral king is desirous of combining with the Madhyama king, then the conqueror should so attempt as to frustrate the desire of the neutral king to over-reach an enemy or to help a friend or to secure the services of the army of another neutral king. Having thus strengthened himself, the conqueror should reduce his enemies and help his friends, though their position is inimical towards him.

Those who may be inimical to the conqueror are, a king who is of wicked character and who is therefore always harmful, a rear-enemy in combination with a frontal enemy, a reducible enemy under troubles, and one who is watching the troubles of the conqueror to invade him.

Those who may be friendly with the conqueror are, one who marches with him with the same end in view, one who marches with him with a different end in view, one who wants to combine with the conqueror to march (against a common enemy), one who marches under an agreement for peace, one who marches with a set purpose of his own, one who rises along with others, one who is ready to purchase or to sell either the army or the treasury, and one who adopts the double policy (*i.e.* making peace with one and waging war with another).

Those neighbouring kings who can be servants to the conqueror are, a neighbouring king under the apprehension of an attack from a powerful king, one who is situated between the conqueror and his enemy, the rear-enemy of a powerful king, one who has voluntarily surrendered oneself to the conqueror, one who has surrendered oneself under fear, and one who has been subdued. The same is the case with those kings who are next to the territory of the immediate enemies of the conqueror.

Of these kings, the conqueror should, as far as possible, help that friend who has the same end in view as the conqueror in his conflict with the enemy, and thus hold the enemy at bay.

When, after having put down the enemy, and after having grown in power, a friend becomes unsubmissive, the conqueror should cause the friend to incur the displeasure of a neighbour and of the king who is next to the neighbour.

Or the conqueror may employ a scion of the friend's family or an imprisoned prince to seize his lands; or the conqueror may so act that his friend, desirous of further help, may continue to be obedient.

The conqueror should never help his friend when the latter is more and more deteriorating; a politician should so keep his friend that the latter neither deteriorates nor grows in power.

When, with the desire of getting wealth, a wandering friend (*i.e.* a nomadic king) makes an agreement with the conqueror, the latter should so remove the cause of the friend's flight that he never flies again.

When a friend is as accessible to the conqueror as to the latter's enemy, the conqueror should first separate that obstinate friend from the enemy, and then destroy him, and afterwards the enemy also.

When a friend remains neutral, the conqueror should cause him to incur the displeasure of his immediate enemies; and when he is worried in his wars with them, the conqueror should oblige him with help.

When, owing to his own weakness, a friend seeks protection both from the conqueror and the latter's enemy, the conqueror should help him with the army, so that he never turns his attention elsewhere.

Or having removed him from his own lands, the conqueror may keep him in another tract of land, having made some previous arrangements to punish or favour the friend.

Or the conqueror may harm him when he has grown powerful, or destroy him when he does not help the conqueror in danger and when he lies on the conqueror's lap in good faith.

When an enemy furiously rises against his own enemy (*i.e.* the conqueror's friend) under troubles, the former should be put down by the latter himself with troubles concealed.

When a friend keeps quiet after rising against an enemy under troubles, that friend will be subdued by the enemy himself after getting rid of his troubles.

Whoever is acquainted with the sense of polity should clearly observe the conditions of progress, deterioration, stagnation, reduction, and destruction, as well as the use of all kinds of strategic means.

Whoever thus knows the inter-dependence of the six kinds of

policy plays at his pleasure with kings, bound round, as it were,
in chains skilfully devised by himself. . . .

2. THE POLITICS *

Aristotle's Politics *is not a unified work but rather a collection
of political essays concerned with the nature and function of the*
polis. *Its unstructured nature raises both chronological and logical
questions regarding the order of the eight books of the treatise.
Oversimplified, the work can be divided into two basic parts.
Part One, consisting of Books II, III, VII and VIII, is concerned with the ideal state and its ethical role in producing the
good man and the good citizen. Part Two, consisting of Books
IV, V and VI, is concerned with the development of a more general science of politics based on empirical examination of actual
forms of the* polis.

*In Chapters IX and XI of Book IV, Aristotle discusses the
various constitutional forms which a* polity *may take. The "best
constitution," he concludes, consists of a mean between democracy and oligarchy or, in other words, the best* polity *is one
which is based on the middle class as the natural mean between
the rich and the poor.*

In arguing for a polity *based on the middle class, Aristotle
seeks to construct the best constitution on a balance of power
between those "who are ignorant how to rule" and those "who
are ignorant how to obey." Such a balance would prevent the
political instability engendered by the conflict between the
"haves" and "have nots." The middle class, says Aristotle, must
be "larger, if possible, than both of the other classes, or at any
rate than either singly; for the addition of the middle class turns
the scale, and prevents either of the extremes from becoming
dominant."*

The selection that follows is from Chapter IX.

* Aristotle, *The Politics*, Book IV, pp. 99–104, trans. Benjamin Jowett,
Willey Book Co., New York, 1899. To make reading easier, footnotes
have been omitted from the text and excisions are not indicated.

ARISTOTLE

Next we have to consider how by the side of oligarchy and democracy the so-called polity or constitutional government springs up, and how it should be organized. The nature of it will be at once understood from a comparison of oligarchy and democracy; we must ascertain their different characteristics, and taking a portion from each, put the two together, like the parts of an indenture. Now there are three modes in which fusions of government may be effected. The nature of the fusion will be made intelligible by an example of the manner in which different governments legislate, say concerning the administration of justice. In oligarchies they impose a fine on the rich if they do not serve as judges, and to the poor they give no pay; but in democracies they give pay to the poor and do not fine the rich. Now (1) the union of these two modes is a common or middle term between them, and is therefore characteristic of a constitutional government, for it is a combination of both. This is one mode of uniting the two elements. Or (2) a mean may be taken between the enactments of the two: thus democracies require no property qualification, or only a small one, from members of the assembly, oligarchies a high one; here neither of these is the common term, but a mean between them. (3) There is a third mode, in which something is borrowed from the oligarchical and something from the democratical principle. For example, the appointment of magistrates by lot is democratical, and the election of them oligarchical; democratical again when there is no property qualification, oligarchical when there is. In the aristocratical or constitutional State, one element will be taken from each—from oligarchy the mode of electing to offices, from democracy the disregard of qualification. Such are the various modes of combination.

There is a true union of oligarchy and democracy when the same State may be termed either a democracy or an oligarchy; those who use both names evidently feel that the fusion is complete. Such a fusion there is also in the mean; for both extremes appear in it. The Lacedæmonian constitution, for example, is often described as a democracy, because it has many democratical features. In the first place the youth receive a democratical education. For the sons of the poor are brought up with the sons of the rich, who are educated in such a manner as to make it possible for the sons of the poor to be educated like them. A similar equality prevails in the following period of life, and when the citizens are grown up to manhood the same rule is observed; there is no distinction between the rich and the poor. In like manner they all have the same food at their public tables, and the rich wear only such clothing as any poor man can afford. Again, the people elect to one of the two greatest offices of State, and in the other they share; for they elect the Senators and share in the ephoralty. By others the Spartan constitution is said to be an oligarchy, because it has many oligarchical elements. That all offices are filled by election and none by lot, is one of these oligarchical characteristics; that the power of inflicting death or banishment rests with a few persons is another; and there are others. In a well attempered polity there should appear to be both elements and yet neither; also the government should rely on itself, and not on foreign aid, nor on the goodwill of a majority of foreign States—they might be equally well disposed when there is a vicious form of government—but on the general willingness of all classes in the State to maintain the constitution.

CHAPTER XI

We have now to inquire what is the best constitution for most States, and the best life for most men, neither assuming a standard of virtue which is above ordinary persons, nor an education which is exceptionally favored by nature and circumstances, nor yet an ideal State which is an aspiration only, but having regard to the life in which the majority are able to share, and to the form of government which States in general can attain. As to those aristocracies, as they are called, of which we were just now speaking, they either lie beyond the possibilities of the greater number of States, or they approximate to the so-called constitutional government, and therefore need no separate discussion. And in fact the conclusion at which we arrive respecting all these forms rests upon the same grounds. For if it has been truly said in the "Ethics" that the happy life is the life according to unimpeded virtue, and that virtue is a mean, then the life which is in a mean, and in a mean attainable by everyone, must be the best. And the same principles of virtue and vice are characteristic of cities and of constitutions; for the constitution is in a figure the life of a city.

Now in all States there are three elements; one class is very rich, another very poor, and a third in a mean. It is admitted that moderation and the mean are best, and therefore it will clearly be best to possess the gifts of fortune in moderation; for in that condition of life men are most ready to listen to reason. But he who greatly excels in beauty, strength, birth or wealth, or on the other hand who is very poor, or very weak, or very much disgraced, finds it difficult to follow reason. Of these two the one sort grow into violent and great criminals, the others into rogues and petty rascals. And two sorts of offences correspond to them, the one committed from violence, the other from roguery. The petty rogues are disinclined to hold office, whether military or civil, and their aversion to these two duties is as great an injury to the State as their tendency to crime. Again, those who have too much of the goods of fortune, strength, wealth; friends, and the like, are neither willing nor able to submit to authority. The evil begins at home: for when they are boys, by reason of the luxury in which they are brought up, they never learn, even at school, the habit of obedience. On the other hand, the very poor, who are in the opposite extreme, are too degraded. So that the one class cannot obey, and can only rule despotically; the other knows not how to command and must be ruled like slaves. Thus arises a city, not of freemen, but of masters and slaves, the one despising, the other envying; and nothing can be more fatal to friendship and good-fellowship in States than this: for good-fellowship tends to friendship; when men are at enmity with one another, they would rather not even share the same path. But a city ought to be composed, as far as possible, of equals and similars; and these are generally the middle classes. Wherefore the city which is composed of middle-class citizens is necessarily best governed; they are, as we say, the natural elements of a State. And this is the class of citizens which is most secure in a State, for they do not, like the poor, covet their neighbors' goods; nor do others covet theirs, as the poor covet the goods of the rich; and as they neither plot against others, nor are themselves plotted against, they pass through life safely. Wisely then did Phocylides pray, "Many things are best in the mean; I desire to be of a middle condition in my city."

Thus it is manifest that the best political community is formed by citizens of the middle class, and that those States are likely to be well administered, in which the middle class is large, and larger if possible than both the other classes, or at any rate than either singly; for the addition of the middle class turns the scale, and prevents either of the extremes from being dominant. Great then is the good fortune of a State in which the citizens have a moderate and sufficient property; for where some possess much, and the others nothing, there may arise an extreme democracy, or a pure oligarchy; or a tyranny may grow out of either extreme—either out of the most rampant democracy, or out of an oligarchy; but it is not so likely to arise out of a middle and nearly equal condition. I will explain the reason of this hereafter, when I speak of the revolutions of States. The mean condition of States is clearly best, for no other is free from faction; and where the middle class is large, there are least likely to be factions and dissensions. For a similar reason large States are less liable to faction than small ones, because in them the middle class is large; whereas in small States it is easy to divide all the citizens into two classes who are either rich or poor, and to leave nothing in the middle. And democracies are safer and more permanent than oligarchies, because they have a middle class which is more numerous and has a greater share in the government; for when there is no middle class, and the poor greatly exceed in number, troubles arise, and the State soon comes to an end. A proof of the superiority of the middle class is that the best legislators have been of a middle condition; for example, Solon, as his own verses testify; and Lycurgus, for he was not a king; and Charondas, and almost all legislators.

These considerations will help us to understand why most governments are either democratical or oligarchical. The reason is that the middle class is seldom numerous in them, and whichever party, whether the rich or the common people, transgresses the mean and predominates, draws the government to itself, and thus arises either oligarchy or democracy. There is another reason—the poor and the rich quarrel with one another, and whichever side gets the better, instead of establishing a just or popular government, regards political supremacy as the prize of victory, and the one party sets up a democracy and the other an oligarchy. Both the parties which had the supremacy in Hellas looked only to the interest of their own form of government, and established in States, the one, democracies, and the other, oligarchies; they thought of their own advantage, of the public not at all. For these reasons the middle form of governments has rarely, if ever, existed, and among a very few only. One man alone of all who ever ruled in Hellas was induced to give this middle constitution to States. But it has now become a habit among the citizens of States, not even to care about equality; all men are seeking for dominion, or, if conquered, are willing to submit.

What then is the best form of government, and what makes it the best is evident; and of other States, since we say that there are many kinds of democracy and many of oligarchy, it is not difficult to see which has the first and which the second or any other place in the order of excellence, now that we have determined which is the best. For that which is nearest to the best must of necessity be better, and that which is furthest from it worse, if we are judging absolutely and not relatively to given conditions: I say "relatively to given conditions," since a particular government may be preferable for some, but another form may be better for others.

---

3. THE ORATION FOR THE
MEGALOPOLITANS *

Freed from subjugation by the Theban defeat of Sparta, the Arcadian people founded the city of Megalopolis in 371 B.C., as the center of their newly independent dominion. By 353 B.C., how-

---

* From *The Olynthiac of Demosthenes*, trans. Charles Rann Kennedy, Vol. I, pp. 204–218, George Bell and Sons, London, 1880. Footnotes in the selection are omitted.

ever, Sparta was again strong enough to attempt to recapture her former possessions. It was evident by Sparta's warlike preparations that an attack on the Arcadian city was imminent. Two delegations, one from Megalopolis and one from Sparta, arrived in Athens each seeking its support in the approaching war.

Demosthenes, in this famous oration, espoused the cause of the Megalopolitans against Sparta on the grounds that it was in the interest of Athens to prevent Spartan expansion. The Athenian interest, argued Demosthenes, was in maintaining a balance of power between Thebes and Sparta. The defeat of the Arcadians would be the beginning of Sparta's resurgence thereby upsetting the existing balance which now favored Athens. He advocated, therefore, the maintenance of the status quo by preventing the destruction of Megalopolis.

DEMOSTHENES

. . . I see how vexatious a thing it is to advise for the best. For when you are carried away by delusion, some taking one view and some another, if any man attempts to advise a middle course, and you are too impatient to listen, he will please neither party and fall into disgrace with both. However, if this be my case, I will rather myself be thought a babbler, than leave you to be misled by certain people, contrary to my notion of Athenian interests. On other points I will speak, with your permission, afterwards; but will begin with principles admitted by all, and explain what I consider your wisest course.

Well then: no man will deny it to be good for Athens, that both the Lacedæmonians and our Theban neighbours should be weak. But things are in this sort of position, if we may form a conjecture from the statements repeatedly made in our assembly—the Thebans will be weakened by the reestablishment of Orchomenus, Thespiæ, and Platæa; the Lacedæmonians will grow powerful again, if they subdue Arcadia and take Megalopolis. We must mind therefore, that we suffer not the one people to wax mighty and formidable, before the other has become weak; that the power of the Lacedæmon do not increase (unremarked by us) in a greater degree than it is well for that of Thebes to be reduced. For we shall hardly say this, that we

should like to have Lacedæmonians instead of Thebans for
our rivals. It is not this we are anxious for, but that neither
may have the means of injuring us: so shall we enjoy the best
security.

But granting this ought to be so—it were scandalous forsooth,
to take those men for allies, against whom we were arrayed at
Mantinea, and then to assist them against the people, with whom
we shared the peril of that day. I think so too, but with one
addition—"provided the others are willing to act justly." If all
will choose to observe peace, we shall not help the Megalopolitans; for there will be no necessity; and thus we shall be in no
opposition to our fellows in arms: one people are, as they
profess, our allies already, the other will become so now. And
what more could we desire? But should they attempt injustice
and determine on war—then—if this be the only question,
whether we ought or ought not to abandon Megalopolis to the
Lacedæmonians, although it would be unjust, I concede the
point; let things take their course, don't oppose your former
partners in danger: but if you all know, that after taking that
city they will march to attack Messene, let any of the speakers
who are now so hard upon the Megalopolitans tell me, what in
that case he will advise us to do. None will declare. However,
you all know, that you would be obliged to support them, whether
these men recommend it or not, both by the oaths that we
have sworn to the Messenians, and because it is expedient that
their city should be preserved. Reflect therefore in your minds,
whether it would be more noble and generous, to begin your
resistance to Lacedæmonian aggression with the defence of Megalopolis, or with that of Messene. You will now be considered
as protectors of the Arcadians, and striving for the maintenance
of that peace, for which you exposed yourselves in the battle-
field: whereas then it will be manifest to the world, that you
desire Messene to stand not so much for the sake of justice, as
for fear of Lacedæmon. Our purposes and our actions should
always be just; but we must also be careful, that they are at-
tended with advantage. . . .

I am sure—to judge from rational observation—and I think
most Athenians will agree with me, that, if the Lacedæmonians

take Megalopolis, Messene will be in danger; and, if they take that also, I predict that you and the Thebans will be allies. Then it is much better and more honourable for us, to receive the Theban confederacy as our friends, and resist Lacedæmonian ambition, than, out of reluctance to preserve the allies of Thebes, to abandon them now, and have afterwards to preserve Thebes herself, and be in fear also for our own safety. I cannot but regard it as perilous to our state, should the Lacedæmonians take Megalopolis, and again become strong. For I see, they have undertaken this war, not to defend themselves, but to recover their ancient power: what were their designs, when they possessed that power, you perhaps know better than I, and therefore may have reason to be alarmed.

I would fain ask the men, who tell us and say, they detest the Thebans and the Lacedæmonians, whether they detest whom they detest respectively out of regard to you and your interests, or detest Thebans for the sake of Lacedæmonians, and Lacedæmonians for the sake of Thebans. If for their sakes, to neither as rational beings ought you to listen: if they say for your sake, wherefore do they exalt either people unduly? It is possible, surely possible, to humble Thebes without increasing the power of Lacedæmon. Aye; and it is much easier too. I will endeavour to show you how.

It is well known, that up to a certain point all men (however disinclined) are ashamed not to observe justice, and that they openly oppose the transgressors, especially where any people suffer damage: it will be found moreover, that what mars everything, and originates every mischief, is the unwillingness to observe justice uniformly. Therefore, that no such obstacle may arise to the depression of Thebes, let us declare that Thespiæ and Orchomenus and Platæa ought to be reestablished, and let us co-operate with their people and call on others to assist us —just and honourable were this, not to regard with indifference the extermination of ancient cities—but let us not abandon Megalopolis and Messene to the aggressors, nor, on the pretence of Thespiæ and Platæa, suffer existing and flourishing cities to be annihilated. If such be your declared policy, every one will desire, that Thebes should no longer hold her neighbour's dominion. If not—in the first place, we may expect to find these men oppose the other scheme, when they see that the establishment of those towns would be their own ruin: secondly, we shall have an interminable business of it ourselves; for where indeed can it end, if we continually allow existing cities to be destroyed, and require those which are in ruins to be restored?

It is urged by the most plausible speakers, that the pillars of their treaty with Thebes must be taken down, if they mean to be our steadfast allies. These people say, that with them it is not pillars, but interest that binds friendship, and they consider those who assist them to be allies. Granting such to be their views, my notion is this. I say, we should both require of them the destruction of the pillars, and of the Lacedæmonians the observance of peace; if either party refuse to comply, whichever it be, we should side immediately with those that will. Should the Megalopolitans, notwithstanding the maintenance of peace, adhere to the Theban alliance, it will surely be evident to all, that they favour the ambition of the Thebans instead of justice. On the other hand, if the Megalopolitans in good faith espouse our alliance, and the Lacedæmonians do not choose to observe peace, they will surely prove to the world, that they are striving not only for the restoration of Thespiæ, but for an opportunity of conquering Peloponnesus while the Thebans are entangled in this war. One thing in certain men surprises me; that they dread the enemies of Lacedæmon becoming allies of Thebes, and yet see no danger in the Lacedæmonians conquering them; although we have actual experience furnished by the past, that the Thebans always use these allies against Lacedæmon, whereas the Lacedæmonians, whilst they had the same people, used them against us.

I think further, you ought to consider this. If you reject the Megalopolitans—should their city be destroyed and themselves dispersed, the Lacedæmonians at once become powerful: should they chance to escape, (as unhoped-for events do happen,) they will in justice be steadfast allies of the Thebans. If you accept them for allies, the immediate consequence to them will be deliverance by your means—but passing from their case— let us consider what may be looked for and apprehended with reference to Thebes and Lacedæmon. Well then: if the Thebans be vanquished in war, as they ought to be, the Lacedæmonians will not be unduly great, having these Arcadians for their rivals, living near them. If the Thebans chance to recover and come off safe, they will at all events be the weaker for these men having become our allies and been preserved through us. So that in every point of view it is expedient, that we should not abandon the Arcadians, and that they should not appear (in case they do escape) to have owed their deliverance to themselves, or to any other people but you.

I have spoken, O Athenians, (Heaven is my witness,) not from private affection or malice towards either party, but what I consider advantageous for you: and I exhort you not to abandon the Megalopolitans, nor indeed any other of the weaker states to the stronger.

II

The Balance of Power
as a System

Our contemporary picture of international politics as a system of sovereign states inside a "society of nations" had its origins in the European pattern of politics set in the sixteenth and seventeenth centuries. The territorial state, with claims to sovereign power, came into being as the Western medieval order (a pale political residue of the Roman Empire,) began finally to crumble. This medieval world had been based, in theory at least, upon a twofold separation of power profoundly antithetic to later conceptions of state sovereignty: a separation of spiritual and temporal power between a universal church and an empire which, though perhaps neither Holy nor Roman nor imperial, also had claims to universality as successor to and survivor of the Roman Empire itself. In the temporal world, political power and authority had been hierarchically distributed among Emperor, kings, independent or quasi-independent city-states, duchies and other fiefdoms. But as political power in Western and Central Europe began to focus upon several integral and territorially distinct centers, these centers began to defy both the will and the authority of traditional universalist institutions.

The Reformation and the religious wars which followed it in the seventeenth century shattered the temporal power of the church in many parts of Europe, and nationalized Christianity according to the preferences of individual temporal rulers. These new leaders of Europe, defying universalist authorities, turned also against those parochial centers of power within their new societies which were resisting the encroachments of central authority. By the middle of the seventeenth century, the Treaty of Westphalia, which brought the religious wars of Europe to an end, established a new constitutional pattern for the continent: Europe's political affairs were henceforth to be governed by sovereign territorial states and their rulers; in turn, these states' authority within a system of international politics now lacking any supreme authority would henceforth depend upon the vicissitudes of power politics.

While we have seen that the idea of the balance of power was not invented by modern Europeans, the idea was reborn in this modern European state system. The formal unity of Europe, which the authority of Church and Emperor once provided, certainly served as façade in its time for the power clashes of European rulers; yet it had lent justification to their rule. What now could justify the new political architecture of Europe after the authority of both church and empire had been challenged and overthrown, and decentralized power was in the hands of individual monarchs, and their civil and military bureaucracies? We see that the concept of balance of power provided a new theoretical construct describing the new order of the state system.

If universal political authority had now disappeared, then mechanical laws derived from the natural world might serve to provide a sense of regularity and order in what otherwise would have been political chaos. Statesmen, engaged in balance-of-power politics, would obtain their cues to strategy and action in foreign policy from impersonal laws. If Europe henceforth was to be composed of separate, independent entities of sovereign states which acknowledged no common human authority over them, then the system of balance might provide impersonal laws as guidelines to action. Thus power replaced authority as the governor of Europe.

The following selections treat with this profound transformation of European politics and describe the workings of the new balance in the state system. In retrospect, we can see that the Age of Power, of which Professors Friedrich and Blitzer speak, owed its "powerfulness" to the political dynamism which ensued when both authority and power were decentralized. Would Europe's subsequent impact upon the world have been greater, had European political unity been reestablished? Probably not; the competition for prestige and survival among the new states may actually have served to greatly augment Europe's collective power to conquer the outside world. Ironically, this struggle for power ultimately hastened Europe's downfall in the twentieth century as the center of world politics.

4. OF THE BALANCE OF POWER *

David Hume's classic essay on the concept of a balance of power attempts to show that the "idea" of a balance has existed throughout Western history. Tracing the concept from the ancient Greeks to the eighteenth century, he argues that the idea of preserving a balance of power among states "is founded so much on common sense and obvious reasoning" as to be beyond dispute.

In the wars with France, Hume cites the indispensable role played by Great Britain in preserving a European balance. At the same time he warns that too much zeal on the part of France's enemies in weakening her can be as damaging to a correct balance of power in Europe as is the aggressiveness of France itself.

The selection that follows is from Essay VII.

DAVID HUME

It is a question whether the *idea* of the balance of power be owing entirely to modern policy, or whether the *phrase* only has been invented in these later ages? It is certain, that Xenophon, in his Institution of Cyrus, represents the combination of the Asiatic powers to have arisen from a jealousy of the encreasing force of the Medes and Persians; and though that elegant composition should be supposed altogether a romance, this sentiment, ascribed by the author of the eastern princes, is at least a proof of the prevailing notion of ancient times.

In all the politics of Greece, the anxiety, with regard to the balance of power, is apparent, and is expressly pointed out to us, even by the ancient historians. Thucydides represents the league, which was formed against Athens, and which produced the Peloponnesian war, as entirely owing to this principle. And after the decline of Athens, when the Thebans and Lacedemonians disputed for sovereignty, we find, that the Athenians (as

---

* David Hume, *Essays,* ed. T. Green and T. Grose, Vol. I, 1882. "Of the Balance of Power," pp. 348–356. Footnotes omitted.

well as many other republics) always threw themselves into the lighter scale, and endeavoured to preserve the balance. They supported Thebes against Sparta, till the great victory gained by Epaminondas at Leuctra; after which they immediately went over to the conquered, from generosity, as they pretended, but in reality from their jealousy of the conquerors.

Whoever will read Demosthenes's oration for the Megalopolitans, may see the utmost refinements on this principle, that ever entered into the head of a Venetian or English speculatist. . . . But whether we ascribe the shifting of sides in all the Grecian republics to *jealous emulation* or *cautious politics,* the effects were alike, and every prevailing power was sure to meet with a confederacy against it, and that often composed of its former friends and allies.

The same principle, call it envy or prudence, . . . naturally discovered itself in foreign politics, and soon raised enemies to the leading state, however moderate in the exercise of its authority.

The Persian monarch was really, in his force, a petty prince, compared to the Grecian republics; and therefore it behoved him, from views of safety more than from emulation, to interest himself in their quarrels, and to support the weaker side in every contest. This was the advice given by Alcibiades to Tissaphernes, and it prolonged near a century the date of the Persian empire; till the neglect of it for a moment, after the first appearance of the aspiring genius of Philip, brought that lofty and frail edifice to the ground, with a rapidity of which there are few instances in the history of mankind.

The successors of Alexander showed great jealousy of the balance of power; a jealousy founded on true politics and prudence, and which preserved distinct for several ages the partition made after the death of that famous conqueror. . . . And in subsequent times, we find, that, as the Eastern princes considered the Greeks and Macedonians as the only real military force, with whom they have any intercourse, they kept always a watchful eye over that part of the world. . . .

The reason, why it is supposed, that the ancients were entirely ignorant of the *balance of power,* seems to be drawn from the

Roman history more than the Grecian . . . It must be owned,
that the Romans never met with any such general combination
or confederacy against them, as might naturally have been expected from the rapid conquests and declared ambition; but
were allowed peaceably to subdue their neighbours, one after
another, till they extended their dominion over the whole known
world. . . .

The only prince we meet with in the Roman history, who seems
to have understood the balance of power, is Hiero king of
Syracuse. Though the ally of Rome, he sent assistance to the
Carthaginians, during the war of the auxiliaries: 'Esteeming it
requisite,' says Polybius, 'both in order to retain his dominions
in Sicily, and to preserve the Roman friendship, that Carthage
should be safe; lest by its fall the remaining power should be
able, without contrast or opposition, to execute every purpose
and undertaking. And here he acted with great wisdom and
prudence. For that is never, on any account, to be overlooked;
nor ought such a force ever to be thrown into one hand, as to
incapacitate the neighbouring states from defending their rights
against it.' Here is the aim of modern politics pointed out in
express terms.

In short, the maxim of preserving the balance of power is
founded so much on common sense and obvious reasoning, that
it is impossible it could altogether have escaped antiquity, where
we find, in other particulars, so many marks of deep penetration
and discernment. If it was not so generally known and acknowledged as at present, it had, at least, an influence on all the
wiser and more experienced princes and politicians. And indeed,
even at present, however generally known and acknowledged
among speculative reasoners, it has not, in practice, an authority much more extensive among those who govern the world.

After the fall of the Roman empire, the form of government,
established by the northern conquerors, incapacitated them, in a
great measure, for farther conquests, and long maintained each
state in its proper boundaries. . . . But the power of the house
of Austria, founded on extensive but divided dominions, and
their riches, derived chiefly from mines of gold and silver, were
more likely to decay, of themselves, from internal defects, than
to overthrow all the bulwarks raised against them. . . . A new

power succeeded, more formidable to the liberties of Europe, possessing all the advantages of the former, and labouring under none of its defects . . .

In the general wars, maintained against this ambitious power, Great Britain has stood foremost; and she still maintains her station. Beside her advantages of riches and situation, her people are animated with such a national spirit, and are so fully sensible of the blessings of their government, that we may hope their vigor never will languish in so necessary and so just a cause. On the contrary, if we may judge by the past, their passionate ardour seems rather to require some moderation; and they have oftener erred from a laudable excess than from a blameable deficiency.

In the *first* place, we seem to have been more possessed with the ancient Greek spirit of jealous emulation, than actuated by the prudent views of modern politics. Our wars with France have been begun with justice, and even, perhaps, from necessity; but have always been too far pushed from obstinacy and passion. . . .

In the *second* place, we are so declared in our opposition to French power, and so alert in defence of our allies, that they always reckon upon our force as upon their own; and expecting to carry on war at our expence, refuse all reasonable terms of accommodation. . . .

In the *third* place, we are such true combatants, that, when once engaged, we lose all concern for ourselves and our posterity, and consider only how we may best annoy the enemy. To mortgage our revenues at so deep a rate, in wars, where we were only accessories, was surely the most fatal delusion, that a nation, which had any pretension to politics and prudence, has ever yet been guilty of. . . .

These excesses, to which we have been carried, are prejudicial; and may, perhaps, in time, become still more prejudicial another way, by begetting, as is usual, the opposite extreme, and rendering us totally careless and supine with regard to the fate of Europe. . . .

Enormous monarchies are, probably, destructive to human nature; in their progress, in their continuance, and even in their downfall, which never can be very distant from their establishment. The military genius, which aggrandized the monarchy, soon leaves the court, the capital, and the center of such a government; while the wars are carried on at a great distance, and interest so small a part of the state. The ancient nobility, whose affections attach them to their sovereign, live all at court; and never will accept of military employments, which would carry them to remote and barbarous frontiers, where they are distant both from their pleasures and their fortune. The arms of the state, must, therefore, be entrusted to mercenary strangers, without zeal, without attachment, without honour; ready on every occasion to turn them against the prince, and join each desperate malcontent, who offers pay and plunder. This is the necessary progress of human affairs: Thus human nature checks itself in its airy elevation: Thus ambition blindly labours for the destruction of the conqueror, of his family, and of every thing near and dear to him. The Bourbons, trusting to the support of their brave, faithful, and affectionate nobility, would push their advantage, without reserve or limitation. These, while fired with glory and emulation, can bear the fatigues and dangers of war; but never would submit to languish in the garrisons of Hungary or Lithuania, forgot at court, and sacrificed to the intrigues of every minion or mistress, who approaches the prince. The troops are filled with Cravates and Tartars, Hussars and Cossacs; intermingled, perhaps, with a few soldiers of fortune from the better provinces . . .

And the melancholy fate of the Roman emperors, from the same cause, is renewed over and over again, till the final dissolution of the monarchy.

---

5. TOWARD A NEW BALANCE
OF POWER *

In this selection from The Age of Power, *Carl J. Friedrich and*

---

* Carl Friedrich & Charles Blitzer, *The Age of Power,* 1962. Excerpts pp. 151–153, 175–188. Cornell University Press, Ithaca, N. Y. Footnotes incorporated into text.

Charles Blitzer discuss the development of international politics in the seventeenth century. They maintain that it was in the latter part of this century that the concept of raison d'etat *became the motivating force in the relations between European states. International politics in the seventeenth century is, therefore, the "story of the creation of the modern European state system."*

Their analysis is based on the key role played by France in creating a balance of power system in Europe during the seventeenth century. The wars of expansion waged by Louis XIV established the basic patterns of international relations to the present time. The European balance of power which resulted from this half century of warfare was, they conclude, the final achievement of the "age of power."

CARL FRIEDRICH AND CHARLES BLITZER

. . . Certain far-reaching general developments and broad patterns are discernible within the field of international politics in the seventeenth century; it is to these that we must turn before examining in any detail the relations among the states of Europe. Perhaps most striking of all, in terms of the great sweep of European history, was the decline of Spain. Formerly the most powerful nation in Europe as well as the leader in the colonization of the non-European world, Spain during the seventeenth century fell to a position of minor—but not negligible—importance among the great powers. Although the process of decline had begun in the sixteenth century and was to continue through the eighteenth, its influence was most deeply felt during this period. If one accepts the notion of "power vacuums," lacunae which must somehow be filled, it is easy to view the meteoric rise of France as a corollary of Spanish weakness; on the other hand, it may also be argued that the spectacular successes of France were a contributing cause of the weakness of Spain. Be that as it may, the fact remains that under Richelieu, Mazarin, and especially Louis XIV, the French monarchy achieved a position of unquestioned supremacy on the continent. Alliance after alliance was formed with the explicit purpose of containing the expansive force of the Grand Monarchy, and some of these alliances achieved considerable success; but their very existence

serves to dramatize the crucial importance of France's role in
the international politics of the age of power. By default of
the Spanish, the task of opposing French designs on the continent
fell primarily to the two leading commercial powers of the age,
England and the Netherlands. Despite the fact that both were
Protestant countries, their conflicting mercantile interests led them
often to open hostility. Finally, however, under William III they
were united to form a bulwark against the aggressive designs of
Louis XIV. From this time forward England was a factor to be
reckoned with in the politics of the continent, pursuing with
remarkable consistency and success a policy designed to maintain
the European balance of power. In central and eastern Europe, too, revolutionary changes were occurring. Following upon
the virtual disappearance of the Holy Roman Empire as a significant factor in international politics, Prussian and Russia
rose to the position of great powers under the guidance of two
extraordinarily able leaders, the elector Frederick William of
Brandenburg (1620–1688) and the tsar Peter I (1672–1725).
In the second half of the seventeenth century these two new
powers came to dominate the area around the Baltic Sea, dis-
placing Sweden, Denmark, and Poland. Finally, the success of
the Austrian Hapsburgs in stemming the westward expansion of
the Turkish Empire laid the foundations for their future hegemony in the southeast.

Even this bare outline suggests certain conclusions about
the pattern of international politics in the seventeenth century.
In the first place, it is clear that religion played a constantly
diminishing role in the relations among nations during this period.
It is noteworthy, for instance, that the papacy, which had formerly been such a potent participant in affairs of state throughout Europe, had virtually nothing to do with the developments
which we have traced. Similarly, religious allegiances and con-
troversies, which had been at the very heart of the Thirty Years'
War, played an exceedingly minor role in the complex international drama of the later seventeenth century. It is customary to
describe this change by saying that the age of religious wars
had ended and that it was replaced by the age of power politics.
In a sense, this is a perfectly true and accurate statement. It is

perhaps more useful, however, to say that the successor to the age of religious wars was the age of "reason of state." For the crucial fact is that the participants in the international relations of the later seventeenth century—the dramatis personae in this vast European drama—were neither religious sects nor royal dynasties, but rather secular, territorial states, the products, at least in part, of the political genius of such figures as Richelieu, Wallenstein, and Gustavus II Adolphus. In their tradition, the objectives for which these new states fought and negotiated were defined—albeit not always overtly—in terms of their secular interests, or "reasons of state." Thus, in a very real sense, it may be argued that the history of international politics in the seventeenth century is the story of the creation of the modern European state system. Furthermore, it should be noted that the word European is used here deliberately. In this period—for the first time—the area stretching from Russia and Turkey on the east to England on the west, from Scandinavia on the north to the Iberian peninsula on the south, became truly a political unit, in the sense that the nations included in it acted within a common frame of reference and were aware always of the interrelations of their actions. . . .

THE WARS OF LOUIS XIV

The Thirty Years' War in Germany, the wars of the Fronde in France, and the English civil wars of 1642–1648 had signaled the emergence of the modern state as the characteristic political institution of western Europe. It was inevitable that such a truly revolutionary development in domestic politics should have far-reaching repercussions in the realm of international politics. On the one hand, as we have noted, the declining importance of dynastic and religious questions created a situation in which sheer power came increasingly to dominate the relations among states. On the other hand, the centralized bureaucratic institutions of the modern state placed in the hands of monarchs and parliaments alike new techniques—economic, diplomatic, and military—which were peculiarly appropriate to the pursuit of their states' interests in the international "war of all against all." Nowhere are these parallel forces more vividly illustrated than in the history of the reckless expansionism of Louis and the opposition which it aroused during the last fifty years of our period. Here, in the so-called "wars of Louis XIV," were established the basic patterns that have characterized international relations down to our own century.

The wars whose collective title stands as a fitting monument to the aggressive designs of the Sun King were four in number: the War of Devolution (1667–1668), concluded by the Treaty of Aix-la-Chapelle; the Dutch War (1672–1678), concluded by the Treaty of Nimwegen (Spelled also Nijmwegen, Nijmegen, and Nimeguen); the War of the League of Augsburg (1688–1697), concluded by the Treaty of Ryswick; and, finally, the War of the Spanish Succession (1701–1714), concluded by the Peace of Utrecht and the Treaty of Rastadt and Baden. Together, these wars filled more than thirty of the fifty-five years of Louis' personal reign, bankrupting his kingdom and causing the deaths of hundreds of thousands of his subjects—in a single battle (Malplaquet in 1709) the French suffered more than 12,000 casualties. A generation brought up on socioeconomic or geopolitical explanations of the phenomenon of war may well view with suspicion any attempt to argue that these wars were in fact the direct consequence of the megalomania of a single man, urged on by an ambitious minister and by his own insatiable ambition. A brief examination of the wars themselves, and of the events leading to them, however, may perhaps provide evidence in support of just this argument.

The international position of France at the beginning of the period of Louis XIV's personal rule was defined by two recently concluded treatises: by the terms of the Peace of Westphalia (1648) her eastern frontier was established on the Rhine, a bastion against the alleged hostile designs of the Hapsburg emperor and (more realistically) a convenient base for further operations in Germany; under the Treaty of the Pyrenees (1659) she received territories in the Spanish Netherlands, and, more important, she demonstrated her ascendancy over the Spanish Hapsburgs, symbolized by the marriage between Louis XIV and the eldest daughter of Philip IV, Maria Theresa. Thus, in 1661 the territories of France stretched from the Atlantic Ocean to the

Rhine, from Flanders to the Pyrenees; rich in natural resources and with a population far exceeding that of her neighbors, she was the unquestioned mistress of western Europe. To contemporaries, and notably to her ruler, there seemed to be no limits to the greatness which she might achieve.

Louis' first opportunity for positive action came with the death of his wife's father, Philip IV of Spain, in 1665. Previously, his role in the Anglo-Dutch commercial war of 1665–1667—in which the British seized the city of New Amsterdam and renamed it New York—had been ambiguous in the extreme. Although bound to the Dutch by an alliance (1662), and actually providing them with troops, he concluded a secret treaty with Charles II of England in 1667, under which he promised to withold all naval assistance from the Dutch. The fact is that Louis was interested in this war only as a prelude to the fulfillment of his own designs in the Spanish Netherlands. It will be recalled that, upon her marriage to Louis XIV, Maria Theresa of Spain had renounced all claim to her Spanish inheritance, upon condition that Louis was to receive a dowry of 500,000 crowns from Spain. The dowry had never been paid, and now in 1665 Louis published his claim to all Spanish possessions in the Belgian provinces; this claim he justified in terms of a provision of private law known as the "right of devolution," by which the daughters of a first marriage had priority over the sons of a second. When the Spanish refused to accept his demands, Louis coolly proceeded with the military occupation of all the territories in question; by May of 1667, as a result of the skill of Turenne and the overwhelming superiority of the French armies, all of the Spanish Netherlands lay open to the Sun King. Confronted with so formidable a threat, the states of western Europe began, characteristically, to forget the differences that divided them. The war between the English and the Dutch was replaced by an alliance, which was soon joined by the Swedes —the Triple Alliance of 1668. Negotiations were at the same time begun between Spain and Portugal, with a view to freeing the Spanish for action against France. Louis' immediate response to the formidable coalition that was being formed against him was an attempt to conciliate the Dutch by turning his attention eastward. Having successfully occupied the Spanish territory of Franche-Comté, on the Swiss border, he then announced his willingness to negotiate a settlement of the war. By the terms of the Treaty of Aix-la-Chapelle (May 1668), he restored Franche-Comté to the Spanish but was allowed to retain twelve forti-fied towns in the Netherlands. The events of the brief, incon-clusive War of Devolution are of particular interest for three reasons: (1) they represent the first of Louis XIV's attempts to extend the frontiers of France by any and all available means, legalistic, diplomatic, or military; (2) the Triple Alliance was the first instance of a combination of traditionally hostile European powers on the basis simply of their common fear of French power; (3) by ordering the destruction of all fortifica-tions in Franche-Comté before returning it to Spain, by insist-ing on the retention of fortresses in the Netherlands, and by con-cluding a secret treaty with the emperor Leopold for the future division of Spanish territories (January 1668), Louis XIV gave clear indication that he regarded the Treaty of Aix-la-Chappelle as no more than a temporary truce. Thus, while the War of Devolution was still in progress, the Sun King was already lay-ing his plans for the next war.

Quite apart from his continuing determination to win the Spanish Netherlands, Louis was now motivated by a profound hatred of the Dutch, who had frustrated his ambitions in 1668. He immediately set about to achieve the diplomatic isolation of Holland, concluding treaties with England (The secret Treaty of Dover 1670) and Sweden (1672); as French gold was used to buy English neutrality in the forthcoming war, so too it was used to buy active German support in the cities of Cologne and Münster. The years between 1668 and 1672 were years of prep-aration which Lionne, the secretary of state, spent laboring with all his might to secure allies, Colbert to find money, and Louvois to raise soldiers for Louis. By May of 1672 the prepara-tions were complete and French armies were once more loosed upon the United Provinces. Again they met with immediate and overwhelming success; only the opening of the dikes saved Am-sterdam from capture. In August an enraged mob murdered the brothers John and Cornelius De Witt, leaders of the Dutch aristocratic republican party; William III (1650–1702), prince of the House of Orange, the future king of England, took over the leadership of the United Provinces and in time became the chief organizer of European resistance to France. Almost immediately the fortunes of the Dutch improved; alliances with the Great Elector, with the emperor, and with Spain ended their position of diplomatic and military isolation, so carefully created by Louis XIV. As the French squandered their initial advantage through their passion for siege warfare, the conquest of the Netherlands became an ever more remote possibility. Once again Louis' eyes turned toward the east: he personally led the force that recaptured Franche-Comté, while Turenne waged a campaign of stunning brilliance in the Palatinate and along the upper Rhine. For years the war dragged on, marked by stiffening opposition—diplomatic and military—to the designs of France. Finally, in 1678 and 1679, a series of treaties among the participants brought the war to a close. The results of the Franco-Dutch War were strikingly similar to those of the War of Devolution: once again Louis had failed to win the Spanish Netherlands; once again his actions had stimulated the formation of an anti-French coalition, this time under the extremely able leadership of William of Orange; and once again his chief gains were on France's eastern border, this time including Franche-Comté. Although largely unseen by the participants, a continuing pattern was beginning to emerge in the relations among the states of western Europe.

The Treaty of Nimwegen is often said to mark the zenith of the power of Louis XIV and the nadir of that of his enemies. This being the case, it is clear that even at the height of his success the Sun King was unable to achieve the objects of his ambition, while from this time forward his fortunes could only decline. Like most men of overweening pride and ambition, Louis was the architect of his own destruction.

By 1678 the French monarch had learned that overt aggression was not an entirely satisfactory means of achieving his aims; for the next four years he pursued a brilliantly conceived and skillfully executed policy of diplomatic and quasi-legal aggrandizement. By the treaties of Westphalia, the Pyrenees, Aix-la-

Chapelle, and Nimwegen, France had acquired during the past thirty years a great number of towns and territories along her borders. Louis now announced that any territories that had in the past belonged to any of these newly acquired possessions should rightfully belong to France. A number of French courts, known as Chambers of Reunion, were established to investigate these claims, and their "findings"—inevitably pro-French—were executed by the armies of France. By a combination of this highly dubious "legal" proceeding and a judicious use of military power, Saarbrücken, Strasbourg, Luxembourg, Alsace and Lorraine (to name only the most important territories) were "reunited" into the kingdom of France. The climax of the success of this policy came in August of 1684 when the emperor Leopold, weakened by his struggle against the Turks, signed the Truce of Ratisbon (Regensburg), acknowledging French possession of all territories gained by the process of "reunion" prior to August 1, 1681. Soon, however, the fortunes of diplomacy were to turn against the Sun King.

The seizure of Strasbourg (1681), and even more the revocation of the Edict of Nantes (1685) and the subsequent persecution of French Protestants, aroused European opinion against Louis XIV as never before. Under the leadership of William of Orange, the explicitly anti-French League of Augsburg was formed in July 1686; its signatories were the emperor, the kings of Sweden and Spain, and the electors of Saxony, Bavaria, and the Palatinate. When the Glorious Revolution placed William on the English throne, England too became associated with the League, as did Holland and Savoy. Although the war which followed originally broke out over the question of the succession to the electorship of the Palatinate and the archbishopric of Cologne, it was actually fought on five fronts: the Netherlands, the Rhine valley, the Pyrenees, Savoy, and Ireland. Apart from his ambitions along the Rhine, Louis had two chief aims: to hold the territories which he had previously taken in Flanders, and to restore James II to the English throne. Considering the cost to France of ten years of war (1688–1697), his gains were at best modest. Standing virtually alone against all of Europe, he managed to retain what he had gained at Nimwegen, as well as both Alsace and Strasbourg. On the other hand, he was forced to return to Spain and the empire the vast bulk of the territories won by "reunion" and by conquest since Nimwegen; he was obliged to acknowledge William III as king of England; and he was made to renounce the claims of his candidate for the see of Cologne. Although he arrogantly claimed to have written the terms of the Treaty of Ryswick, it is clear that these very terms placed severe limitations on the ambitions of Louis XIV. The strengthened position of the emperor and the increasing unification of Protestant Europe made it almost inevitable that in the years to come his attention would be focused on the possessions of the Spanish Hapsburgs.

The succession to the Spanish throne of the sickly, impotent Charles II in 1665 had raised political and diplomatic issues of the first importance for all of Europe. By the time of the Treaty of Ryswick it was apparent to all that this mentally and physically feeble monarch had not many years to live; the inheritance of his vast territories was generally recognized as a problem that demanded an international solution. In purely dynastic terms, there were three contenders for the Spanish succession: (1) Louis XIV claimed the right of inheritance through both his mother and his wife, the eldest daughters respectively of Philip III and Philip IV, both of whom, however, had explicitly renounced all rights to the Spanish throne; (2) the emperor Leopold claimed the right through *his* mother and *his* wife who, although younger daughters of Philip III and Philip IV, had never renounced their rights; (3) Joseph Ferdinand, the electoral prince of Bavaria, put forward his claim as great-grandson of Philip IV and grandson of the sister of Charles II. In addition to the dynastic aspect of the question, however, there was the further fact that neither Holland nor England, the two great naval powers of Europe, was prepared to allow the unification of the Spanish possessions with those of France *or* the Austrian Hapsburgs. Largely for this reason, Louis XIV put forward his claim in the name of his grandson, Philip of Anjou, while the emperor claimed on behalf of his second son, Charles.

In the year 1698, while Charles II of Spain was still living, the powers of Europe met to arrange the division of his possessions upon his death. By the Treaty of Partition of that year it was agreed: (1) that the bulk of the inheritance—Spain, the

Indies, and the Netherlands—would go to the electoral prince of Bavaria; (2) that Naples, Sicily, and various other Italian territories would go to the son of Louis XIV; (3) that the duchy of Milan would go to the emperor's second son, the archduke Charles. This rather high-handed proceeding enraged the dying Charles II, who thereupon bequeathed the entire inheritance to the elector of Bavaria, then a child of seven; this attempt to punish both Louis XIV and the emperor met with the approval of England and Holland, since it tended to maintain the balance of power on the continent. No sooner had this acceptable settlement been achieved than the prince elector of Bavaria died (February 1699), opening the entire vexing question afresh. Once again negotiations among the powers were opened and, in March 1700, a second Treaty of Partition was written. By its terms, Spain, the Netherlands, and the Indies were to be given to the archduke Charles; Naples, Sicily, and the duchy of Lorraine went to the dauphin; and Milan was given to the duke of Lorraine in compensation for the loss of his duchy. With the balancing "third force" of Bavaria removed, agreement proved more difficult to achieve in 1700 than it had been in 1698. The terms of the second Treaty of Partition were rejected by both the emperor, who greedily claimed the entire inheritance for his son, and Charles II, who proceeded to bequeath all his possessions to Philip of Anjou, the grandson of Louis XIV. Louis now found himself in an odd position: he was a party to a treaty which divided the Spanish inheritance, but he was also the grandfather of the chosen heir to the entire inheritance. What was he to do? Characteristically, he decided to scrap the treaty and support the claims of Philip of Anjou. It must be added, however, that he was motivated less by the desire to gain the Spanish possessions for the House of Bourbon than by the fear that any other policy would cause Charles II to change his will and make the archduke his sole heir. Foreseeing that war with Austria was inevitable, he realistically preferred to have Spain on his side and hoped that the naval powers would remain neutral. On November 1, 1700, Charles II died and Philip of Anjou was proclaimed as Philip V of Spain. The stage was set for an international collision of unequaled magnitude.

Once again, despite his skillful maneuvers to assure the neutrality of England and Holland, Louis XIV's ambition and arrogance soon united the great powers in opposition to his designs. In February 1701 he sent French troops into the Spanish Netherlands, immediately arousing the suspicions of England and the United Provinces. His announcement that this was done simply to protect the Netherlands until Spain should be able to take over did nothing to allay these suspicions. When the French began systematically to undermine the colonial trade of England and Holland, and when Louis negotiated an alliance between Spain, Portugal, and France (June 1701), the immediate response was the formation of a Grand Alliance of England, Holland, and Austria (September 1701), later joined by Prussia, Portugal, and Savoy. Although his opposition to the Austrian Hapsburgs was originally viewed with sympathy by England and Holland, Louis had made the fatal mistake of threatening both the commercial interests of the maritime powers and the continental balance of power, which they viewed as essential to their security. During the next fifteen years France was to pay heavily for this mistake.

The War of the Spanish Succession began in 1701, with the invasion of Italy by the imperial general, Prince Eugene of Savoy. The strategy of Louis XIV was to hold the English and the Dutch in the Netherlands, while he proceeded to attack Eugene and march on to Vienna. This plan was frustrated by the great English general, the duke of Marlborough (born John Churchill) who brought his army safely from the lower Rhine to the upper Danube, where he joined Eugene in time to meet the combined French and Bavarian forces at Blenheim; the battle of Blenheim (August 13, 1704) was the first great allied victory of the war. It was soon followed by others, as the tide turned definitely against France: in Flanders, Marlborough defeated the duc de Villeroi at Ramillies (May 1706), Marlborough and Eugene bested both Vendôme and the duke of Burgundy at Oudenarde (July 1708), and, in the bloodiest battle of the war, Marlborough and Eugene won a Pyrrhic victory at Malplaquet (September 1709); in Spain, Philip V was twice driven from Madrid by British, Portuguese, and Austrian forces; in Italy, an Austro-Prussian army under Eugene won a victory at Turin (September 1706) that effectively broke French power in the entire country.

By 1708, when peace negotiations began, Louis XIV was prepared to make great concessions. He was willing to recognize Charles of Austria as king of Spain, to surrender the border fortresses of the Netherlands to Holland, to restore the empire to the state prevailing at the Peace of Westphalia, and to accept the succession of Anne to the English throne. Unfortunately, the allies insisted upon one further condition: they demanded that Louis should send French armies to drive his grandson from the Spanish throne. Although virtually exhausted militarily, economically, and diplomatically, Louis still retained his pride, and this last ignominious demand proved too much for him to swallow. Rallying his people with a magnificent appeal to the glorious memories of French power he determined to continue the war. Again in 1709, after the holocaust of Malplaquet, negotiations were opened. At this time Louis went so far as to offer to pay mercenary troops to fight against his grandson in Spain, but again the allies insisted that French soldiers should be used and again hostilities were renewed. This time, however, the tide began to run against Louis' enemies. One is tempted to say that fate had stepped in to punish them for their arrogance, but in any case three events occurred which upset the existing political and military balance of Europe, vastly improving the position and the bargaining power of Louis XIV. In August 1710 the Whig government of England was overthrown—partly as a reaction against the slaughter of troops at Malplaquet—in the first regular and peaceful change of government under the new English party system; the Tory government that came to power was made up of Marlborough's enemies. In 1711 the archduke Charles, the allies' candidate for the Spanish throne, inherited the throne of Austria, creating a situation in which allied victory would unite all the Hapsburg territories, an event quite unacceptable to the other powers of Europe. Finally, in 1712, the French general Villars won a signal victory over Lord Albemarle at Denain. As a result of these three events, negotiations were again reopened, this time on a much more even footing.

The terms of the settlements reached at Utrecht (1713) and at Rastadt (1714) can hardly be described as a victory for either side in the war. Philip of Anjou was recognized as king of Spain at the price of renouncing all claims to the French throne and surrendering to England Gibraltar, Minorca, and certain trading rights in Latin America (the *Asiento*). The Spanish Netherlands, Milan, Sardinia, and Naples were given to Austria, despite the emperor's refusal to recognize Philip V. France ceded Newfoundland, Acadia (Nova Scotia), and the Hudson's Bay territory to England, but was allowed to maintain its frontiers intact; Louis recognized the Hanoverian succession in England and gave up his championship of the Stuart pretenders.

Certain things, however, can be said about the settlements reached at Utrecht and Rastadt. At the very least, they clearly represented the final shattering of Louis XIV's dream of European hegemony. When Louis died in 1715, his country was internally weakened to the point of bankruptcy and externally confined by the new European balance of power. It was the creation of this balance, involving all the states of Europe, and through them all the colonial areas of the world, that represented the final achievement of internal politics in the seventeenth century. Wrought on the battlefields of Flanders, Germany, and Italy, this complex pattern of relations among independent, bureaucratically organized states persisted through two centuries until its destruction by the cataclysmic events of our own age.

6. THE PRINCIPLES AND THE PRACTICE

OF METTERNICH*

Metternich, the Austrian Foreign Minister (1809–1849), could rightfully claim to have been both architect and manager of Eu-

---

* Ernest L. Woodward, *Three Studies in European Conservatism*. Excerpts, pp. 37–43. London: Constable and Company, Ltd., 1929. Footnotes omitted.

ropean equilibrium after the Napoleonic wars. In 1813, when Na-
poleon's armies had been forced back into France by a cumber-
some coalition of European states, the allies sought to establish
by diplomacy a new European order in which France and
French military power would be checked but not destroyed. In
the diplomatic process (which lasted two years) of constructing
a postwar Europe, Metternich's wish was both to restore France
as a viable element in the European order, and to establish
among and within all European states a viable constitutional
order. Had his wish been fulfilled (and it was not), Europe
would have been governed indefinitely by a confederal quadrum-
virate of the Great Powers—Austria, Russia, Prussia and Great
Britain. Acting in concert, they would have seen to it that in
France and indeed in all of Europe a status quo of conservative
regimes would be maintained. The British foreign secretary
Castlereagh shrank from such grandiose confederal proposals; to
him, the principal object of the Vienna Congress in 1815 had
been to restore a multiple balance, including territorial arrange-
ments favorable to Britain; Metternich's three-dimensioned con-
cept of equilibrium, among and within all European states, was
irrelevant to British security interests.

To Metternich, however, European stability hinged on the ca-
pacity of statesmen to prevent a recurrence of both major war and
revolution. His system, the principles of which are analyzed by
Professor Woodward in the following essay, came as close as
any to a coherent conservative theory of political stability.

ERNEST L. WOODWARD

In face of the revolutionary theories of his political enemies
Metternich always claimed to act upon a reasoned view of
society. His enemies said that he acted upon a "system." He
denied that he had a "system," and took care to distinguish
"system" from "principles." His "principles" led him now to this,
now to that course of action, as the needs of the day might
determine. The view of society, from which the "principles"
were drawn, must be true because it took account of the un-
changing nature of man—"the French Revolution did not make
men nobler"; because it was based upon history, and could
be tested by history. He contrasted his own "principles" with
the generalisations of passion or doctrinaire inexperience.

What were these "principles"? How did Metternich apply them? Did he really believe in them, or were they only a means of making a hand-to-mouth policy look respectable, and of cloaking local and temporary expedients with an appearance of universality? The "principles" were not original: nor did Metternich develop them; they remained as little changed by time as his own handwriting. He had little cause to change them. They were based upon the experience of his early life, and the philosophy of history which he had learned from his professors at Strasbourg and Mainz. The events of his youth seemed to justify the conclusions of this philosophy; the events of his long political life only confirmed them; his views were formed before he came into the service of the Hapsburgs; the conditions of the Austrian empire would have led him to the conclusions which he already held. Finally, the "principles" opposed to his own seemed to him never to change, in whatever local or temporal form they might manifest themselves. If the principles of the revolution remained the same, why should the principles of the counter-revolution alter?

The basis of Metternich's philosophy was the idea of the balance of power as a cosmic principle, for so it seemed to eighteenth-century philosophers who drew their analogies from the mechanistic science of their age. The idea of a stability, a balance between extremes, was applied to man as to the forces of nature, and was a more scientific statement, or a statement in more modern scientific terms, of the Aristotelian doctrine of the mean. The political lesson was obvious. The ineluctable laws of the universe compelled men and things to seek repose as the only way of escape from dissolution; a repose which was an equilibrium between conflicting forces. In the political world stability could only be found in a balance of power between the different states which were the units of the great human society, between the different classes and interests in particular states. As in the physical, so in the political world the balance could easily be disturbed; a disturbance of equilibrium would mean civil war within a state, external war between states, just as it would mean calamities in the physical world or moral anarchy in the nature of man. This doctrine is doubly pessimistic because it leads to a belief in stability rather than progress and finds in history no more than a variation upon a single theme; a recurrent cycle of repression and anarchy, with only a few intervals of repose. There seems no lasting alternative between chaos and stagnation. Apply the doctrine to the life of man, and the same melancholy conclusion is inevitable. The balance of opposing forces is maintained rarely, and for a short time; while death may come at any hour and destroy the balance for ever. None the less death must always win in the end; nor is a view of human society necessarily false because it is unpleasing to comfortable men.

Under the domination of this conception of the physical laws which govern the world and of the consequent philosophy of history—a philosophy shared by the greatest of Greek historians—Metternich found the balance badly upset in his own time; the pendulum had swung in the direction of anarchy. Hence it was the duty of statesmen to act upon the defensive; to counter exuberance by repression and to oppose stability to movement. It must be the continual work of those in power to secure a redress of the balance in the direction of repose; such action was in accordance with an instructed conception of natural law. This is why Metternich called himself "tout à terre, tout historique," and objected to the claim of his opponents that they alone were "socialist." For this reason he insisted always that the duty of statesmen was to "govern."

If it were the duty of statesmen to lean towards the side of strong government when the unscientific thought of the time was driving European society towards anarchy, it followed that a co-operation between governments was necessary. Experience proved this. The mischievous indifference of Austrian and Prussian statesmen to the common danger of the French Revolution had resulted in the unexpected victories of the French armies, the rise of Napoleon, and long years of war and tyranny. Firm and united action at the outset, a coalition based upon common principles, would have prevented untold miseries. Only after bitter lessons did the European powers really act together; then at last their action, borne on the stream of favouring circumstances, brought about Napoleon's fall. Yet the "principles" of the revolution could not be burnt out of men's minds by victories in the field. The Peace of Paris had brought material, not moral, tranquillity. A generation of repose was needed in which the young might learn the true laws governing the life of man in society. The transition from a period of movement to a period of repose was always difficult. During these years of morale education the incurable revolutionaries of an older time must be held down by force. For this work the co-operation of all the states of Europe was essential. Co-operation implied intervention. The "principle of non-intervention" was purely arbitrary, and was not based upon natural law. It was not recognised by the revolutionaries themselves, however often they might appeal to it in times of distress. "The revolution reckoned upon the separation of states."

Metternich repeated Burke's remark that a man has an interest in putting out the flames when his neighbour's house is on fire. Revolution was a kind of disease, and measures of public health ought to be international. Intervention must be on the side of authority. Therefore support must be given to the monarchial principle as such, however unworthy its representatives. A Neapolitan or a Spanish Bourbon, a Dom Miguel in Portugal, were to be supported not because of their personal merits—they had but few—nor because of any divine right of kings, whatever the Bourbons might think, but because the right of hereditary succession was a guarantee of other rights, and, as a consequence, a guarantee of the whole social order. Metternich never thought that the "principle of legitimacy" belonged of itself to the moral order. Kingship was not the only form of government; hereditary monarchy was not the only form of kingship. Napoleon had no predecessor. The monarchical principle was to be upheld because in the Europe of the early nineteenth century it happened to be the constituted source of authority; the visible sign of the rule of law. In short, it must be defended not because it was inevitable but because it was attacked by those who wished to overthrow more than monarchy.

Popular sovereignty was set over against monarchy. Popular sovereignty as set forth by its supporters must have led ultimately to an attack upon all forms of property. Its fancied justification was the equality of all men. But men are equal only before God and the law; there is no equality apart from this. Any society which based authority upon the general equality of men was

building upon the fallacy, widespread among eighteenth-century
philosophers, that man could reach perfection, or upon the
simple rule: "ôte-toi, que je m'y mette." It is an indication of
the limits of his reading that Metternich never quoted Aristotle's
wise analysis of "the universal and chief cause of revolutionary
feeling . . . the desire of equality when men think they are
equal to others who have more than themselves; or, again, the
desire of inequality and superiority, when conceiving themselves
to be superior they think that they have not more but the same
or less than their inferiors." In other words equality is of two
kinds, numerical and proportional; and from the confusion between the two arise wars, tumults, and confusions.

If popular sovereignty was a conception likely to destroy the
balance of states, and hence to lead to calamity, monarchy
based upon popular sovereignty must be a contradiction in terms.
For this reason Metternich was bound to regard the monarchy
of July as a sham from the beginning. The English monarchy
was an apparent exception; but it was only possible because of
an historical tradition which did not exist on the continent of
Europe. The American constitution was a perpetual *tour de
force;* in any case American conditions were more local even
than those of England. As a rule invented constitutions, or
chartes, as the French liked to call them after 1815, were of
no value in themselves, nor was there any universal receipt for
their composition. To Metternich a constitution was much more
than a written document, as marriage was something more than
a marriage contract. He agreed with Burke that a constitution
was the sum of the conditions of the life of a state, the product
of the national character, not of a moment of excitement. Magna
Charta in English history was a beginning, and not an end, and
was followed by centuries of bloodshed and civil disturbance. To
make a constitution was to give legislative shape to a revolution.
In fact the constitutions asked for by revolutionary agitation
were "representative constitutions," based upon popular sovereignty. Here was the great distinction; the form was indifferent,
so long as the monarchical principle was maintained. Once the
idea of the sovereignty of the people was accepted, the life of
the state, the working of its institutions, would be hampered by
talk, corruption, disputes. Inefficiency would lead to chaos; the

only escape from anarchy would be despotism. The cycle leading from 1793 to 18 brumaire was of the order of nature. "Like Saturn, revolutions always devour their own children."

These were, in outline, the "principles" of Metternich. Such a philosophy may be superficial; it was certainly "doctrinaire," and certainly based upon the "half-truths" and the shallow learning which Metternich claimed to despise. Much of it was commonplace enough; though a reading of the eighteenth-century political writers, whose work made history a generation later, shows that one generation may easily forget the commonplaces of another. The so-called generalisations from experience were out of date when the romantic revival led to a restoration of the belief in the "manifoldness" of history. They ignored—could it have been otherwise?—the psychological basis of popular sovereignty, the evolutionary value of the instincts, impulses, dispositions, be the word what it may, to give a lead, to play a part in the social group. Liberty is more than the "certitude du lendemain." In the long struggle of human creatures with an unkind environment, no horde, no group, no society could live where the members did not have their say or contribute their ideas to the common stock. We are the heirs of a hardly-won inheritance, and we cannot throw away the weapons by which it was won, for these weapons are part of ourselves. Metternich was fighting against the dead, the one battle in which the living must always be the losers.

7. THE IMPERIAL CHANCELLOR *

After German unification had been attained under Prussian leadership and power in 1870, the system of European politics became radically altered. Metternich's post-Napoleonic "system" had been based upon a concert of conservative powers intent

* C. G. Robertson, *Bismarck,* Chapter VI, "The Imperial Chancellor," pp. 408–423. New York: Henry Holt and Company, 1919. Quoted by permission of Constable and Company, London, and the executors of the C. G. Robertson estate. Footnotes omitted.

upon the double task of checking French power and maintaining European stability through concerted policies of status quo regimes. After 1870, this old European system was irretrievably dead. Prussia had crushed Austria in war, in 1866, to seize authority in the Germanies; had defeated France in 1870; and stood unchallenged as the principal continental European state. For two decades, between 1870 and 1890, European equilibrium seemingly hung on the capacities of Otto von Bismarck, the Imperial German Chancellor; having wrought a precarious new order in Central Europe, Bismarck as German Chancellor became legatee of that which he as Prussian Chancellor had wrought by force and diplomacy. The complex management of that equilibrium lay in his hands. Fearful of French revenge, and anxious lest combinations of European powers be established to reduce the power of the new Germany, Bismarck erected a complicated structure of alliances and sought to divert French ambitions away from Central Europe into colonial areas. It is hard to find, at any point in the history of the European society of nations, any parallel to Bismarck's brilliant yet foredoomed effort to control the entire system, not by war but by highly centralized balancing diplomacy. The following selection, from C. G. Robertson's Bismarck, analyzes and recounts this extraordinary strategy. The Bismarckian system did not outlast its founder. When he was removed by the new Emperor in 1890, it quickly crumbled; within fifteen years, Imperial Germany found itself surrounded by the "nightmare of coalitions" which the Iron Chancellor had sought to avoid.

C. G. ROBERTSON

. . . The German hegemony of the European State system rested on the power and prestige of Prussia, but it was a power and prestige interpreted by, and reflected in, the personality of a single man; and if the revolving years strengthened the political ascendency consummated by the Treaty of Frankfurt, the Congress of Berlin, and the Dual Alliance—the main terms of which were known before the ink was dry on the signatures—they also emphasised the egoism and vanity of the ministerial autocrat. Bismarck demanded homage, and he expected incense, from all the statesmen and all the courts. Ambassadors at Berlin informed their governments that they would do well always to consult Bismarck on every step, for if they acted without asking his advice, even in matters in which Germany could not be regarded as directly interested, they would soon discover that the jealous, suspicious, and vain Chancellor intended to make them pay for the neglect and the implied personal insult. . . .

An element of grandeur sublimated this vanity. More and more the Chancellor absented himself from Berlin and conducted the foreign affairs of Europe from Friedrichsruhe or Varzin, and the men who combined business and homage in a visit to Bismarck enjoyed a patrician hospitality from the hands of a great patrician, who tried to forget on his own hearth or in the glades of the avenues he had planted, the methods so congenial in the Wilhelmstrasse. If, in addition, the visitor could prove that in his arteries ran the red blood of a fierce virility—that rich meat and drink, physical exuberance, and joy in the carnal framework of life and the passions of nature, appealed as much as the conclusion of a hard bargain—Bismarck was ready to make concessions that were not for the anæmic and the bookworms of the Chancery. . . . Statecraft was an excrescence on the natural life of the healthy man, but as it was inevitable, let men bring into it not the weaknesses of the physical unfit but the qualities that made man the lord of the universe and of his own hearth.

Bismarck was never on the side of the angels—for in a dirty and sordid world he held that the angels by Divine wisdom prudently kept clear of human affairs—but he was never on the side of the apes. He was always 'on the side of the white man,' not 'the blonde beast,' of which so much has been written with so much profound ignorance, but the white man who represented 'his idol, Authority,' the man of the master races whose very vices and brutality were the necessary correlatives of his virtues, and were a proof of his strength of brain, physical vitality, and appetite for order and discipline.

But beneath the elements of grandeur in Bismarck lay an inferno of personal feeling as passionate and intense as the manhood that he admired. . . .

The Dual Alliance of 1879 had been intended to solve the critical dilemma thrust upon him between 1876 and 1879, and

to provide a firm foundation for his system. But Bismarck doubt-
less felt that his object was identical with that expressed in 1872
when he pronounced that he had 'thrown a bridge across to
Vienna, without breaking down that older one to Petersburg.'
In 1879 'the older bridge' was hardly safe for traffic; but Bismarck was determined to reconstruct it. The Dual Alliance
steeled this determination, while it provided an immovable point
from which to work. After 1879 a new method is distinctly
discernible, caused by the unexpected introduction of wholly
new elements. The position and problems of Russia, to begin
with, were fundamentally altered after 1878. The effort to effect
by diplomacy and intrigue what the Treaty of San Stefano would
have established by war and a treaty—the Balkan States controlled by Petersburg, and a Constantinople living under the fiat
of the Tsar—the policy of Kutchuk-Kainardji (1774) and of
Unkiar Skelessi (1833) gave a wholly new turn to the Near
Eastern question. Such a policy, with Pan-Slavism behind it, cut
right across the Austrian line of development and was wholly
opposed to the ambitions of Germany, masked behind the Dual
Alliance. It involved Russia in desperate and tortuous courses
in which the weakness of her statesmanship was continuously
revealed, witness the folly and blindness of her treatment of
Roumania and Bulgaria, but it made a new and torturing problem for Bismarck. The antagonism of Great Britain and Russia
was superimposed on the antagonism of Austria and Russia;
it had been recreated by the events of 1876–8, and henceforward
was a standing menace to both countries. Russian expansion
eastwards into the heart of Asia inflamed the old quarrel of the
Crimean War and of 1875–8, and for Russia the expansion eastwards into Central Asia was inevitable, apart from its merits as a
riposte to Great Britain, though it imposed a fresh drain on her
resources, while it restated the old problem: Was Russia to concentrate on her Eastern Empire, or on establishing her position
in Europe? . . .

. . . Alexander, swayed by Nationalism, religion, and ambition, was continually breaking away from the principle of a
modern Holy Alliance of the Three Monarchies, and continually
being lured back by the fear of revolution into the charmed

circle of the magician at Berlin. Well-informed statesmen were convinced that in 1880 Russia was on the point of returning to the *entente* of 1872, when the assassination of Alexander II. and the confusion caused by a change on the throne and the internal peril to the autocracy, snapped for the time the 'new wire' between Berlin and Petersburg. The opposing schools of policy strove round the person of Alexander III., but it was not until death removed Gortschakov, Skobeleff, and Katkoff, and the Nihilist danger had been comparatively mastered, that Russia and the Tsar had both ears for Bismarck's arguments. Through all the evidence available runs a persistent principle— the desirability of uniting the monarchies on a common basis of resistance to democracy and revolution—the old principles of the historic Holy Alliance in a modern form. Apart from the political considerations underlying a German hegemony of Central Europe, this dynastic unity was a bulwark of the existing social order, and no one felt more strongly than Bismarck that his system at bottom in Germany and without rested on the maintenance of a defined social structure correlated to, and a guarantee of a distribution of political authority and defined political principles. He could and did cordially agree with Alexander III. that the political evolution of France and the ideas underlying the Republic, together with the continuous lapse of Great Britain from aristocratic grace to democracy, constituted a real peril and set up a perpetual antithesis between the Liberal west and the Conservative and Monarchical centre and east. The danger of infection from the west was serious. For all the facts went to prove that the west might inoculate and sap the centre and east, but there was small prospect of the centre and the east curing democratic Great Britain and France of their deplorable heresies. Dual or Triple Alliances were of no avail unless they aimed at ends deeper and more substantial than a nicely and perpetually readjusted political equilibrium. A coalition of ideas and principles could be more fatal to German supremacy than a coalition of fleets or armies. The return, therefore, to a reactionary Conservatism, . . . was partly the reflex, partly the inspiration, of Bismarck's foreign policy.

The disturbing elements in the situation were not confined to

Russia. Europe in 1880 was on the threshold of an era with a very different outlook and ambition. Five other characteristics can be broadly disentangled—the Eastern Question, the problem of the Mediterranean, the renaissance of France, the revived activity and policy of Great Britain, and the colonial movement. Their combination provided the problem for Bismarck, and his exploitation of them makes the history of his foreign policy from 1879 to his fall. . . .

If we may judge from events, everything strengthened his conclusion in 1879 that safety lay in a firm control of Austria-Hungary. He could pivot on the Dual Alliance more securely than on any other nodal, strategic, and diplomatic point. The remarkable analysis at the end of his Memoirs, with all its obvious omissions and veiled allusions, shows how continuously and with what microscopic diligence he watched and weighed every symptom in Austrian policy. Austria was essential to Germany, for if Austria collapsed the Near Eastern Question threatened a catastrophe. The heart of the problem lay therefore in this issue: if it was easier to control Austria than to control Russia —and to secure Russia if Austria had been first secured—to what extent could Germany 'back the Austrian bill'? That Berlin must back the bill drawn at Vienna broadly was clear. But the analysis in the Memoirs and the crisis of 1890 reveal that Bismarck fully recognised very precise limits to the German credit placed behind the Austrian draft, and showed that he was not prepared to support 'an unreasonable Austria' at the price of a complete rupture with Russia. He decided, in effect, that Germany and Austria might at some future date have to part company, under the pressure of events: and the decision brought him into sharp antagonism with the new school of policy which made an Austro-German alliance, *coûte que coûte,* the basis of German policy in the Near East. . . .

The main argument of that school was profoundly influenced by the growing ambition to substitute, also *coûte que coûte,* a German ascendancy at Constantinople (with all its illimitable possibilities) for a Russian, a British, or French ascendancy; or, in other words, the integrity and the revival of the shrinking Ottoman Empire could and ought to be made a primary German interest. The Mayor of the Sultan and the Sublime Porte was to be the German Emperor, in close alliance with Austria. Bismarck between 1879 and 1890 was not prepared to go that length. He recognised that it involved, for all its advantages, an irreconcilable breach with Russia, and a serious antagonism to Great Britain. To the end, while recognising a deepening German interest in Constantinople and Turkey in Europe, he had his eyes on the West and France. The 'Austrian School' at Berlin was really interpreting Centralism in a way that, in Bismarck's view, might imperil not merely Germany's interest in the East but the fundamental basis of German supremacy in Europe. For Bismarck an alliance of Russia and France, and the closing of the breach between Great Britain and Russia, spelled the ruin of a true system of European policy. The younger generation, in short, was distinguishing between Bismarckian Centralism and a *Weltpolitik*. They aspired to make Germany a *Weltmacht*—a World-Empire—and not merely a Continental Power, and they saw the main road winding from Hamburg through Berlin across the Balkans, through a Constantinople controlled by Germany to Mesopotamia and the Persian Gulf, with an entry to the seas not so closely controlled as the routes down the Channel or north of the Shetlands; they also saw it reaching across the Atlantic to the Pacific, expressed in the formula 'ships, colonies, and commerce . . .'

In a more concrete form, the Near Eastern Question from 1879 to 1890 was summed up in the antagonism of Austria and Russia in the Balkans, and in the rivalry between Great Britain and France in Egypt. These two problems brought the Mediterranean into the main diplomatic theatre, and kept it there.

By 1878 the isolation of France was proving exceedingly difficult. The crisis of 1875 had shown that the European Powers would not tolerate a further reduction of France or French power; the International Exhibition of 1878 picturesquely mirrored the remarkable extent of France's recovery from the collapse in 1870. Paris, as in 1867, was still a great, if not the great, *foyer de civilisation,* the attraction of which was inextinguishable. The new France, working so hard to make good the blunders of the Second Empire, would soon be, if she was not already, an ally worth having. But the Germany that had failed to crush her or to isolate her completely, and that must fail to reconcile her because of Alsace and Lorraine, might divert her gathering strength into directions that would involve her in a collision with all the possible allies of the new France. There were three such possible allies—Great Britain, Russia, and Italy. The colonial movement combined with the situation in the Mediterranean to give Bismarck a fine chance of checkmating the *rapprochement* so necessary to France and his diplomacy was equal to it.

After 1879 Colonial questions moved sharply and suddenly into the forefront of European controversy and ambition. Africa and the Pacific kept the chancelleries busy. For Africa was the one great area, of vast extent, and unlimited possibilities, a continent not yet properly explored, and not yet finally allotted to, or occupied by, any great European Power. With 1880 'the scramble for Africa' seriously began, and it behove the Powers that had started late in the foundation of colonies to be quick, or the one fine field left in a limited world would be overrun and mastered by the Powers which had started early, and were already settled at various points on the rim of the Continent. . . .

. . . The diversion, as distinct from the isolation, of France, began in 1878. . . . [It] is tolerably certain that France understood after 1878 that, if she did go to Tunis, Germany and Great Britain would not combine to make the occupation a *casus belli,* or an occasion for a humiliating rebuff. In 1881 France accordingly went to Tunis—with the results that Bismarck at any rate had foreseen and intended. Great Britain was already hard pressed by difficulties in Egypt; her relations with France were becoming strained, and the new Foreign Secretary at London regretted the virtual pledge of his predecessor.

That France should quarrel with Great Britain was just what Bismarck desired, and the causes of quarrel could be extended by judicious diplomacy inflaming further French Colonial ambitions in Africa, in Siam, Cochin-China, and the Pacific. The more that France spent in men or money on colonial expansion, the less she would have for her eastern frontier in Europe; the

more she stared across the seas the less she would be 'hypno-
tised by the gap in the Vosges'; she would not find European
allies by expeditions to the Nile, the Mekong, or the Niger, but
European rivals, whose ambitions would be reflected and
refracted at London, Paris, Rome, Petersburg, Brussels, and the
Hague: colonial policy and colonial failures have, moreover, always been since 1660 a fine dissolvement of ministries in most
European states. French and British ministeries would come to
grief at home because French or British expeditions met with
reverses on the Nile or the Niger: France must therefore be encouraged to suffer a perpetual *angina pectoris,* in which colonial-
ism would be an irritant, very shattering to the Republic.

No less beneficial to Berlin and Central Europe, Tunis and
French Mediterranean ambitions brought France at once into
sharp collision with the sister Latin race in Italy. The kingdom
of Italy desired colonies and a sure grip on the Mediterranean.
The French occupation of Tunis was a bitter blow. How was
France to be prevented from adding Tripoli to Tunis? And if she
had a *condominium* in Egypt, what was there left in the Mediterranean for Italy? An isolated Italy studied the map and the
diplomatic constellations. Her position was becoming desperate.
She could not stand alone. But with whom could she act? A con-
fidential explanation from Berlin of the terms and meaning of
the Dual Alliance of 1879, made one certainty absolutely clear.
'Unredeemed Italy' (*Italia irredenta*)—Trieste and Istria, the
Alpine frontier of the Napoleonic kingdom of Italy of 1810, the
Balkan littoral of the Adriatic were now postponed to the German Kalends. If Italy could not get these from Austria single-
handed, she assuredly could not get them by a war in which
Germany stood behind Austria. The Dual Alliance sponged from
the screen of the future the Italian dream of rounding off the
unification of 1859 and 1866 by the incorporation of unredeemed Italy or securing the Dalmatian coast of the Adriatic.
And the exposed shores of the peninsula were vulnerable to sea-
power and to French sea-power, located at Toulon, Corsica,
Tunis, Bizerta—perhaps Egypt. Given the conditions of 1882, the
accession of Italy to the Dual Alliance was—if the invitation
were held out from Berlin—a foregone conclusion.

On May 20, 1882, Italy's accession turned the Dual into the Triple Alliance. The text of the treaty has never been officially published; but it is certain that in 1882 Italy joined for five years, and that the treaty was renewed in 1887 and at subsequent intervals, with which Bismarck was not concerned. It is practically certain that the three signatory Powers gave a reciprocal guarantee for the integrity of their respective territories, undertook to assist each other in the case of attack by any European Power (*i.e.* France), and (probably by secret conventions) agreed to allot with precision the nature and amount of their respective military contribution to a joint effort. It is practically certain that no guarantee was given to Italy either by Germany or Austria of support in a colonial policy in the Mediterranean or elsewhere, and that Italy was in no way bound to support Balkan or other adventures of Germany or Austria. The maintenance of the existing balance of power in the Mediterranean, or the nature of any future rearrangement of the Mediterranean situation, probably did not fall within the scope of the engagements undertaken in 1882. . . .

To Bismarck the concusion of the Treaty of May 20, 1882, was the culmination of his system. Henceforward German hegemony in Central Europe moved securely on the pivotal point of the Triple Alliance, which gradually and naturally grew into the one grand combination in the European State system, with which all other possible combinations or *ententes* had to reckon. And for Bismarck the accession of Italy had every advantage and no disadvantages. Italy from 1878 to 1882 was in a restless and excited state. She might indeed precipitate a crisis which would upset the carefully poised equilibrium of Europe. Crises that arise from the action of strong States are often not as dangerous as the crises provoked by the recklessness of weak States. Italian policy in 1882 came under the control of the Wilhelmstrasse, and control was stealthily and relentlessly followed by the moral and economic penetration of the German bankers, cartels, syndicates, and commercial travellers. After 1878 the Ottoman Empire was similarly 'penetrated.' How deeply the penetration had pierced in both cases—how enmeshed had become the finance and the springs of trade by German wheels and cogs and 'controls'—Italy and the world learned in 1914. 'Trade followed the alliances, and the alliances followed trade.' . . .

But Bismarck, in concluding the Triple Alliance, was not thinking so much of the Vatican or the British fleet, as of Central Europe and France. The Triple Alliance completed Central Europe; it closed the Alpine passes; it barred the great gate to Vienna through which Napoleon had marched in 1796; it opened the Mediterranean to Germany; it rent away from France the ally of the sister Latin race and made it henceforward necessary for her to keep two of her best corps to guard against invasion through the Maritime Alps. Best of all, it shivered the serious menace of 1869 and 1871. France, Austria and Italy, bound in a common war of revenge, had been a real danger. Austria had been secured as an ally in 1879; Italy was secured in 1882. It would take genius on the one side or bungling on the other to undo the Triple Alliance. Where were now the possible allies of France? Great Britain? Russia?

In 1882, with the bombardment of Alexandria, the rebellion of Arabi, the fall of Gambetta (January 26), and the Anglo-Egyptian Campaign, war was more likely than an alliance between France and Great Britain. The Triple Alliance, in fact, largely undid the benefits to France of the benevolent hint to take Tunis and to take it at once. In the future Italy's claims in the Mediterranean might be much more serious, if Berlin found it convenient to give them 'moral' support. Bismarck's 'moral' support was unlike that of most European Powers. It was only given because he had decided that, if need be, behind it lay 'the immoral' support of German force. . . .

III

Perceiving and Redressing an Imbalance of Power

In 1823, when President Monroe unilaterally announced a "Monroe Doctrine" for the Americas, the British foreign secretary Canning proudly boasted in Parliament that he had "called the New World into existence to redress the balance of the Old." In actuality, American power never was employed to redress the European balance until the first World War; Canning thus was nearly a century premature in his remark. A more modest and accurate claim would have been that henceforth Britain and America would act in parallel policies to prevent other European states from extending their influence in the Americas.

As used by statesmen, the idea of balance and balancing is as loosely employed as any other political concept of such generality. In this instance, Canning was less concerned to re-establish an equilibrium in the Old World than to acquire what Mr. Dean Acheson much later was to call a "comfortable surplus of power" in the New. Yet the idea of redressing an imbalance of power by conscious strategy is an important one.

66

Statesmen, politicians and political writers spend much of their time attempting to discern shifts in the distribution of power and influence among states and within their own. Such conclusions as they make, whether prophetic or faulty, may be grounds for highly significant action. It makes a great deal of difference whether one acts on the assumption that the distribution of power and influence in society is essentially unchanged, or whether it is changing favorably or unfavorably to one's nation. Hitler's eagerness to launch an aggressive campaign to dominate Europe in the late 1930's sprang in part from his belief that time was not on Germany's side; delay would lessen chance of success. So also, in 1941, Japanese political and military leaders made their fateful decision to attack Pearl Harbor, knowing full well the superiority of American power in an ensuing war, yet believing also that delay would permit the imbalance of power to become even more unfavorable, to their plans for a new order in Asia.

The following selections—both memoranda and political essays—are presented to show the kinds of intellectual speculation which political leaders and thinkers may make about a condition of present or incipient imbalance of power in international politics.

8. THE UNITED STATES AND ANGLO-GERMAN RIVALRY *

In 1913, when this essay appeared, Europe enjoyed its last year of peace, and America experienced the 100th anniversary of its last involvement in European conflict, the Napoleonic wars. But the post-Napoleonic equilibrium established by Metternich, Castlereagh and Alexander had long since vanished. The Vienna "system" of 1815 had had two principal objects—to enable Europe as a whole peaceably to coexist with a still-powerful France, and to enable Europe also to maintain its existing social structure and its conservative political institutions. By 1913, this equilibrium which some had called the "Concert of Europe," had been replaced by two rival alliance systems, the Triple Alliance and the Triple Entente. Imperial Germany, not Republican France, was the principal threat to Europe's international stability. Domestically, Socialist and nationalist-chauvinist movements such as Pan-Slavism and Pan-Germanism had replaced the liberal, constitutional movements of Metternich's time as disrupters of the internal equilibrium of all major European states.

These two features of European politics, so ominous in themselves, were not the direct concern of David Einstein, author of the following essay. An American foreign-service officer, Einstein foresaw threats to an equilibrium which, seen from America, was of much larger scope than the European Continent alone. For German power, reaching out beyond Europe, now directly challenged a global politicoeconomic system in which Britain had long been supreme. A future war between these two great powers, resulting perhaps in British defeat, would wreck the fortunate global environment which had surrounded America for more than a century. The Monroe Doctrine and British sea power together had permitted America, in isolation from Europe, to pursue its destiny virtually unimpeded in the Western Hemisphere and in the Pacific basin. To Einstein, America's objective interest was to see that such a German victory did not

---

* D. L. Einstein, "The United States and Anglo-German Rivalry," *The National Review*, Jan. 1913, pp. 736–750.

come about; American power should be employed to maintain
or redress an equilibrium which no longer was an affair of Con-
tinental Europe alone, but was worldwide.

D. L. EINSTEIN

. . . The European balance of power has been such a permanent factor since the birth of the republic that Americans have
never realised how its absence would have affected their political status. The national existence was first brought about by
European dissension. When Pitt resisted Napoleon, the justi-
fiable irritation felt against British high-handedness at sea caused
Americans to forget that England's fight was in reality their own,
and that the undisputed master of Europe would not have been
long in finding pretexts to reacquire the Louisiana territory
which, except for England, he would never have relinquished.
When the Holy Alliance endeavoured to concentrate the power
of Europe under the banner of legitimacy and divine right,
Canning, by inspiring the Monroe Doctrine, interposed an
effective restraint in the Western Hemisphere, and in the often-
quoted phrase, "called in the New World to redress the balance
of the Old."

Fifty years later, had England joined France in recognising
the Confederacy or in her abortive Mexican adventure, the history of the United States might have run a different course.
At no time since the foundation of the Republic could a change
materially altering the ancient European balance of power have
been brought about without perceptibly affecting American interests and the position of the United States. Even to-day, in
spite of the enormous increase in the country's resources and
population, this political axiom holds as true as it did in the
period of national formation and weakness. The undisputed para-
mountcy of any nation, both by land and sea, must inevitably
make that Power a menace and a peril to every other country.
In the words of a distinguished Secretary of State, Mr. Olney,
were the career of a Napoleon ever again to approach or even to
threaten repetition, not merely sentiment and sympathy, but the
strongest consideration of self-preservation and self-defence might

compel the United States to take sides. It may therefore be of
interest to survey the forces of war and peace to-day at work in
Europe and see if there lies any menace to that balance of
power, the preservation of which is essential to its national
security. . . .

. . . A wave of renewed militarism and nationalism has
spread over Europe. France, where it had lain dormant for
years, is now witnessing an intense revival provoked by the
recent difficulties with Germany over Morocco, and excited by its
splendid success in aviation. In Russia the painful awakening
after the Manchurian War, has led to a reorganised Army and
the construction of a new Navy. In Austria-Hungary the difficulties attending the late annexation prompted a military reform, while gratitude to Germany for the assistance rendered
during that crisis, has led to an extensive battleship programme
and awakened for the first time naval ambition. Italy again,
whatever be the future of her newly designed African Empire,
realises that she has condemned herself during many years to
come to a vastly increased expenditure for armaments._

The sources of European unrest could, however, be more
lightly dismissed without the antagonism between Great Britain
and Germany. In spite of the attempts made on both sides to
explain it away, and to dwell on the pacific disposition animat-
ing the construction of new "Dreadnaughts," this remains as an
irreducible fact obscuring the political horizon. Nor should it be
regarded as a mere contest for commercial supremacy on the
part of two countries, one seeking to preserve, the other to gain
new markets. Intelligent Germans are the first to recognise that
neither their merchants nor their trade suffer in British Colonies.
Beneath it lies the deeply conscious rival ambition of two great
nations, the one to maintain undiminished the heritage conquered
by its forebears, the other to obtain the place "under the sun"
which it regards as its right. And the magnitude of this issue
is enhanced by the hardly lesser constellations gravitating around
the rivals, each with its own historic traditions and interests, but
who have realised comparative security in a system which finds
its political expression in the series of alliances and understandings forming the balance of modern Europe. . . .

. . . But there is serious danger lest in an atmosphere as surcharged as is the present, with the deep-rooted feeling of hostility existing on both sides, some petty cause of friction, or some paltry colonial quarrel, inflaming public opinion, should induce either Government to prefer a foreign contest which it might regard as inevitable to domestic humiliation. . . .

Whatever be the future of this situation a far-sighted statesmanship compels the United States, as it does every other nation, to take cognisance of the possibility of a conflict breaking out in the near future between Great Britain and Germany, and to consider in what manner its interests would be affected. It is an easy remedy to repeat the old adage about American proverbial non-interference in European affairs. With all respect toward a policy which in the past has been thoroughly sound, it cannot be said in this instance to offer a complete panacea. A struggle between the two nations, even though it did not set ablaze the rest of Europe, cannot leave America indifferent. In too many regions of the world would its interests be affected by such reality.

It would withal be absurd to deduce from this, that the United States would be dragged into a war against all inclination. The alternative of arms is no necessary consequence of diplomatic interest, and in such a conflict direct participation would with proper precautions be most unlikely. This should not, however, excuse any neglect on the part of Americans to consider the various political, strategic, and economic points of view in different regions of the world, where such struggle would react upon them, or how the balance of power, which it should be the policy of the United States to preserve in Europe, would be affected by the contest. An indication of its wide-reaching nature independent of the actual field of hostilities, would, for instance, be presented in the Far East, where the even temporary withdrawal of European influence would leave America face to face with a commensurately more powerful Japan. To say nothing of the Philippines the situation thus created depends on the degree of stability and strength attained by China. It is not difficult, however, to conceive of circumstances where to ensure respect for the often pledged integrity of that State would lead the United States toward a course of action which it would be obliged to adopt single-handed, and without the benefit of such diplomatic support as in the past it has received from friendly Powers.

Omitting from consideration the extent to which the almost inevitable conflagration would affect the world in a conflict between Great Britain and Germany, three general possibilities are open: (1) The victory of the former; (2) The reverse; (3) A war of indefinite result.

So far as America is concerned, the first alternative would be the least likely to materially alter the existing status. England might conceivably recover a pecuniary indemnity and deal a death-blow to German oversea commerce. But the German Colonies are not such as to sensibly attract a conqueror, nor would a change in their title affect other nations in any way. While the predominant position of Germany upon the European Continent would be shattered, the balance of power would hardly be affected, even though the disposition of its weight were altered. The insular position of Great Britain debars her from continental ambitions, and any attempt to assert herself in such manner would both run counter to all her traditions and be stoutly resisted by former allied States. It is fortunate that in modern times no nation has succeeded in being paramount on both land and sea. Great Britain has hitherto refrained from unduly developing her military strength and there is no reason to anticipate that flushed by victory she would adopt a different course. Her naval superiority, which is a matter of life and death, menaces no one though it bars the way to Germany already supreme on land. But for America it represents an essential element in the maintenance and stability of the European balance of power.

If the terms of peace after such a war were to be dictated in London, the situation as it affected the United States would be radically reversed. While defeat for Germany might prove disastrous to the dynasty, for Great Britain it would be fatal to the Empire whose disintegration would almost inevitably ensue. It is apparent that the fate of Canada and the British possessions in

America immediately concern the Republic. Of Canadian loyalty
to the Empire there is here no question. It is certain that like the
other self-governing British Colonies, she would to the best of
her ability support the Mother Country. But if the fortune of
war prove adverse, there is no reason to suppose that Canada
would long continue under the control, however nominal, of a
parent State deprived of prestige and authority, and ruined by
an unsuccessful war. . . .

Without going to the length of such extreme conclusions, a
. . . more likely possibility would be that of a contest long
drawn out between the two countries wherein neither could obtain decisive advantage. In spite of the paper proof that a lengthy
war presents to-day an economic impossibility there is no practical evidence to substantiate this theory, and there are distinguished economists who believe that the modern system of
credit is peculiarly adopted to facilitate the prolongation of war.
When poor countries, like Japan and Russia, have been able to
maintain in the field for a considerable duration armies of
almost unprecedented size, there is no reason to suppose that
the pinch of poverty alone would materially hasten the conclusion of a contest between England and Germany. The financial
aspect of this is also likely to concern America. If the struggle
should be protracted, extensive borrowing will have to be undertaken, and New York is more and more becoming one of the
money markets of the world. It is probable that it will be called
upon, possibly by both sides, to furnish pecuniary assistance,
even though the obligations of strict neutrality are somewhat
questionable on this point. . . .

An Anglo-German conflict would . . . affect the United States
at various points and in various ways. There is hardly a branch
of American national activity, governmental or economic, which
would not feel its consequences in varying degree or be concerned by its outcome. While the American attitude in such
contest would in the beginning be one of strict neutrality, which
would be maintained as long as possible, this does not mean that
a far-sighted policy might not under certain contingencies impose
a different course of action. However considerable the respon-

sibility incurred, however great the bait offered, it would hardly be wise statesmanship to remain passive if England should by any series of disasters be crushed. Even though the immediate consequence would be to throw Canada and the British Antilles into the lap of the United States, it would leave the latter confronted by an Empire supreme on land and sea, and would force it to pursue a preparation of armaments which for its own preservation could not be inferior to what it might be called upon to face. Unperceived by many Americans, the European balance of power is a political necessity which can alone sanction on the Western Hemisphere the continuance of an economic development unhandicapped by the burden of extensive armaments. At no time, even unknown to the United States, were European politics a matter of indifference to its vital interests. But if hitherto it was impotent to alter their march, a fortunate destiny preserved the existing balance.

Seeking, as little as in the past, any selfish benefit in the Old World, even though it were possible, America has to-day a distinct and legitimate duty in the family of great nations in contributing to preserve those elements which compose the balance of power, and to which it can only be blind at a later cost. The disappearance or diminution of any one State in Europe would be a calamity, varying with its degree. But while the importance of such extinction might not in most instances be sufficiently close to warrant or provoke active intervention, this would not be true with Great Britain. The disintegration of the British Empire would be a defeat for America by the erection of a Power supreme on land and sea. . . .

. . . Great Britain, by upholding the European balance of power, has contributed toward American development. If misfortune in arms await her it would be as politically unwise as it would be ungenerous to allow her to suffer unduly. A disastrous defeat inflicted by an opponent unwilling to use moderation in his victory should invite on the part of America a friendly mediation which in the last extremity might have to be converted into more effective measures. Hence the advisability for the United States of preserving its strength in such a way as ever to make its counsel welcome and its action unnecessary.

9. NOTES ON REICHSCHANCELLERY CONFERENCE, NOVEMBER 10, 1937 *

Hitler and the Nazi movement, seizing power in 1933, were pledged to smash the brittle political equilibrium of Europe established by the victorious Allies at Versailles in 1919. Germany, once free from these shackles, would rearm and then proceed to redraw the map of Europe; the Third Reich would expand territorially into Eastern Europe, incorporating ethnically Germanic areas into a Greater Germany and establishing German control over the Slavic nations further East. An economically self-sufficient New Order, unchecked by any countervailing power would thenceforth dominate the European continent.

In 1933 this pledge had been programmatic and lacking in necessary power. German military strength still was severely limited by the Versailles Treaty. Hitler's Germany, situated in the heart of the Continent, inherited the classic strategic problem of Frederick the Great and Bismarck: the threat of military encirclement and the nightmare of a two-front war. Yet by 1937 the strategic picture for Nazi Germany seemed vastly improved; Hitler, reoccupying the Rhineland in 1936 and repudiating the disarmament provisions of the Treaty, commenced with impunity a series of defiant acts which culminated in aggressive war in 1939. In 1937—the year in which the following document was written—the Western powers and Soviet Russia, while remonstrating against these actions, were still unable and unwilling to use force in concert to check Germany's expansion.

Yet Hitler, as the following selection dramatically shows, sensed that the strategic opportunity presented Germany by Western weakness of purpose and power was at best temporary. Time was not on Germany's side; the projected demographic, economic and military potential of non-German Europe was far greater than that of the Third Reich; a distribution of power now favorable to Germany would probably be reversed by 1943. For this reason it was necessary to plan for major war before that date, if Hitler's goals were to be attained.

---

* Hossbach Memorandum, International Military Tribunal, *Trial of Major War Criminals*, Vol. II, pp. 262–273.

The Hossbach memorandum, so named after the rapporteur at the conference where Hitler discussed these problems with his generals in November 1937, classically illustrates one mode of response to an unfavorably changing balance of power: that of planning to strike before the situation becomes even more unfavorable. The text is as it was read into the record of the International Military Tribunal on November 26, 1945.

ADOLF HITLER

One of the most striking and revealing of all the captured documents which have come to hand is a document which we have come to know as the Hossbach notes of a conference in the Reich Chancellery on 5 November 1937 from 1615 to 2030 hours, in the course of which Hitler outlined to those present the possibilities and necessities of expanding their foreign policy, and requested—I quote: "That his statements be looked upon in the case of his death as his last will and testament." And so with this document we shall present to the Tribunal and to the public the last will and testament of Adolf Hitler as he contemplated that last will and testament on 5 November 1937. The document comes to hand through the United States Department of State and it is authenticated by the seal of the Secretary of State of the United States. It is Document Number 386-PS in our series of numbered documents. I offer it in evidence as Exhibit USA-25.

Before reading it, I note at the start that the recorder of the minutes of this meeting, then Colonel Hossbach, was the Führer's adjutant. I note also the presence at this conspiratorial meeting of the Defendant Erich Raeder. The Defendant Constantin von Neurath was present. The Defendant Hermann Wilhelm Göring was present. The minutes of this meeting reveal a crystalization towards the end of 1937 in the policy of the Nazi regime. Austria and Czechoslovakia were to be acquired by force. They would provide Lebensraum (living space) and improve Germany's military position for further operations. While it is true that actual events unfolded themselves in a somewhat different manner than that outlined at this meeting, in essence the purposes stated at the meeting were carried out. The document destroys any possible doubt concerning the Nazis' premeditation of their Crimes against Peace. This document is of such tremendous importance that I feel obliged to read it in full into the record:

"Berlin, 10 November 1937. Notes on the conference in the

Reichskanzlei on 5 November 1937 from 1615 to 2030 hours.

"Present: The Führer and Reich Chancellor; the Reich Minister for War, Generalfeldmarschall Von Blomberg; the C-in-C Army, Generaloberst Freiherr Von Fritsch; the C-in-C Navy, Generaladmiral Dr. H. C. Raeder; the C-in-C Luftwaffe, Generaloberst Göring; the Reichsminister for Foreign Affairs, Freiherr Von Neurath; Oberst Hossbach" (the adjutant who took the minutes).

"The Führer stated initially that the subject matter of today's conference was of such high importance that its detailed discussion would certainly in other states take place before the Cabinet in full session. However, he, the Führer, had decided not to discuss this matter in the larger circle of the Reich Cabinet, because of its importance. His subsequent statements were the result of detailed deliberations and of the experiences of his 4½ years in government; he desired to explain to those present his fundamental ideas on the possibilities and necessities of expanding our foreign policy, and in the interests of a far-sighted policy he requested that his statements be looked upon, in the case of his death, as his last will and testament.

"The Führer then stated: The aim of German policy is the security and the preservation of the nation and its propagation. This is consequently a problem of space. The German nation comprises 85 million people, which, because of the number of individuals and the compactness of habitation, form a homogeneous European racial body, the like of which cannot be found in any other country. On the other hand it justifies the demand for larger living space more than for any other nation. If there have been no political consequences to meet the demands of this racial body for living space, then that is the result of historical development spread over several centuries and should this political condition continue to exist, it will represent the greatest danger to the preservation of the German nation"— The German word used there, is not "nation"; it is "Volkstum" —"at its present high level. An arrest of the decrease of the German element in Austria and in Czechoslovakia is just as little possible as the preservation of the present state in Germany itself."

I interpolate that I can but think that this is not a good translation of the German because to me the sentence seems meaningless.

"Instead of growth, sterility will be introduced, and as a consequence, tensions of a social nature will appear after a number of years, because political and philosophical ideas are of a permanent nature only as long as they are able to produce the basis for the realization of the actual claim of the existence of a nation. The German future is therefore dependent exclusively on the solution of the need for living space. Such a solution can be sought naturally only for a limited period, about one to three generations.

"Before touching upon the question of solving the need for living space, it must be decided whether a solution of the German position with a good future can be attained, either by way of an autarchy or by way of an increased share in universal commerce and industry.

"Autarchy: Execution will be possible only with strict National Socialist State policy, which is the basis"—that is the basis of autarchy—"Assuming this can be achieved the results are as follows:

"A. In the sphere of raw materials, only limited, but not total autarchy can be attained:

"1. Wherever coal can be used for the extraction of raw materials, autarchy is feasible.

"2. In the case of ores the position is much more difficult. Requirements in iron and light metals can be covered by ourselves. Copper and tin, however, cannot.

"3. Cellular materials can be covered by ourselves as long as sufficient wood supplies exist. A permanent solution is not possible.

"4. Edible fats—possible.

"B. In the case of foods, the question of an autarchy must be answered with a definite capital NO.

"The general increase of living standards, compared with 30 to 40 years ago, brought about a simultaneous increase of the demand and an increase of personal consumption among the producers, the farmers themselves. The proceeds from the production increase in agriculture have been used for covering the increased demand, therefore they represent no actual increase in production. A further increase in production by making greater demands on the soil is not possible because it already shows signs of deterioration due to the use of artificial fertilizers, and it is therefore certain that, even with the greatest possible increase in production, participation in the world market could not be avoided."

I interpolate, that if I understand him he means by that, "no autarchy; we must participate in world trade and commerce."

"The considerable expenditure of foreign currency to secure food by import, even in periods when harvests are good, increases catastrophically when the harvest is really poor. The possibility of this catastrophe increases correspondingly to the increase in population, and the annual 560,000 excess in births would bring about an increased consumption in bread, because the child is a greater bread eater than the adult.

"Permanently to counter the difficulties of food supplies by lowering the standard of living and by rationalization is impossible in a continent which has developed an approximately equivalent standard of living. As the solving of the unemployment problem has brought into effect the complete power of consumption, some small corrections in our agricultural home production will be possible, but not a wholesale alteration of the standard of food consumption. Consequently autarchy becomes impossible, specifically in the sphere of food supplies, as well as generally.

"Participation in world economy: There are limits to this which we are unable to transgress. The market fluctuation would be an obstacle to a secure foundation of the German position; international commercial agreements do not offer any guarantee for practical execution. It must be considered on principle that since the World War (1914–18) an industrialization has taken place in countries which formerly exported food. We live in a period of economic empires, in which the tendency to colonies, again approaches the condition which originally motivated colonization; in Japan and Italy economic motives are the basis of their will to expand, and economic need will also drive Germany to it. Countries outside the great economic empires have special difficulties in expanding economically.

"The upward tendency, which has been caused in world economy, due to armament competition, can never form a permanent basis for an economic settlement, and this latter is also hampered by the economic disruption caused by Bolshevism. There is a pronounced military weakness in those states which base their existence on export. As our exports and imports are carried out over those sea lanes which are dominated by Britain, it is more a question of security of transport rather than one of foreign currency and this explains the great weakness of our food situation in wartime. The only way out, and one which may appear imaginary, is the securing of greater living space, an endeavor which at all times has been the cause of the formation of states and of movements of nations. It is explicable that this tendency finds no interest in Geneva and in satisfied states. Should the security of our food situation be our foremost thought, then the space required for this can only be sought in Europe, but we will not copy liberal capitalistic policies which rely on exploiting colonies. It is not a case of conquering people, but of conquering agriculturally useful space. It would also be more to the purpose to seek raw material-producing territory in Europe directly adjoining the Reich and not overseas, and this solution would have to be brought into effect for one or two generations. What would be required at a later date over and above this must be left to subsequent generations. The development of great worldwide national bodies is naturally a slow process and the German people, with its strong racial root"—I interpolate, there is that German word "Rassekern" again (the racial root)—"has for this purpose the most favorable foundations in the heart of the European continent. The history of all times—Roman Empire, British Empire—has proved that every space expansion can only be effected by breaking resistance and taking risks. Even setbacks are unavoidable; neither formerly nor today has space been found without an owner; the attacker always comes up against the proprietor."

[*A recess was taken.*] MR. ALDERMAN: May it please the Tribunal, after the somewhat jumbled discussion which I have just read of geopolitical economic theory and of the need for expansion and Lebensraum, Adolf Hitler, in these Hossbach notes, posed this question—and I quote:

"The question for Germany is where the greatest possible conquest could be made at lowest cost.

"German politics must reckon with its two hateful enemies, England and France, to whom a strong German colossus in the center of Europe would be intolerable. Both these states would oppose a further reinforcement of Germany, both in Europe and overseas, and in this opposition they would have the support of all parties. Both countries would view the building of German military strong points overseas as a threat to their overseas communications, as a security measure for German commerce, and retroactively a strengthening of the German position in Europe.

"England is not in a position to cede any of her colonial possessions to us, owing to the resistance which she experiences in the Dominions. After the loss of prestige which England has suffered owing to the transfer of Abyssinia to Italian ownership, a return of East Africa can no longer be expected. Any resistance on England's part would at best consist in the readiness to satisfy our colonial claims by taking away colonies which at the present moment are not in British hands, for example, Angola. French favors would probably be of the same nature.

"A serious discussion regarding the return of colonies to us could be considered only at a time when England is in a state of emergency and the German Reich is strong and well armed. The Führer does not share the opinion that the Empire is unshakeable."—Meaning, I take it, the British Empire.—

"Resistance against the Empire is to be found less in conquered territories than amongst its competitors. The British Empire and the Roman Empire cannot be compared with one another in regard to durability; after the Punic Wars the latter did not have a serious political enemy. Only the dissolving effects which originated in Christendom, and the signs of age which creep into all states, made it possible for the ancient Germans to subjugate ancient Rome.

"Alongside the British Empire today a number of states exist which are stronger than it. The British mother country is able to defend its colonial possession only allied with other states and not by its own power. How could England alone, for example, defend Canada against attack by America, or its Far Eastern interests against an attack by Japan?

"The singling out of the British Crown as the bearer of Empire unity is in itself an admission that the universal empire cannot be maintained permanently by power politics. The following are significant pointers in this respect:

"(a) Ireland's struggle for independence.

"(b) Constitutional disputes in India where England, by her half measures, left the door open for Indians, at a later date, to utilize the non-fulfilment of constitutional promises as a weapon against Britain.

"(c) The weakening of the British position in the Far East by Japan.

"(d) The opposition in the Mediterranean to Italy which—by virtue of its history, driven by necessity and led by a genius —expands its power position and must consequently infringe British interests to an increasing extent. The outcome of the Abyssinian war is a loss of prestige for Britain which Italy is endeavoring to increase by stirring up discontent in the Mohammedan world.

"It must be established in conclusion that the Empire cannot be held permanently by power politics by 45 million Britons, in spite of all the solidity of their ideals. The proportion of the populations in the Empire, compared with that of the motherland, is nine to one, and it should act as a warning to us that if we expand in space, we must not allow the level of our population to become too low."

I take it he meant by that: "Keep the population of occupied territories low in comparison with ours."

"France's position is more favorable than that of England. The French Empire is better placed geographically; the population of its colonial possessions represents a potential military increase. But France is faced with difficulties of internal politics. In the life of the nations, parliamentary governments ruled only 10 per cent of the time, approximately; whereas, totalitarian governments ruled 90 per cent of the time. Nevertheless, we have to take the following into our political consideration as power factors:

"Britain, France, Russia, and the adjoining smaller states.

"The German question can be solved only by way of force, and this is never without risk. The battles of Frederick the Great for Silesia, and Bismarck's wars against Austria and France had been a tremendous risk and the speed of Prussian action in 1870 had prevented Austria from participating in the war. If we place the decision to apply force with risk at the head of the following expositions, then we are left to reply to the questions 'when' and 'how'. In this regard we have to decide upon three different cases."

I interpolate: The Tribunal will recall the specific allegation in the Indictment that at this meeting there emerged three different plans, any of which might be utilized.

"Case 1. Period 1943–45: After this we can only expect a change for the worse. The rearming of the Army, the Navy, and the Air Force, as well as the formation of the Officers' Corps, are practically concluded."

I remind the Tribunal that this meeting was on 5 November 1937, but he is contemplating the period 1943–45.

"Our material equipment and armaments are modern; with further delay the danger of their becoming out-of-date will increase. In particular, the secrecy of 'special weapons' cannot always be safeguarded. Enlistment of reserves would be limited to the current recruiting age groups and an addition from older untrained groups would be no longer available.

"In comparison with the rearmament, which will have been carried out at that time by other nations, we shall decrease in relative power. Should we not act until 1943–45, then, dependent on the absence of reserves, any year could bring about the food crisis, for the countering of which we do not possess the necessary foreign currency. This must be considered a point of weakness in the regime. Over and above that, the world will anticipate our action and will increase counter-measures yearly. Whilst other nations isolate themselves, we should be forced on the offensive.

"What the actual position would be in the years 1943–45, no one knows today. It is certain, however, that we can wait no longer.

"On the one side the large armed forces, with the necessity for securing their upkeep, the aging of the Nazi movement and of its leaders, and on the other side the prospect of a lowering of the standard of living and a drop in the birth rate, leaves us no other choice but to act. If the Führer is still living, then it will be his irrevocable decision to solve the German space problem no later than 1943-45. The necessity for action before 1943-45 will come under consideration in cases 2 and 3.

"Case 2.   Should the social tensions in France lead to an internal political crisis of such dimensions that it absorbs the French Army and thus renders it incapable for employment in war against Germany, then the time for action against Czechoslovakia has come.

"Case 3.   It would be equally possible to act against Czechoslovakia if France should be so tied up by a war against another state that it cannot proceed against Germany.

"For the improvement of our military political position it must be our first aim, in every case of entanglement by war, to conquer Czechoslovakia and Austria, simultaneously, in order to remove any threat from the flanks in case of a possible advance westwards. In the case of a conflict with France it would hardly be necessary to assume that Czechoslovakia would declare war on the same day as France. However, Czechoslovakia's desire to participate in the war will increase proportionally to the degree to which we are being weakened. Its actual participation could make itself felt by an attack on Silesia, either towards the north or the west.

"Once Czechoslovakia is conquered—and a mutual frontier, Germany-Hungary is obtained—then a neutral attitude by Poland in a German-French conflict could more easily be relied upon. Our agreements with Poland remain valid only as long as

Germany's strength remains unshakable; should Germany have any setbacks then an attack by Poland against East Prussia, perhaps also against Pomerania, and Silesia, must be taken into account.

"Assuming a development of the situation, which would lead to a planned attack on our part in the years 1943–45, then the behavior of France, England, Poland, and Russia would probably have to be judged in the following manner:

"The Führer believes personally, that in all probability England and perhaps also France, have already silently written off Czechoslovakia, and that they have got used to the idea that this question would one day be cleaned up by Germany. The difficulties in the British Empire and the prospect of being entangled in another long, drawn-out European war, would be decisive factors in the non-participation of England in a war against Germany. The British attitude would certainly not remain without influence on France's attitude. An attack by France, without British support, is hardly probable, assuming that its offensive would stagnate along our western fortifications. Without England's support it would also not be necessary to take into consideration a march by France through Belgium and Holland, and this would also not have to be reckoned with by us in case of a conflict with France, as in every case it would have, as a consequence, the enmity of Great Britain. Naturally, we should in every case have to bar our frontier during the operation of our attacks against Czechoslovakia and Austria. It must be taken into consideration here that Czechoslovakia's defense measures will increase in strength from year to year and that a consolidation of the inside values of the Austrian Army will also be effected in the course of years. Although the population of Czechoslovakia in the first place is not a thin one, the embodiment of Czechoslovakia and Austria would nevertheless constitute the conquest of food for 5 to 6 million people, on the basis that a compulsory emigration of 2 million from Czechoslovakia, and of 1 million from Austria could be carried out. The annexation of the two States to Germany, militarily and politically, would constitute a considerable relief, owing to shorter and better frontiers, the freeing of fighting personnel for other purposes, and the possibility of reconstituting new armies up to a strength of about 12 divisions, representing a new division per 1 million population.

"No opposition to the removal of Czechoslovakia is expected on the part of Italy; however, it cannot be judged today what would be her attitude in the Austrian question, since it would depend largely on whether the Duce were alive at the time or not.

"The measure and speed of our action would decide Poland's attitude. Poland will have little inclination to enter the war against a victorious Germany, with Russia in the rear.

"Military participation by Russia must be countered by the speed of our operations; it is a question whether this needs to be taken into consideration at all, in view of Japan's attitude.

"Should case 2 occur—paralyzation of France by a civil war—then the situation should be utilized at any time for operations against Czechoslovakia, as Germany's most dangerous enemy would be eliminated.

"The Führer sees case 3 looming nearer; it could develop from the existing tensions in the Mediterranean, and should it occur, he has firmly decided to make use of it any time, perhaps even as early as 1938.

"Following recent experiences in the course of the events of the war in Spain, the Führer does not see an early end to hostilities there.

"Taking into consideration the time required for past offensives by Franco,"—the English text says "France"; it means "Franco"—"a further 3 years' duration of war is within the bounds of possibility. On the other hand, from the German point of view, a 100 per cent victory by Franco is not desirable; we are more interested in a continuation of the war and preservation of the tensions in the Mediterranean. Should Franco be in sole possession of the Spanish peninsula, it would mean the end of Italian intervention and of the presence of Italy in the Balearic Isles. As our interests are directed towards continuing the war in Spain, it must be the task of our future policy to strengthen Italy in her fight to hold on to the Balearic Isles. However, a solidification of Italian positions in the Balearic Isles cannot be tolerated either by France or by England and could lead to a war by France and England against Italy, in which case Spain, if entirely in White (that is, Franco's) hands, could participate on the side of Italy's enemies. A subjugation of Italy in such a war appears very unlikely. Additional raw materials could be brought to Italy via Germany. The Führer believes that Italy's military strategy would be to remain on the defensive against France on the western frontier and carry out operations against France from Libya, against the North African French colonial possessions.

"As a landing of French and British troops on the Italian coast can be discounted, and as a French offensive via the Alps to upper Italy would be extremely difficult, and would probably stagnate before the strong Italian fortifications, French lines of communication by the Italian fleet will, to a great extent, paralyze the transport of fighting personnel from North Africa to France, so that at its frontiers with Italy and Germany, France will have at its disposal solely the metropolitan fighting forces."

There again I think that must be a defective English translation. "French lines of communication by the Italian fleet," must mean "fresh lines," or something in that connection.

"If Germany profits from this war by disposing of the Czecho-slovakian and the Austrian questions, the probability must be assumed that England, being at war with Italy, would not decide to commence operations against Germany. Without British support, a warlike action by France against Germany is not to be anticipated.

"The date of our attack on Czechoslovakia and Austria must be made depending upon the course of the Italian-French-English war and would not be simultaneous with the commencement of military operations by these three States. The Führer, was also not thinking of military agreements with Italy, but in complete independence and by exploiting this unique favorable opportunity, he wishes to begin to carry out operations against Czechoslovakia. The attack on Czechoslovakia would have to take place with the speed of lighting."—The German words are "blitzartig schnell." . . .

10. SOVIET EXPANSION
THE END OF AN ILLUSION*

After Russia and America entered the war against Nazi Germany in 1941, covert Anglo-American fears of a separate peace between Stalin and Hitler were amply reciprocated by Stalin, who, distrusting the Western powers' motives in delaying a second front on the Continent, feared especially that for political reasons they would welcome a war to the death in the East between Russia and Germany. Such mutual distrust, however, was coupled with a common fear of German power; and for this reason, Allied unity in the European theater came to rest on one goal and doctrine: the total defeat and unconditional surrender of Nazi Germany. This policy, pressed in 1942 by President Roosevelt, was reluctantly accepted by Churchill at the Casablanca Conference; for the Western powers at least, it meant that the respective military advances made by each element of the wartime coalition on both Western and Eastern fronts, aimed at Germany's defeat, would establish in an otherwise nonpolitical manner the equations of power and politics in postwar Europe.

Perhaps because of this "win-the-war" doctrine, few Westerners—even those with misgivings about Soviet aspirations—publicly speculated at the time about the aftereffects of Germany's disappearance as a European power, and especially about the political effects of Soviet military penetration of Eastern and Central Europe. To do so then, so it was argued, would only strengthen the cause of Nazi Germany, the common enemy.

The following essay is by a disillusioned German ex-Communist and Comintern agent and is an exception to this general rule of silence. Written by Arthur Koestler in 1943, it was published in his The Yogi and the Commissar. *It anticipates*

---

* Arthur Koestler, *The Yogi and the Commissar*, pp. 202–217. New York: The Macmillan Company, 1944.

*with candor and surprising accuracy the future geographic lo-
cation of the postwar Iron Curtain between the West and Communist Eastern Europe, and also the political effects of the
ensuing disequilibrium of power between Russia and a shattered
Western Europe.*

ARTHUR KOESTLER

The Perspective of Soviet Expansion

1

Before the war, the European field was dominated by the
triangle: Great Britain—Germany—Russia. Each of the three
protagonists tried to manoeuvre in such a way as to split the
other two and, in case of war, to remain the laughing third.

If we abstain from wishful thinking and look into the future
beyond the short period of elations and illusions which victory
will bring, we see a similar triangle on a larger scale design itself:
the triangle Britain—U.S.A.—U.S.S.R. Already the tensions
along the three sides make themselves felt: economic and financial tensions across the Atlantic, political across the Pacific
and along the Arctic; political and territorial across Europe and
the Middle East.

Of the three powers, Britain will obviously be on the defensive, intent, in Churchill's words, to "hold what we have." To
neutralise the centrifugal tendencies within the Empire, the ties
with the Dominions will probably have to become even more
elastic and the Colonies will have to be given more rope. This
inevitable loosening of the Empire's texture will invite pressure
on the more vulnerable points by her competitors. Among
these, the United States will be mainly interested in economic
expansion and in securing strategical bases on nodal points. The
second tendency need not lead to conflict with Great Britain,
as the United States does not seek new living spaces but rather
a series of strategic footholds. Economic competition, however,
will probably prevent the formation of a really stable Anglo-
Saxon bloc and give the third partner ample scope for triangular
manoeuvring.

Russia, among the three, represents the most vigorous expansive force. As a world power it arrives on the stage young and full of ruthless dynamism. With its nationalised economy, centralised power, and totalitarian methods, the U.S.S.R. presents an aspect of massive compactness compared with the loosely knit, extended and decentralised British Empire—rather like a giant battering ram facing the long, crumbling walls and moats of an ancient fortress. This does not mean that the ram will actually attack the wall; it only means that the men behind the ram and the men behind the moat, however amicable their relations, both know at the back of their minds the potentialities of the situation. And these potentialities must inevitably translate themselves into latent pressure.

According to the laws of least resistance, this pressure will be the stronger the more exposed and vulnerable the point of attack: that is, in the Middle East, the Mediterranean and on the Continent of Europe. Expressed by a polite euphemism, the aim of this pressure is to procure "zones of influence." But the definition of this term depends entirely on the balance of forces. Where the balance is nearly equal such zones merely mean trading facilities and political treaties; e.g., Britain and Portugal. A tilt of the scales, and the same term means the use of airfields and strategic bases; the zone of influence has become a satellite country. One further tilt, and we get puppet governments and all but official incorporation into the bigger state: e.g., Japan and Manchukuo. Finally direct incorporation either by military conquest or by terror referendum: eg., Eastern Poland and the Baltic States.

When people talk of "expansion," even the politically educated are apt to think in static and antiquated terms. The Nazis spoke of the Russians as "Asiatic hordes" and tried to scare us with the anachronistic picture of Stalin-Genghis Khan riding with his Cossacks to Boulogne; in Conservative clubland the Russian conquest of Czechoslovakia is conceived of in the old-fashioned terms of straightforward military conquest. Hence the general incredulity regarding the real perspectives of Russian expansion on the Continent. The possibilities of modern political warfare by internal disruption and vassalisation were by no means exhausted by Hitler and are not yet appreciated in their true significance. . . .

The question "how far Stalin intends to go" is naïve and meaningless. The expansion of great Empires follows certain dynamic laws. A great power surrounded by a political vacuum will expand its zones of influence until it feels a growing pressure of resistance. The greater density of communications, higher industrialisation and living standard of the countries west of Russia exert the pull; the desire for more and more security and power provide the push; the traditions of Panslavism and the century-old aspirations at hegemony over Poland, the Balkans and Constantinople provide the historical background. The drive for access to the world trade-lines through the Mediterranean, the Baltic and North Atlantic must inevitably follow. There is no possibility of saturation in a vacuum.

On the other hand, each new increase in power means an increase in attraction towards the small states, unable to maintain their independence without outside aid. They have to become protegés of the big neighbour, to be gradually transformed into satellites and knit closer and closer into his framework. . . . Germany became unified by the most militant, autocratic and spartan of its states. The Soviets occupy today the same position towards Eastern and Central Europe as Prussia did towards the other German states in the middle of last century.

3

For centuries Central and Eastern Europe were under Germanic domination. The break-up of the Austrian Empire disturbed the balance and created a vacuum. The Treaty of Versailles replaced one of the great European power centres by an unstable mosaic of small states, each of them an ethnical mosaic in itself, without the capacity for economic and political independence. The Balkans and the Danube Basin were crowded with potential satellites in search of a sun.

Three great Powers made their bids for including them in their zone of influence: Russia through the Comintern; France through the Little Entente; Germany through the barter-trade system and through fifth-column tactics. Germany succeeded—only to be broken up in turn by military defeat; thus the unstable situation created in 1918 was re-established on an even larger scale. Europe east of the Alps is atomised and in a state of political, economical, ideological chaos as never before. But this time Russia stands without a rival as a great power on the Continent. She has a crushing superiority in every respect over the next single competitor, France. Never since the days of Charles V has the European balance been so profoundly tilted in favour of one single power.

The outstanding feature in this situation is the collapse of Germanic hegemony over the eastern half of Europe. One may object that Germany lost the last war, too, and yet recovered. But this time conditions are radically different. After the last war Germany's eastern neighbours, Poland and Russia, were fighting each other, while her western neighbour France, with only half the population of Germany and a much weaker industrial potential, could never dream of permanently dominating the bigger neighbour. But this time Germany's victorious neighbour is the Russian giant; her industry is a shambles, her territory will for the first time suffer total occupation and partial dismemberment. East Prussia beyond Koenigsberg will go to Russia; West Prussia, Pomerania and Silesia along the line Stettin-Breslau will probably go to Poland which will be no longer Russia's rival but her satellite. The boundary of the Russian zone of influence will thus run about fifty miles east of Berlin. But temporarily it will extend much further to the west, about halfway between Berlin and the Rhine, where the Russian zone of occupation ends.

How long this occupation will last we do not know; but we may rest assured that if and when it ends, the occupied country and people will have undergone profound and irremediable changes. The probabilities are that the temporary partitioning of Germany into zones of occupation will lead to a permanent break-up; "Red Saxony" for example with its strong revolutionary traditions may have a communist government and vote itself into the Soviet federation, while the Catholic Rhineland with its easy-going, civilised and liberal traditions may become a French-sponsored autonomous republic. The details of this development during the next five years are difficult to foresee; further south, however, the process is both quicker and clearer in its outlines.

Great Britain's hopes to redress the balance by the creation of an Eastern European Federation collapsed with Beneš's journey to Moscow and the signing of the Soviet-Czechoslovak alliance. By the time of writing—September, 1944—the Soviet conquest of the Balkans is in full swing and Russia's intentions towards Poland have become visible even to the politically snow-blind. Instead of arguing about Stalin's intentions we should endorse the facts; and the facts are that *the demarcation line between the Russian and Western zones of influence has already shifted from the Vistula to the Elbe; from the Black Sea to the Adriatic and Mediterranean, from east of Warsaw to west of Prague.*

THE WEANING OF THE LEFT

1

How far will Russian expansion go? The only possible answer is that it will continue until the European balance, upset by the fall of the two great Germanic empires and the weakening of France, is restored.

But the potential forces which may one day restore the balance are chaotic and confused compared to Russia's compact dynamism. . . .

. . . How can the European vacuum be filled with new contents? A mere political alliance of Great Britain, France and other countries of Western Europe is not enough. It is true that those countries of the West which went through the public school of Roman colonisation have a great tradition in common, and that two thousand years of Judeo-Christian ethics and a century of western liberalism have left in them a sediment which is not easily washed away by political storms on the surface. But deep and lasting though this moral substratum is, it is buried by layers of rubble. No inspiration can be derived from it until the rubble is cleared away. In other words, the traditional values can only be revived by the forces of progress.

2

. . . The next few years will bring a gradual awakening to Soviet reality. Russia's advance into the footlights of the European stage will make it increasingly difficult for her to deceive the world about her interior regime, though she will do her best to isolate newly conquered territories as thoroughly as Poland and the Baltic states were isolated after the first conquest in 1939–41. The truth will filter through, but only slowly and gradually; it is well to remember how the Nazi regime succeeded in keeping the majority of the British and French in ignorance about the German terror for six whole years from 1933 to 1939, although Germany was wide open to tourist traffic and much nearer than Russia. Those who knew the truth about Germany and kept on shouting it into the ears of the deaf were accused of war- and atrocity-mongering; to tell the truth about Russia is today an equally ungrateful and equally necessary task. . . .

. . . In the case of Russia as in that of Germany, appeasement is based on the logical fallacy that an expanding Power if left alone will automatically reach a state of saturation. But history proves the contrary. A yielding environment acts as a vacuum, a constant incentive to further expansion, and gives the aggressor no indication how far he can go without risking a major conflict; it is a direct invitation to him to overplay his hand and stumble into war by sheer miscalculation. Both world wars actually arose from such miscalculations. Appeasement transforms the field of international politics from a chessboard into a poker table: in the first case both partners know where they are, in the second they don't. Thus the opposite of appeasement is not bellicosity, but a clearly outlined, firmly principled policy which leaves the partner in no doubt how far he can go. It does not eliminate the possibility of war but prevents the danger of stumbling blindly into it; and that is as much as political wisdom can achieve. It is highly unlikely that any great Power will commit an act of aggression against a small nation if it is clearly and definitely understood by all concerned that a new world war will be the inevitable consequence. In other words: the point of saturation of an expanding Power depends not on its own appetites which are unlimited, but on the forces of potential resistance in the environment.

The balance of Europe can only be restored through a revival of the values on which Western civilisation is based. But this is a task beyond the powers of the conservative rear-guard, and can only be achieved if the socialist movement sheds its illusions and regains its vigour and independence, both in the national and the international sphere. . . .

The weaning of the Left, the breaking up of the false emotional compounds, is one half of the task. The other half is the creation of a new fraternity in a new spiritual climate, whose leaders are tied by a vow of poverty to share the life of the masses, and debarred by the laws of the fraternity from attaining unchecked power. If this seems utopian, then socialism is a utopia.

The age of enlightenment has destroyed faith in personal survival; the scars of this operation have never healed. There is a vacancy in every living soul, a deep thirst in all of us. If the socialist idea cannot fill this vacancy and quench our thirst, then it has failed in our time. In this case the whole development of the socialist idea since the French Revolution has been merely the end of a chapter in history, and not the beginning of a new one.

IV

Justifying and Rejecting the Balance of Power

During the eighteenth and nineteenth centuries, two general atti-
tudes developed in European thought toward the idea of the
balance of power. One viewpoint, which often today is called
"realistic," continued to accept the notion of balance as intrinsic
to the state system; the other, which we might loosely term an
"idealistic" view, regarded the notion of balance of power politics
as immoral, and a product of a defective yet reparable system
of political relationships. In the late eighteenth century, the pre-
tensions of balance theory to maintain the security of states had
been shattered by the partitioning of Poland. Engaging in bal-
ance politics, Austria, Prussia and Russia each had annexed slices
of the Polish kingdom and thus effectively removed from the in-
ternational scene one major power. If a sovereign state could
be so cavalierly sacrificed on the altar of the balance, how
then could equilibrium theory be reconciled with the idea of
political freedom?

From another quarter, harsh criticism of the balance system
appeared when the American colonies, liberating themselves from
British rule, sought to liberate themselves as well from the Euro-
pean balance system, and to develop a wholly different inter-
national system in the New World. Finally, the French Revolu-

tion in 1789, with its threat to overthrow the ancien régime *both in France and the rest of Europe, posed a massive ideological challenge to the very territorial states which were the classic practitioners of balance politics. In England especially, liberal philosophers began to look anew at the nature of international society, and to demand that governments ground their foreign policies on principles of international law and morality.*

The following writings represent both moral and ideological attempts to justify or reject the concept of balance. To some, like the German historian Ranke, the process of balancing was deemed essential to the maintenance of cultural vitality and pluralism in European civilization; to others, like the English liberal Cobden, and Woodrow Wilson, the balance constituted nothing less than a mode of power politics antithetic to human progress and to international peace.

11. THOUGHTS ON FRENCH AFFAIRS *

In 1791, Marie Antoinette appealed to her brother Leopold, Emperor of Austria, to intervene and thus save Louis XVI and the French monarchy from the revolution. Frederick William II of Prussia promised to aid Leopold should he attempt this venture. In spite of these developments, Great Britain under Pitt continued to maintain a neutralist position toward the French Revolution.

Edmund Burke, in his Thoughts on French Affairs, *clearly saw the dangers posed both by the revolution and by this new possibility of a Prussian-Austrian combination. The universalist ideologies of the revolution—which already had made deep inroads into European thought—endangered a continental equilibrium, especially in the Germanies, by weakening and distracting "the locality of patriotism." As in the earlier religious wars of Europe, "the warm parties in each state were more affectionately attached to those of their doctrinal interest in some other country than to their fellow citizens or to their natural government." In such circumstances, equilibrium politics among territorial states was virtually impossible. Burke feared that Revolutionary France, in abandoning (for messianic reasons) France's historic role as guarantor of order in Central Europe, would thus invite its partition between Austria and Prussia; but he also feared Austro-Prussian intervention in France itself, an action which might permanently shatter French power. Britain should intervene on the continent, not to defeat France but to destroy French Jacobinism. Only in this way could the European equilibrium be maintained.*

EDMUND BURKE

. . . The Germanic body is a vast mass of heterogeneous states, held together by that heterogeneous body of old principles which formed the public law positive and doctrinal. The modern laws and liberties, which the new power in France pro-

---

* Edmund Burke, *The Works of Edmund Burke*, Vol. IV, pp. 328–335. Boston: Little, Brown and Co., 1866.

poses to introduce into Germany, and to support with all its force of intrigue and of arms, is of a very different nature, utterly irreconcilable with the first, and indeed fundamentally the reverse of it: I mean the *rights and liberties of the man,* the *droit de l'homme.* That this doctrine has made an amazing progress in Germany there cannot be a shadow of doubt. They are infected by it along the whole course of the Rhine, the Maese, the Moselle, and in the greater part of Suabia and Franconia. It is particularly prevalent amongst all the lower people, churchmen and laity, in the dominions of the Ecclesiastical Electors. It is not easy to find or to conceive governments more mild and indulgent than these Church sovereignties; but good government is as nothing, when the rights of man take possession of the mind. Indeed, the loose rein held over the people in these provinces must be considered as one cause of the facility with which they lend themselves to any schemes of innovation, by inducing them to think lightly of their governments, and to judge of grievances, not by feeling, but by imagination.

It is in these Electorates that the first impressions of France are likely to be made; and if they succeed, it is over with the Germanic body, as it stands at present. A great revolution is preparing in Germany, and a revolution, in my opinion, likely to be more decisive upon the general fate of nations than that of France itself,—other than as in France is to be found the first source of all the principles which are in any way likely to distinguish the troubles and convulsions of our age. If Europe does not conceive the independence and the equilibrium of the Empire to be in the very essence of the system of balanced power in Europe, and if the scheme of public law, or mass of laws, upon which that independence and equilibrium are founded, be of no leading consequence as they are preserved or destroyed, all the politics of Europe for more than two centuries have been miserably erroneous.

If the two great leading powers of Germany do not regard this danger (as apparently they do not) in the light in which it presents itself so naturally, it is because they are powers too great to have a social interest. That sort of interest belongs only to those whose state of weakness or mediocrity is such as to give

them greater cause of apprehension from what may destroy
them than of hope from anything by which they may be aggrandized.

As long as those two princes are at variance, so long the
liberties of Germany are safe. But if ever they should so far
understand one another as to be persuaded that they have a more
direct and more certainly defined interest in a proportioned
mutual aggrandizement than in a reciprocal reduction, that is,
if they come to think that they are more likely to be enriched
by a division of spoil than to be rendered secure by keeping to
the old policy of preventing others from being spoiled by either
of them, from that moment the liberties of Germany are no more.

That a junction of two in such a scheme is neither impossible nor improbable is evident from the partition of Poland in
1773, which was effected by such a junction as made the inter-
position of other nations to prevent it not easy. Their circumstances at that time hindered any other three states, or indeed
any two, from taking measures in common to prevent it, though
France was at that time an existing power, and had not yet
learned to act upon a system of politics of her own invention.
The geographical position of Poland was a great obstacle to any
movements of France in opposition to this, at that time, un-
paralleled league. To my certain knowledge, if Great Britain had
at that time been willing to concur in preventing the execution of
a project so dangerous in the example, even exhausted as France
then was by the preceding war, and under a lazy and un-
enterprising prince, she would have at every risk taken an active
part in this business. But a languor with regard to so remote
an interest, and the principles and passions which were then
strongly at work at home, were the causes why Great Britain
would not give France any encouragement in such an enterprise.
At that time, however, and with regard to that object, in my
opinion, Great Britain and France had a common interest.

But the position of Germany is not like that of Poland, with
regard to France, either for good or for evil. If a conjunction
between Prussia and the Emperor should be formed for the
purpose of secularizing and rendering hereditary the Ecclesiastical Electorates and the Bishopric of Münster, for settling two

of them on the children of the Emperor, and uniting Cologne and Münster to the dominions of the king of Prussia on the Rhine, or if any other project of mutual aggrandizement should be in prospect, and that, to facilitate such a scheme, the modern French should be permitted and encouraged to shake the internal and external security of these Ecclesiastical Electorates, Great Britain is so situated that she could not with any effect set herself in opposition to such a design. Her principal arm, her marine, could here be of no sort of use.

France, the author of the Treaty of Westphalia, is the natural guardian of the independence and balance of Germany. Great Britain (to say nothing of the king's concern as one of that august body) has a serious interest in preserving it; but, except through the power of France, *acting upon the common old principles of state policy,* in the case we have supposed, she has no sort of means of supporting that interest. It is always the interest of Great Britain that the power of France should be kept within the bounds of moderation. It is not her interest that that power should be wholly annihilated in the system of Europe. Though at one time through France the independence of Europe was endangered, it is, and ever was, through her alone that the common liberty of Germany can be secured against the single or the combined ambition of any other power. In truth, within this century the aggrandizement of other sovereign houses has been such that there has been a great change in the whole state of Europe; and other nations as well as France may become objects of jealousy and apprehension.

In this state of things, a new principle of alliances and wars is opened. The Treaty of Westphalia is, with France, an antiquated fable. The rights and liberties she was bound to maintain are now a system of wrong and tyranny which she is bound to destroy. Her good and ill dispositions are shown by the same means. *To communicate peaceably* the rights of men is the true mode of her showing her *friendship;* to force sovereigns to *submit* to those rights is her mode of *hostility.* So that, either as friend or foe, her whole scheme has been, and is, to throw the Empire into confusion; and those statesmen who follow the old routine of politics may see in this general confusion, and in

the danger of the *lesser* princes, an occasion, as protectors or
enemies, of connecting their territories to one or the other of the
two great German powers. They do not take into consideration
that the means which they encourage, as leading to the event they
desire, will with certainty not only ravage and destroy the Empire, but, if they should for a moment seem to aggrandize the
two great houses, will also establish principles and confirm tem-
pers amongst the people which will preclude the two sovereigns
from the possibility of holding what they acquire, or even the
dominions which they have inherited. It is on the side of the
Ecclesiastical Electorates that the dikes raised to support the
German liberty first will give way.

The French have begun their general operations by seizing
upon those territories of the Pope the situation of which was the
most inviting to the enterprise. Their method of doing it was by
exciting sedition and spreading massacre and desolation through
these unfortunate places, and then, under an idea of kindness and
protection, bringing forward an antiquated title of the crown of
France, and annexing Avignon and the two cities of the Comtat,
with their territory, to the French republic. They have made an
attempt on Geneva, in which they very narrowly failed of
success. It is known that they hold out from time to time the
idea of uniting all the other provinces of which Gaul was an-
ciently composed, including Savoy on the other side, and on this
side bounding themselves by the Rhine.

As to Switzerland, it is a country whose long union, rather
than its possible division, is the matter of wonder. Here I know
they entertain very sanguine hopes. The aggregation to France of
the democratic Swiss republics appears to them to be a work half
done by their very form; and it might seem to them rather an
increase of importance to these little commonwealths than a
derogation from their independency or a change in the manner
of their government. Upon any quarrel amongst the Cantons,
nothing is more likely than such an event. As to the aristocratic republics, the general clamor and hatred which the French
excite against the very name, (and with more facility and success than against monarchs,) and the utter impossibility of their
government making any sort of resistance against an insurrection,

where they have no troops, and the people are all armed and trained, render their hopes in that quarter far indeed from unfounded. It is certain that the republic of Bern thinks itself obliged to a vigilance next to hostile, and to imprison or expel all the French whom it finds in its territories. But, indeed, those aristocracies, which comprehend whatever is considerable, wealthy, and valuable in Switzerland, do now so wholly depend upon opinion, and the humor of their multitude, that the lightest puff of wind is sufficient to blow them down. If France, under its ancient regimen, and upon the ancient principles of policy, was the support of the Germanic Constitution, it was much more so of that of Switzerland, which almost from the very origin of that confederacy rested upon the closeness of its connection with France, on which the Swiss Cantons wholly reposed themselves for the preservation of the parts of their body in their respective rights and permanent forms, as well as for the maintenance of all in their general independency. . . .

---

12. THE GREAT POWERS *

Leopold von Ranke (1795–1886), the great German historian, wrote the following essay on "the Great Powers" in 1833, shortly after the defeat of Napoleon had ended the threat of French hegemony over Europe. To him, the "genius" of European politics had been the capacity to meet "pressure on the one side with resistance on the other"; thereby the "freedom and separate existence of each state" had been preserved. This systemic guardian spirit, as he saw it, guaranteed to all European peoples the cultural freedom and diversity necessary to a vigorous and flourishing civilization. Political dominion by one brought cultural extinction to all others. To prevent this, European na-

* T. H. Von Laue, *Leopold Ranke*, pp. 181–218. Princeton, N.J.: Princeton University Press, 1950. Footnotes omitted.

tionalities had constructed countervailing power to guard a
pluralistic Europe against French cultural dominion. The balance
was thus justified on moral grounds: "out of separation and
independent development will emerge . . . true harmony."

LEOPOLD VON RANKE

THE PERIOD OF LOUIS XIV

Let our starting point be the fact that in the sixteenth century
the freedom of Europe was seen to rest upon the opposition and
balance between Spain and France. Those who were over-
powered by the one would find refuge with the other. The fact
that France was for a long time weakened and disorganized by
civil war was considered a general misfortune. That Henry IV
should have been so eagerly welcomed was not only because
he put an end to the anarchy in France but principally because
he thereby restored a stable European order.

It happened, however, that in the course of dealing dangerous
blows to her rivals everywhere, in the Netherlands, in Italy, on
the Iberian Peninsula, and of defeating Spain's allies in Germany, France herself obtained a preponderance of power greater than Spain had possessed even at her height.

. . . It was not only through military power, however, but
also through diplomacy and alliances that the French had succeeded in overcoming the Spaniards. They expanded their new
position into a kind of supremacy. . . .

In such a situation it was certainly England, above all other
European nations, who would have had the mission and also the
power to oppose the French. But it is well known by what
strange combination of politics and love, of luxury and religion,
of personal interest and intrigue Charles II was bound to Louis
XIV. . . .

In the face of France Europe was indeed divided and impotent, "without heart," as a Venetian remarked, "and without
gall." One can imagine the condition of European politics if Louis
XIV was suffered to set up the Chambers of Reunion at Metz
at the suggestion of one of his legal councillors. He summoned
mighty princes to these chambers in order that their rights to

territories and populations, rights guaranteed by treaties of state, might be determined by his judges as though they were private rights. The German Empire must have been in a sorry plight that it should have allowed Strassburg to be torn from it so violently and unnaturally. . . . Yet Germany put up with such an insult and concluded an armistice. . . .

[Against] such an increase in strength and in political predominance the lesser powers could band together. And they did indeed form alliances and associations. The concept of the European balance of power was developed in order that the union of many other states might resist the pretensions of the "exorbitant" court, as it was called. The forces of resistance gathered around Holland and William III. By a common exertion they warded off attack and waged war. One would have erred, however, in assuming that this afforded a permanent remedy. Despite the European alliance and a successful war, a Bourbon became King of Spain and the Indies. In the course of events the dominion of this House even spread over part of Italy.

In great danger one can safely trust in the guardian spirit (*Genius*) which always protects Europe from domination by any one-sided and violent tendency, which always meets pressure on the one side with resistance on the other, and, through a union of the whole which grows firmer from decade to decade, has happily preserved the freedom and separate existence of each state. As the supremacy of France rested upon the superiority of her military forces and upon her inner strength, so it could only be really challenged if other opposing powers either regained or attained inner unity, independent strength, and general importance. Let us review in a few swift strokes how this occurred.

ENGLAND, AUSTRIA AND RUSSIA

England was the first to awake to a realization of her strength. . . .

The power of the purse, over which most of the previous quarrels between king and parliament had arisen, now commenced to unite them instead. During the quarter century of his rule Charles II had collected 43 million pounds altogether. Within the space of thirteen years William received 72 million pounds; and these revenues increased tremendously thereafter. They increased for the very reason that they were voluntary, because the people perceived that they served, not the luxury of a few courtiers, but the common good. Under these conditions the predominance of the English navy did not long remain in doubt. In 1678 the flourishing condition of the royal fleet was indicated by the fact that it already numbered 83 warships, including fireships, with a complement of 18,323 men. Yet in contrast to this there were 184 ships in 1701, from first to sixth class, excluding fireships and smaller vessels, with a complement of 53,921 men. . . .

In this manner Louis XIV was opposed by the rival whom he had hoped to overcome by diplomacy or the influence of religion, a more powerful, magnificent, and dangerous rival than one could ever have expected. The balance of seapower and the whole condition of western Europe were thereby radically changed.

In the meantime the East was also being transformed. . . . Austria first became an independent and important European power through the reconquest of Hungary. So long as Budapest was in the hands of the Turks, the French could threaten and gravely endanger Austria whenever they chose to exert their influence upon the Porte to this end. If they did not actually incite the expedition of Kara Mustapha in 1683, they at least knew about it. Their intention was not to ruin Germany or Christendom; they did not go that far. But they wanted to let the Turks take Vienna and even press on to the Rhine. Then Louis XIV would have appeared in the role of sole protector of Christendom. In the confusion which such an event would have produced, he could not have failed to gain control of the German crown and, if he wished, to take it for himself.

This plan was defeated outside the walls of Vienna. It was the last great effort of the Turks, which reacted the more disastrously upon them because they had thrown all their strength into it in a savage excess of effort. After that the disorderly Turkish hordes, which, according to an Italian, had advanced like "a strong, impenetrable wall," gave way everywhere before the German armies. In vain did a *fetva* of the Mufti declare Budapest to be the key to the Empire and its defense the duty of the Faithful. It was lost all the same. All of Hungary was reconquered and made into a hereditary kingdom. The discontented elements submitted. An orthodox Serbian population moved into the borderlands of lower Hungary to defend it in future against the Turks. From then on Austria rested on a wholly different foundation. . . . It was no longer possible for French diplomacy to summon the Turks into the heart of the kingdom upon the slightest occasion. Only once more did France find support and help from the discontented elements. Finally all was quiet. The Emperor afterwards based his power particularly upon that very province which had hitherto been the greatest source of danger to him. It is obvious what a change must have been brought about in the condition of eastern Europe by the strengthening of this stable, rich, well-armed power, which held the Turks in check and even in awe.

Louis XIV experienced at least the beginning of another such change. The situation in Poland, which made it easy for him always to have a faction within that country, and the power of Sweden, which was at least theoretically bound to him by tradition and old alliance, readily gave him a decided predominance in the North. Charles XII [Sweden] made no change in this. . . . While the Spanish succession was to be the means of delivering southern Europe into the hands of the Bourbons, their old allies, the Swedes, were on the point of gaining complete supremacy in the North. After Charles XII had attacked and subdued the Danes, after he had conquered Poland and placed his own king there, after he had marched through half of Germany, which was not much better fortified in the East than in the West, and held Saxony for a long time, nothing more was needed to consolidate his supremacy but to annihilate the Tsar, whom he had already defeated once. He set out to accomplish this with his army which had been reconditioned in Saxony.

In the meantime the Tsar had made strenuous preparations. The decisive battle of 1709 took place. . . . [The] greater future lay with the Tsar's success. While Charles showed little understanding for the true interests of his nation, Peter had taken upon himself the development of his, had personally prepared and commenced it, and had made it his chief aim.

He carried the day. To the report on the battle of Poltava

which he sent to the capital he added a postscript, "With this, the cornerstone for St. Petersburg is laid." It was the foundation for the whole edifice of his state and his politics. From then on Russia began to give orders in the North. . . . [The] Tsar, who had formerly taken orders from the Poles, was now giving them at will and with unlimited authority. Henceforth the French influence in Poland necessarily decreased more and more. The French were no longer able to promote their candidate for the throne, even when they had the Polish nobility on their side.

In the meantime Sweden was weakened and reduced by these events. . . .

Thus the North had come under quite another rule than the indirect one of France; a great nation was commencing a new and truly European development. In the East the French influence had not altogether disappeared, but it had nowhere near its old importance, even though Austria under Charles VI had certainly grown very weak. The sea was in the hands of France's rivals, who permitted or broke off at will the advantageous connection which France had established via Cadiz with Hispanic America.

On the other hand, through the natural agreement of the Bourbon courts, who after a short interruption had resumed their common policy, France kept the preponderance of power in southern Europe and also in Germany. . . .

PRUSSIA

It was a moment of seeming danger to the German fatherland, which at that time possessed neither powerful states nor distinguished men of action nor a pronounced national feeling. It had no literature, no art, no culture of its own, nothing with which it could have opposed the predominating influence of its neighbors. Just then Frederick II appeared upon the scene and Prussia emerged as a power.

This is not the place to describe either the ruler or the state which he inherited and the state which he created. Nor may we lightly venture to show the innate power of the man and of the state and the many aspects of their character. Let us only attempt to make clear their position in the world. . . .

. . . The prestige of Prussia also deeply affected the northern system. Prussia's conclusion of a quite harmless treaty with Sweden and France, in order to maintain a balance of power in the North, aroused the wholehearted hatred of several Russian ministers, who believed their supremacy in the North to be threatened. Frederick might all the more easily have found support in France. But the fact that he, unlike Sweden, was not to be dominated but presumed to follow a free, independent policy, provoked also the indignation of the court at Versailles. Although this court perceived very well what was at stake, it decided nevertheless to change its whole system of alliances and to ally itself henceforth with Austria. . . . Thus the Empress succeeded in uniting both great continental powers with herself. Lesser powers, her neighbors in Saxony and Pomerania, joined with them. An alliance was at work, not very different from that which was formed against Austria after the death of Charles VI, even stronger, in fact, because of the participation of Russia. As one had talked formerly about a partition of Austria, so now of Prussia, and it was only across the sea that Frederick found an ally, the same one who had previously joined with Austria. . . .

. . . If ever an event depended upon a great personality, it was the Seven Years War. The wars of our time are usually brought to an end by a few decisive blows. Formerly they lasted longer. Yet men fought more for limited demands and claims than for their very existence or for that of the state itself. The Seven Years War differed in that throughout its long duration the existence of Prussia was at stake every moment. . . .

If one could establish as a definition of a great power that it must be able to maintain itself against all others, even when they are united, then Frederick had raised Prussia to that position. For the first time since the days of the Saxon emperors and Henry the Lion a self-sufficient power was found in northern Germany, needing no alliance, dependent only upon itself.

It followed that from then on France was able to exert little or no influence on German affairs. The time for an opposition such as she had aroused or favored during the War of the Austrian Succession was now completely past. As Prussia had emancipated herself, so had Bavaria and Saxony allied themselves again to Austria. . . .

As we have seen, it was a necessity of the seventeenth century that France be checked. This had now occurred in a manner that exceeded all expectation. It cannot really be said that an artificial, complex political system had been formed to this end. It merely appeared so, but the fact was that great powers had raised themselves by their own strength and that new independent national states in all their original power had taken over the world stage.

Austria, a Catholic and German nation, was in a stable military condition, full of fresh, inexhaustible vitality, rich, and, in short, a world by itself. The Graeco-Slavic principle appeared more strongly in Russia than ever before in world history. The European forms which it adopted were far from crushing this original element. They penetrated it instead, animated it, and for the first time drew forth its own strength. In England the Germanic maritime interests had developed into a colossal world power which ruled all the seas and before which all memories of earlier sea powers paled. And in Prussia the German Protestants found the support which they had long sought, at once their representation and their expression. "Even if one knew the secret," says a poet, "who would have the courage to tell it?" I shall not presume to put the character of these states into words. But we can see clearly that they were founded upon principles which had grown out of the various great developments of earlier centuries, that they were formed according to these original differences and with varying constitutions, and that they represented those historic demands which in the nature of things were made upon successive generations. In their rise and development, which, understandably enough, could not have occurred without a many-sided transformation of inner conditions, lies the principal event of the hundred years which preceded the outbreak of the French Revolution.

THE FRENCH REVOLUTION

However significant the rise of the continental powers was in itself, it cannot be denied that France was thereby restricted

and that she was right in viewing the success of the other countries as her own loss. She had always vigorously opposed them.
. . . Russia had wrested her influence in the north from the French. When the cabinet at Versailles became aware what position Prussia had assumed and was seeking to maintain in the world, it forgot its American interests in order not only to reduce but actually to annihilate this power. How often had the French undertaken to restore the old relationship with England, to favor the Jacobites and perhaps to foment a Stuart rebellion. In return they made enemies of the English every time, whether they stood with Prussia against Austria or with Austria against Prussia. They waged their wars upon the continent and neglected their navy. During the Seven Years War they lost America, as the elder Pitt said, in Germany.

Thus France stood nowhere near so definitely at the center of the European world as a hundred years earlier. She was forced to witness the partition of Poland without being consulted. In 1772, to her deep resentment, she had to permit an English frigate to appear at the roadstead of Toulon in order to supervise the stipulated disarmament of her fleet. Even the smaller independent states, such as Portugal and Switzerland, had admitted other outside influences.

At the same time it must be remarked that the harm was not so great as has often been represented. France still exerted her old influence over Turkey. Through the Family Compact she had linked Spain to her policy. The Spanish fleet and the riches of the Spanish colonies stood at her disposal. The remaining Bourbon courts, among which Turin may almost be included, allied themselves with France. And the French faction finally won out in Sweden. But this was not nearly enough for a nation who gloried more than any other in the splendor of a universal superiority. She was aware only of the loss of claims which she regarded as rights. She noticed only what the others had conquered, not what she had kept. She eyed with indignation such powerful, well-established rivals, for whom she was no longer a match.

Much has been said about the causes of the Revolution and they have also been sought where they can never be found.

One of the most important, in my opinion, is this change in the international position of France which had brought the government into deep discredit. It is true that the government knew neither how to manage the state correctly nor how to wage war properly. It had allowed the most dangerous abuses to prevail, and the collapse of its European prestige originated in large measure from this. But the French also blamed their government for everything that was really only a product of the changed world situation. They still fed on memories of the days of the all-powerful Louis XIV. All the conditions that resulted from the rise of other vigorous states, who curtailed France's former influence, were attributed by the French to the incapacity of their foreign policy and to the indeed undeniable degeneration of their internal situation. Thus it came about that the reform movement in France, which turned all too soon into a revolutionary one, was also directed from the very beginning against the outside world. . . .

The American Revolution now became a turning-point, not so much through a change in the general balance of power as through its indirect effects. For although the English colonies had been torn loose from the mother country, it was soon apparent that England was in so well-established a position that she did not feel their loss very keenly. And although the French navy had regained a certain prestige, England had still been victorious in the decisive battles and had maintained supremacy over her combined rivals.

By indirect effects I refer not only to the rise of republican tendencies. There was also a more immediate result. . . .

War was declared and waged at an extravagant cost. . . . In 1780 Vergennes already declared to the King that the condition of the finances was truly alarming, that it made peace necessary, and without delay. In the meantime the war dragged on, and only after its conclusion did the confusion become generally apparent. Here again is a striking contrast. England came out of the American war no less exhausted and laden with debts, but Pitt seized the evil by the roots and restored confidence through strict measures. The French finances, on the other hand, passed from weak into ever weaker hands, more untried and at the same time more daring, so that matters grew worse from month to month and not only deprived the government of authority but threatened its very form.

One can imagine how strongly this affected foreign policy. The French no longer had any choice; war must be avoided at all costs. . . .

At all events we can see that French foreign policy was suffering from an insignificance and futility neither commensurate with the natural claims of that country nor corresponding to the interests of Europe as a whole. If this weakness of policy stemmed from the internal confusion, as cannot be denied, then the latter in turn was immensely aggravated thereby. . . .

. . . The national consciousness of a great people demands a fitting position in the European community. International relations depend not on convenience but on actual power, and the prestige of a state will always correspond to the strength of its internal development. Any nation will feel sensitive not to find itself in its rightful position. How much more so the French nation which had so often raised the singular claim of being preeminently *the* great nation!

I shall not go into the multiplicity of causes which led to the fearful development of the French Revolution. I shall only remind the reader that the decline in France's external position was an important factor. . . .

. . . The ideas which Europe had hailed as salutary and liberating to mankind were suddenly transformed before its eyes into the horror of devastation. The volcanic fire, from which one had expected a nourishing, life-giving warmth for the earth, had poured forth a fearful eruption.

Yet even in the midst of this wreckage the French never abandoned the principle of unity. During the confusion of the revolutionary years France proved much more powerful than before in relation to the other European states. One can justly say that this tremendous explosion of all forces extended beyond France's borders. Between the old and the new France there existed the same contrast as between the aristocracy who had controlled the old state—spirited, to be sure, and brave by nature, but accustomed to court life, motivated often by petty ambition, effete and voluptuous—and the wild, violent Jacobins, intoxicated with a few ideas and stained with blood, who ruled the new one. In the course of events the other states had developed an aristocracy not exactly like the French one but still similar to it. Thus it was no wonder that by fiercely straining all forces the Jacobins gained the preponderance of power in Europe. The first victory, won by a coincidence of unexpected circumstances, was all that was needed to awaken the revolutionary enthusiasm which thereupon gripped the French nation and became its life principle for a long time.

It cannot be said, however, that France thus became actually stronger than the other great powers together or even than her nearest neighbors if they remained united. We are sufficiently familiar with the errors of policy and of military strategy which produced so unfavorable a result for these countries. And they could not wean themselves all at once from their previous jealousy. Even the one-sided coalition of 1799 was able to liberate Italy and to assume a very powerful military position, until an unfortunate dissension divided it. But it cannot be denied that the French state, formed in the midst of a struggle with Europe and designed to cope with it, became stronger than any one of the continental states through the new centralization of power.

Although France had always appeared to be seeking freedom, she had advanced through successive revolutions towards a military despotism which far exceeded the development of military systems elsewhere, great as these were. The successful general crowned himself emperor. He had the power to throw all available resources of the nation into the field at any moment. In this way France returned to her old supremacy. She succeeded in excluding England from the Continent, in robbing Austria of her oldest provinces in Germany and Italy during repeated wars, in overthrowing the army and the monarchy of Frederick II, in forcing even Russia into obedience, and finally in penetrating the latter's inner provinces as far as the old capital. The French emperor needed war with only these powers in order to establish direct dominion over both southern and central Europe, not excluding a large part of Germany. Thus everything which had happened in Louis XIV's time had now been far exceeded. The old liberties of Europe were submerged. Europe seemed about to be swallowed up by France. The universal monarchy, which had hitherto seemed only a remote danger, was almost realized. . . .

France had only atttained her supremacy because, in the midst of her turbulence, she had known how to keep the feeling of national unity more alive than ever and how to strain her national resources in an extraordinary expansion for the single purpose of the war.

If anyone wished to oppose her or conceived a hope of once more breaking her predominance, the means which had previously sufficed were no longer enough. Even an improved military organization would not have helped by itself. A more thorough revival was needed in order to concentrate all available resources. It had become necessary to awaken to self-conscious activity those slumbering spirits of the nations by whom life had hitherto been carried on more unconsciously. . . .

It is certain that men for the first time began to fight with some prospect of success when, in 1809, they commenced to fulfill satisfactorily these demands of world destiny: when in well-ordered empires whole sections of the inhabitants lost their hereditary dwellings to which they were tied even by religion and abandoned them to the flames; when whole populations, accustomed for generations to peaceful civilian life, took up arms, man for man; when people finally forgot their hereditary feuds and united themselves in earnest. Then for the first time, and no sooner, did they succeed in defeating the enemy, restoring the old liberties, and restraining France within her borders, driving the flooded stream back into its bed.

If the main event of the hundred years before the French Revolution was the rise of the great powers in defense of European independence, so the main event of the period since then is the fact that nationalities were rejuvenated, revived, and developed anew. They became a part of the state, for it was realized that without them the state could not exist. . . .

. . . They have finally made the public aware how important moral strength and the sense of nationality are for the state.

What would have become of our states if they had not received new life from the national principle upon which they
were based? It is inconceivable that any state could exist without
it.

World history does not present such a chaotic tumult, warring,
and planless succession of states and peoples as appear at first
sight. Nor is the often dubious advancement of civilization its
only significance. There are forces and indeed spiritual, life-
giving, creative forces, nay life itself, and there are moral
energies, whose development we see. They cannot be defined or
put in abstract terms, but one can behold them and observe
them. One can develop a sympathy for their existence. They
unfold, capture the world, appear in manifold expressions, dispute with the check and overpower one another. In their interaction and succession, in their life, in their decline or rejuvena-
tion, which then encompasses an ever greater fullness, higher
importance, and wider extent, lies the secret of world history.

As we are now attacked by a spiritual power, so must we
oppose it with spiritual force. The dominion which another nation threatens to gain over us can only be combatted by developing our own sense of nationality. I do not mean an invented,
illusionary nationality but the real, existing one which is expressed in the state.

But, so people will reply, is not the world developing at this
moment into an ever closer community? Would not this tendency
be impeded and limited by the contrast between different peoples
with their national ways or different states with their individual
principles?

Unless I delude myself, there is a close analogy with literature.
No one spoke of a world literature at the time that French
literature dominated Europe. Once since then has this idea been
conceived, expressed, and propagated, in other words, only after
most of the principal peoples of Europe had developed their
own literature independently and often in sharp contrast. If I
may be allowed to make a trivial comparison, I should like to
remind the reader that the sort of company where one person is
spokesman and leads the whole conversation affords neither
pleasure nor profit, nor does the sort where all the people, being

on the same level or, if you will, of the same mediocrity, only say the same thing. One only feels happy when many-sided personalities, freely developed, meet on a higher common ground or indeed produce this very meeting-place by stimulating and complementing one another. There would be only a disagreeable monotony if the different literatures should let their individual characters be blended and melted together. No, the union of all must rest upon the independence of each single one. Then they can stimulate one another in lively fashion and forever, without one dominating or injuring the others.

It is the same with states and nations. Decided, positive prevalence of one would bring ruin to the others. A mixture of them all would destroy the essence of each one. Out of separation and independent development will emerge the true harmony.

---

13. BALANCE OF POWER *

After 1945, when the power of Continental European states had been smashed in history's most physically destructive war, the two remaining great power centers were on Europe's peripheries: Russia and the United States. Since the Treaty of Westphalia in 1648, the balance of power system had been European-based, and a multiple one. In 1945, it suddenly became both global and bipolar. The Soviet Union, confronting the United States, threatened to overwhelm all of Europe in its totalitarian grasp. In America, there were voices, such as that of the LIFE publisher Henry Luce, who spoke of an American Century— one of American dominion of world politics.

DeWitt C. Poole, a veteran American diplomat and one-time American Embassy Counselor in Russia, undertook in the following essay published shortly after the war, to suggest that

---

* DeWitt C. Poole, "Balance of Power," *Life*, Vol. 23, No. 12, Sept. 22, 1947, pp. 76–94.

neither an American nor Russian "century" was desirable; that only when a state system could be restored with independent concentrations of nearly equal power, could a network of co-operation and interdependence emerge which would ensure world peace. Only through reestablishment of a new world balance of power "to replace the simple confrontation" could world empire, whether Russian or American, be prevented. For even if it were an American empire, "freedom will be destroyed."

DEWITT C. POOLE

WHICH COMES FIRST—FREEDOM OR PEACE?

Events move toward some tighter organization of the world. What kind of world is it going to be? Will it be our kind of world? What *is* our kind of world?

Many Americans will answer: above all, there must be peace; but neither history nor a look into our souls will bear that out. Peace we can most easily have. No nation has to fight. In 1917 and 1941 we could have compounded with the aggressor to good advantage—for the short term; but we would not. We may fight again.

The first specification for our kind of world is not peace but freedom. We have enjoyed freedom so long and take freedom so easily for granted that we have to remind ourselves of that. Next after freedom comes justice, for large numbers can enjoy freedom only in a frame of order. Peace comes third. Peace we need and yearn for, but peace comes third, because, if freedom and justice lack, we shall not ourselves be peaceful.

Freedom, as we shall show shortly, is to be had in only one kind of world. That is a world in which power is widely distributed and balanced; a world of complex balance of power. The most obvious alternative, a world in which power is concentrated at a single point, spells empire and tyranny. But the second alternative is little better; it is what we have now. A good balance of power must be complex. A simple balance, like the present one between the U.S. and Russia (alias: two armed camps) does not serve freedom or justice or peace; it is dangerous and unstable. If a new complex balance does not soon

replace the present simple confrontation, world empire will ensue and freedom be destroyed. Even if it is an American empire,
freedom will be destroyed.

A world of complex balance of power is for us the familiar
world in which we feel at home. This world began with the
Renaissance 500 years ago. Far from perfect, it has been tolerable, exciting and progressive. With balance of power came
freedom and with freedom a flowering of the human spirit unprecedented except in classic Greece, where also there was complex balance of power. In the interval between the Grecian and
the modern world came empire and its aftermath. For 200 years
imperial Rome insured peace, imposed justice but denied freedom. A Dark Age followed, and civilization had to be rebuilt
with pain and sweat.

In 1945 this painfully rebuilt world was again destroyed. The
ultimate and controlling aim of American foreign policy must be
to bring us from the present crisis into a new world of complex
balance and of freedom. How?

OUR KIND OF WORLD AND HOW TO GET IT

Concretely the U.S. must work to have alongside of the U.S.
and the U.S.S.R. six or eight centers of power comparable to
them in weight and independent of them both. The standard of
power is set by the U.S. and Russia. We could not reduce these
power centers if we would. The other power centers (1.6
billion people are in question) must be brought up toward the
American-Russian level. This is neither easy nor impossible.

The practical means is federation. First, federation in EU-
ROPE. Sixteen European nations are at work at Paris concerting
their postwar recovery, following Secretary Marshall's invitation;
three (Netherlands, Belgium, Luxembourg) have already formed
a customs union. The size, shape and nature of any federation
or federations of Europe will be primarily decided, of course,
by the peoples involved. Political hindrances continue formidable, but Europe is under instant economic pressure. It is in
the field of economics that the U.S. can offer the surest help.

Applied first in the Ruhr, going further as requested, American engineering talent can help revitalize all of Western Europe.

Europe may be economically viable only as a whole; but since the Iron Curtain blocks the way at present, we must begin in Western Europe with what is at hand. What concerns us is that there should come into being soon a genuinely European Europe, strong and free.

Next, CHINA. The U.S. needs and desires a strong China, independent of other world powers. Russia seeks a manageable China. As between Communists and Nationalists in China, only the Nationalists can create—if either can create—a strong and independent China. That is why we should be for the Nationalists and their leader, Chiang Kai-shek.

Of all the unawakened countries of the world, China has the greatest potential. By underwriting the Monroe Doctrine the British statesman, George Canning, called in the Americas to redress the European balance after Napoleon; similarly a strong China offers American statesmanship a chance to stabilize the Pacific. Should success in this role someday go to China's head and lead her into imperial adventures as they led Japan, then the U.S. on that day would of course become China's enemy. But at present the opposite is the case: to replace the Japanese unit in the international balance—not against Russia but against anybody—is America's controlling interest.

Now free, INDIA becomes important in the international balance. As India starts her new life divided into Pakistan and Hindustan, the fact (long obscured under British rule) that India is not a unitary nation is made manifest to all. But when India's wounds heal and she proceeds through the next stages of industrialization, she will be compelled toward federal unity in order to protect the independence of her parts. The U.S. should favor and can help in this process, at the moment by taking a direct interest in her industrial development.

Similarly we can and should encourage the renascence of the MOSLEM WORLD. Geographically there are two Moslem worlds and probably two potential Moslem federations. In the Near East the Pan-Arab movement hitherto has been mainly a diplomatic scarecrow. But if the Near Eastern desert is watered and developed by American oilmen and engineers, Arab nationalism could become a serious international political reality.

In INDONESIA, also predominantly Moslem, the old colonial system is in agony, as also in Indo-China. The U.S. should assist the realization of an Indonesian federal state. It may ultimately include Indo-China, Malaya and other strengthening neighbors.

Federal possibilities based on cultural affinity may also be present in the LATIN-AMERICAN WORLD. The cultural movement called Hispanidad is largely a Franco invention, but once Franco is removed and Spain is free the natural links between Spain, Portugal and Latin America may take political form.

A sound statesmanship in North America would not be alarmed by this development nor regard it as an infringement of our hemispheric unity. We shall in general be wise to look with favor on cross-ties and multiple relationships wherever they arise. We aim to bind the world together, not fence it into parcels.

The BRITISH are now in the process of erecting their main overseas bastion in Africa. Field Marshall Smuts talks of a South and Central African federation with its center at Pretoria. On the other hand the British may turn in again toward Europe, sharing and promoting federation there. In either event it is imperative that the U.S. help the British make themselves again a power more nearly equaling the U.S. and Russia. The British command an important physical position. They are for us indispensable coworkers. The more Britain cleaves to Europe, the more Canada, Australia and New Zealand can be counted independent centers.

In sum, then, adding federative possibilities to existing powers, we come out with a total possibility of some 10 power centers of something near the same order of magnitude. That would be a world of complex balance of power, and so of freedom, and so a world in which we could be content. It would be a peace of freedom—an American peace.

THE BALANCE OF POWER AND ORIGINAL SIN

The theory that a complex power balance is the best, perhaps the only, guarantee of freedom begins with Original Sin. Man being imperfect as he is, power concentrated and uncontrolled will *always* be abused. As Alexander Hamilton put it, "The spirit of moderation in a state of overbearing power is a phenomenon which has not yet appeared, and which no wise man will ever expect to see." Conscience is not enough; the safeguards of freedom must be intensely practical. Keep power from concentrating. Find safety in numbers. Separate and make numerous the repositories of power; let them watch and check each other. This our Founding Fathers knew as the theory of checks and balances, though some of them called it balance of power. They would have agreed with Ortega y Gasset: "The *state* of liberty results from a plurality of forces mutually resistant."

Throughout history this hardheaded and skeptical doctrine has had only two foes: 1) those equally hardheaded, the tyrants, who seek power for themselves by overriding checks and safeguards, 2) political idealists. The idealists believe that somehow governors will emerge who are wiser and more virtuous than the generality. Plato, in the *Republic,* would rely on breeding these supermen—his philosopher-kings—eugenically like racehorses. Up to the French Revolution, Europe touched kings with divinity. That experiment ran three centuries, and the kings turned out to be ordinary clay. Following this the German philosopher Hegel enthroned not a flesh-and-blood monarch but an abstraction, "the State" as "the expression of the Divine Will on earth." The secular fruit of that idea has ripened for our time in Hitler's "leadership principle" and the absolutism of the Politburo at Moscow.

Today the political idealists take a slightly different tack: if we all really try to make the United Nations work or turn it into a world government, won't a balance of power be unnecessary? Quite the contrary; a complex balance of power, which does not now exist, is the only basis on which the U.N. could ever work, especially if it is hoped to turn it into a federal government of the world. Swiss, American and other experiences of federation show that the closer the political association, the more necessary balance of power becomes alike to freedom and to justice. Successful federation, A. V. Dicey tells us, requires "approximate equality in the wealth, in the population, and in the historical position" of the participants.

The U.N. is still largely ineffectual because of its suppliant position vis-à-vis both the U.S. and Russia and the client position of too many of its members. Americans expect U.N. to be an association of free nations. Only against a background of complex balance of power can it become so.

THE ATOMIC BOMB AND RUSSIA

But hasn't the atomic bomb changed all this? If the bomb has broken the line of our descent from Patrick Henry, making life indeed so dear and peace so sweet as to be purchased at the price of freedom, then it has; but our course so far suggests nothing of the sort. Technically we hold in our hands the means to wipe freedom from the earth. What do we do? After long prayer and thought we propose to share control of the secret internationally. The Acheson-Lilienthal-Baruch proposals were nothing more nor less than a scheme for putting the balance of power in action. Our temporary and instinctively uncomfortable monopoly of atomic power was to be shared in such a way that no single power would ever again enjoy a monopoly.

Russia's lone refusal of this offer marks her as the principal foe of the balance of power in the world today—whether from tyrannical or idealistic motives matters not. Russia having refused, we have no choice but to maintain a strong defensive posture, remaining trustees of the bomb as long as science permits and maintaining strength equal in all respects to Russia's as long as this direly oversimplified power balance lasts. But for the long term our controlling aim remains a world of complex balance of power in respect also to atomic fission. . . .

BALANCE OF POWER IS AN AMERICAN IDEA

Recent American generations have been disposed to think of balance of power as European. The principle is even more thoroughly American. When the U.S. Constitution was under popular scrutiny in the summer of 1789, John Adams wrote Roger Sherman in defense of the distribution of powers proposed therein: "Power naturally grows. Why? Because human passions are insatiable. But that power alone can grow which already is too great; that which is unchecked; that which has no equal power to control it." And he noted: "Longitude, and the philosopher's stone have not been sought with more earnestness by philosophers than a guardian of the laws has been studied by legislators from Plato to Montesquieu; but every project has been found to be no better than committing the lamb to the custody of the wolf, except that one which is called a balance of power."

In the foreign policy of the U.S. balance of power has alternated with neutrality as a determinant of action. The preferred position, naturally, has been neutrality; but whenever imperialists or adventurers have so far upset the general balance as to menace freedom, the American people have stood ready to intervene or have intervened.

The founders were confronted very soon with a problem of balance of power internationally. French armies were spreading over Europe and might soon subjugate Russia. Napoleon was showing an interest even in the Western Hemisphere. By 1815 even Jefferson, pacifistic and Francophile, was worried over the prospect. "The establishment in our day of another Roman empire, spreading vassalage and depravity over the face of the globe, is not, I hope, within the purpose of Heaven," Jefferson exclaimed to his friend Leiper. "It cannot be to our interest that all Europe be reduced to a single monarchy. . . . And were the consequences even to be the longer continuance of our war," Jefferson did not hesitate to add, "I would rather meet them than see the whole force of Europe wielded by a single hand." Jefferson hoped "that a salutary balance of power may ever be maintained among nations."

The victories of Trafalgar and Waterloo lifted the Napoleonic threat, and five years later the accent had gravitated to neutrality. Now Jefferson writes to President Monroe that European "political interests are entirely distinct from ours." "Their mutual jealousies, their balance of power, their complicated alliances, their forms and principles of government, all are foreign to us," he asserts. "They are nations of eternal war."

Yet Europe with its balance of power was to enjoy a century of peace marred only by relatively brief and localized intervals of campaigning. The two biggest wars of the 19th Century were civil wars, one fought in the U.S. and one in China.

Our Civil War being over and danger of European intervention past, there set in for the U.S. a privileged international position. British naval supremacy, dedicated to economic rather than political imperialism, was one source of our security. Another was the continuance of a complex balance of power on the Continent of Europe. The two combined to yield the American people —free, gratis, and for nothing—the shield and buckler of external freedom; and swift accretions of strength at home put the cap upon a situation certain to lull Americans toward complacency.

At the end of this long, bright interval Theodore Roosevelt cut through to underlying facts. In 1911, being then on the editorial staff of the *Outlook,* T.R. said to a German diplomat, "As long as England succeeds in keeping up the balance of power in Europe, not only on principle, but in reality, well and good; should she, however, for some reason or other fail in doing so, the United States would be obliged to step in at least temporarily, in order to reestablish the balance of power in Europe, never mind against which country or group of countries our efforts may have to be directed."

It was not Roosevelt, however, but Woodrow Wilson who had to meet the situation, and to Wilson as to other Americans of the present century, "balance of power" seemed alien and unclean. To Wilson balance of power meant not freedom's shield and buckler, it recalled instead the abuses which had grown up in the practices of dynastic Europe. To these Wilson was not alone in his aversion.

In Europe also the advancing 19th Century had come to look askance at the accepted doctrine of two centuries preceding. Complex balance of power was still, no less than ever, the indispensable basis of Europe's freedom; but after Napoleon's defeat the danger of any new drive toward empire grew dim. The French cartoonist, Daumier, pilloried balance of power as a source of insecurity and armaments; and indeed these are, at times, the price of freedom. The felony of Poland's partition was compounded in the name of balance of power; in the name of balance of power sovereignty over peoples had been traded among chanceries as if peoples were but cattle. In shying from dynastic abuses of the principle, public spokesmen shied also from the phrase. When Prussian armies invaded France in 1870, Gladstone spoke to Parliament, not of balance of power but of "the common interest against the unmeasured aggrandizement of any Power whatever." On that phrase Sir Edward Grey relied again in August 1914.

Earlier, when Europe was being remade at Utrecht (1713) following Louis XIV's imperial adventure, "balance of power" was the very gospel. Treaties spoke of Europe as "this federal Equilibrium." At Vienna in 1814, balance of power reigned again. But when, in January 1919, the delegates gathered at Paris for Europe's third remaking, Woodrow Wilson expressed the hope that "no odour of Vienna" would be brought into the proceedings. Before leaving the U.S. he had denounced the balance of power in the second of his Four Principles of Feb. 11, 1918. He stipulated therein that "peoples and provinces are not to be bartered about from sovereignty to sovereignty as if they were mere chattels and pawns in a game, even the great game, now forever discredited, of the balance of power." Instead there was to be "self-determination."

The slight duration of the Versailles respite, compared with Utrecht's 80 years and Vienna's century, has elicited some second thoughts on balance of power. The critical point for our cognizance today is this: Though Wilson rejected, as his British cousins in Liberalism, Gladstone and Grey, circumvented, the phrase "balance of power," Wilson held, not less surely than did they, to the conviction that any single domination of Europe must imperil freedom everywhere, and must therefore be resisted.

This capital fact is confirmed to us by Wilson's close friend and advisor, the historian, William E. Dodd. In an article contributed to the New York *Times* magazine, Dec. 27, 1936, Dodd recounted that "when the World War assumed proportions and purposes like those of Napoleon I and Louis XIV, President Wilson began to wonder whether his country could safely witness a dictatorship embracing practically all Europe." On August 15, 1915 Wilson said to Dodd, "I am as much a devotee of peace as any man; but in case Europe falls under the domination of a single militarist group, peace and democracy for our country are going to be in grave danger. In case that seems obvious, I shall have to urge American intervention."

World War II confronted the people of the U.S. once more with the dilemma of neutrality and their own proper interest in the fate of Europe. President F. D. Roosevelt never openly invoked the principle of the balance of power. The attack on Pearl Harbor removed many political uncertainties. However, during 1944 there were published in the *Saturday Evening Post* articles by Forrest Davis based on talks with President Roosevelt, and the latter is said to have reviewed before publication what Davis wrote. The following passage is in point: "Our historic interest, like England's, has demanded a European balance of power wherein no single nation commands all the Continent's resources and manpower to our potential disadvantage. Stripped to the bare essentials, we fought in 1917 and are fighting now to prevent the mastery of Europe by one aggressive power."

In each war we took up the final challenge and spent our blood and treasure in a cause which (as Gladstone once said of England) was not immediately our own. We accepted a fate which others had prepared for us and fulfilled the last cruel necessity of the principle of the balance of power defensively conceived.

The world today is far more compact and explosive than it was in 1941. In order to survive we must advance consciously, without more delay, from the purely defensive into a constructive and preventive stage of our historic quest for freedom through balance of power.

Fruitless negotiations with the Kremlin, whose lack of common purpose was writ large from the outset, have slowed our start. Historical momentum took us some distance nevertheless. At least we have been unable to persevere in policies which pointed *away* from a balance of power, such as the Morgenthau plan for Germany and the Stilwell-Vincent line in China. It is now time to confess explicitly our devotion to the balance of power, and to draw the scattered manifestations of our policy into a worldwide plan. Such a plan would commit us:

1. To support "the common interest against the unmeasured

aggrandizement of any Power whatever," as we have begun to do in Greece and Turkey. And beyond that—

2. To lead the world, if we can do so, toward a new complex balance of power in fact, moving thus from the defensive into a constructive and preventive phase.

Leadership in these regards was until recently with the British. But during four centuries they had never to face a situation so threatening as the present or to act with so little outside help as we may look for. Probably never has a people held the general fate so unequivocally in their hands as do Americans at the present juncture. Upon us has descended, without reversion, guardianship not only of our own ideals but that legacy of the Western World of which our ideals are part. . . .

---

14. POLITICAL WRITINGS *

An English manufacturer and Radical politician in the early nineteenth century, Richard Cobden exemplified both in thought and action the ideals of Victorian liberalism. A man of cosmopolitan views, he effectively espoused policies of free trade for Britain, and, despite the popularity of imperialism in the country, deplored the survival of the colonial system. Cobden's vision of a future world of international politics was one of closely knit, interdependent nations bound together by trade and by the free movement of labor, goods, and services.

Like many British liberals, Cobden scorned the balance of power as guide to British `policy on the Continent. In this scathing attack on the concept, he derided it as "an undescribed, indescribable, incomprehensible nothing." Published in 1836, his polemic centered on England's historical role as "balancer" of European politics. This "chimera," he wrote, had re-

* Richard Cobden, *The Political Writings of Richard Cobden*, Vol. I, 1867, pp. 256–268. Footnotes omitted.

*sulted only in wars of aggrandizement among the power-hungry
states of Europe, and was little more than rationalization for
their "lust for conquest."*

RICHARD COBDEN

. . . British intervention in the state policy of the Continent has
been usually excused under the two stock pretences of maintaining the balance of power in Europe, and of protecting our commerce; upon which two subjects, as they bear indirectly on the
question in hand, we shall next offer a few observations.

The first instance in which we find the "balance of power" al-
luded to in a king's speech, is on the occasion of the last address
of William III. to his parliament, December 31, 1701, where
he concludes by saying—"I will only add this—if you do in good
earnest desire to see England *hold the balance of Europe,* it will
appear by your right improving the present opportunity." From
this period, down almost to our time (latterly, indeed, the phrase
has become, like many other cant terms, nearly obsolete), there
will be found, in almost every successive king's speech, a constant recurrence of the "balance of Europe;" by which, we may
rest assured, was always meant, however it might be concealed
under pretended alarm of the "equilibrium of power" or the
"safety of the Continent," the desire to see England "hold the
balance." The phrase was found to please the public ear; it
implied something of equity; whilst England, holding the balance
of Europe in her hand, sounded like filling the office of Justice
herself to one-half of the globe. Of course, such a post of
honour could not be maintained, or its dignity asserted, without
a proper attendance of guards and officers; and we consequently
find that, at about this period of our history, large standing
armies began to be called for; and not only were the supplies
solicited by the government, from time to time, under the plea
of preserving the liberties of Europe, but, in the annual mutiny
bill (*the same in form as is now passed every year*), the preamble stated, amongst other motives, that the annual army was
voted for the purpose of *preserving the balance of power in
Europe.* The "balance of power," then, becomes an important

practical subject for investigation; it appeals directly to the business and bosoms of our readers, since it is implicated with an expenditure of more than a dozen millions of money per annum, every farthing of which goes, in the shape of taxation, from the pockets of the public.

Such of our readers as have not investigated this subject, will not be a little astonished to find a great discrepancy in the several definitions of what is actually meant by the "balance of power." The theory—for it has never yet been applied to practice—appears, after upwards of a century of acknowledged existence, to be less understood now than ever. Latterly, indeed, many intelligent and practical-minded politicians have thrown the question overboard, along with that of the balance of trade—of which number, without participating in their favoured attributes, we claim to be ranked as one. The balance of power—which has, for a hundred years, been the burden of kings' speeches, the theme of statesmen, the ground of solemn treaties, and the cause of wars—which has served, down to the very year in which we write, and which will, no doubt continue to serve, for years to come, as a pretence for maintaining enormous standing armaments, by land and sea, at a cost of many hundreds of millions of treasure—the balance of power is a chimera! It is not a fallacy, a mistake, an imposture—it is an undescribed, indescribable, incomprehensible nothing; mere words, conveying to the mind not ideas, but sounds like those equally barren syllables which our ancestors put together for the purpose of puzzling themselves about words, in the shape of *Prester John,* or the *philosopher's stone!* We are bound, however, to see what are the best definitions of this theory.

"By this balance," says Vattel, "is to be understood such a disposition of things as that no one potentate or state shall be able, absolutely, to predominate and prescribe laws to the others."—*Law of Nations,* b. 3, c. 3, § 47.

"What is usually termed a balance of power," says Gentz, "is that constitution subsisting among neighbouring states, more or less connected with one another, by virtue of which no one among them can injure the independence or essential rights of another without meeting with effectual resistance on some side, and, consequently, exposing itself to danger."—*Fragments on the Political Balance,* c. 1.

"The grand and distinguishing feature of the balancing system," says Brougham, "is the perpetual attention to foreign affairs which it inculcates; the constant watchfulness over every nation which it prescribes; the subjection in which it places all national passions and antipathies to the fine and delicate view of remote expediency; the unceasing care which it dictates of nations most remotely situated, and apparently unconnected with ourselves; the general union which it has effected of all the European powers, obeying certain laws, and actuated in general by a common principle; in fine, the right of mutual inspection, universally recognised, among civilised states, in the rights of public envoys and residents."—*Brougham's Colonial Policy,* b. 3, § 1.

These are the best definitions we have been able to discover of the system denominated the balance of power. In the first place, it must be remarked that, taking any one of these descriptions separately, it is so vague as to impart no knowledge even of the writer's meaning; whilst, if taken together, one confuses and contradicts another—Gentz describing it to be "a constitution subsisting among neighbouring states more or less connected with each other;" whilst Brougham defines it as "dictating a care of nations most remotely situated, and apparently unconnected with ourselves." Then it would really appear, from the laudatory tone applied to the system by Vattel, who says that it is "such a disposition of things as that no one potentate or state *shall be able* absolutely to predominate and prescribe laws to the others;" as well as from the complacent manner in which Brougham states "the general *union which it has effected* of all the European powers, obeying certain laws, and actuated in general by a common principle"—it would seem, from such assurances as these, that there was no necessity for that "perpetual attention to foreign affairs," or that "constant watchfulness over every nation," which the latter authority tells us, the system "prescribes and inculcates." The only point on which these writers, in common with many other authors and speakers in favour of the balance of power, agree, is in the fundamental delusion that such a sys-

tem was ever acceded to by the nations of Europe. To judge
from the assumption, by Brougham, of a "general *union* among
all the European powers;" from the allusion made by Gentz
to that *"constitution* subsisting among neighbouring states;" or
from Vattel's reference to "a *disposition of things,"* &c.—one
might be justified in inferring that a kind of federal union had
existed for the last century throughout Europe, in which the
several kingdoms had found, like the States of America, un-
interrupted peace and prosperity. But we should like to know
at what period of history such a compact amongst the nations of
the Continent was entered into? Was it previously to the peace
of Utrecht? Was it antecedent to the Austrian war of succession? Was it prior to the seven years' war, or to the American
war? Or did it exist during the French revolutionary wars? Nay,
what period of the centuries during which Europe has (with only
just sufficient intervals to enable the combatants to recruit their
wasted energies) been one vast and continued battle-field, will
Lord Brougham fix upon, to illustrate the salutary working of that
"balancing system" which "places all national passions and antipathies in subjection to the fine and delicate view of remote
expediency?"

Again, at what epoch did the nations of the Continent sub-
scribe to that constitution, "by virtue of which," according to
Gentz, "no one among them can injure the independence or
essential rights of another?" Did this constituton exist, whilst
Britain was spoiling the Dutch at the Cape, or in the East?—or
when she dispossessed France of Canada?—or (worse outrage
by far) did it exist when England violated the "essential
rights" of Spain, by taking forcible and felonious possession of a
portion of her native soil? Had this constitution been subscribed
by Russia, Prussia, and Austria, at the moment when they
signed the partition of Poland?—or by France, when she amal-
gamated with a portion of Switzerland?—by Austria, at the acquisition of Lombardy?—by Russia, when dismembering Sweden,
Turkey, and Persia?—or by Prussia, before incorporating Silesia?

So far from any such confederation having ever been, by
written, verbal, or implied agreement, entered into by the "European powers, obeying certain laws, and actuated in general by

a common principle;" the theory of the balance of power has, we believe, generally been interpreted, by those who, from age to age, have, parrot-like, used the phrase, to be a system invented for the very purpose of supplying the want of such a combination. Regarding it for a moment in this point of view, we should still expect to find that the "balancing system" had, at some period of modern history, been recognised and agreed to by all the Continental states; and that it had created a spirit of mutual concession and guarantee, by which the weaker and more powerful empires were placed upon a footing of equal security, and by which any one potentate or state was absolutely unable "to predominate over the others." But, instead of any such self-denial, we discover that the balance of Europe has merely meant (if it has had a meaning) that which our blunt Dutch king openly avowed as his aim to his parliament—a desire, on the part of the great powers, to *"hold the balance of Europe."* England has, for nearly a century, held the European scales—not with the blindness of the goddess of justice herself, or with a view to the equilibrium of opposite interests, but with a Cyclopean eye to her own aggrandizement. The same lust of conquest has actuated, up to the measure of their abilities, the other great powers; and, if we find the smaller states still, in the majority of instances, preserving their independent existence, it is owing, not to the watchful guardianship of the "balancing system," but to the limits which nature herself has set to the undue extension of territorial dominion—not only by the physical boundaries of different countries, but in those still more formidable moral impediments to the invader—the unity of language, laws, customs, and traditions; the instinct of patriotism and freedom; the hereditary rights of rulers; and, though last not least, that homage to the restraints of justice which nations and public bodies have in all ages avowed, however they may have found excuses for evading it.

So far, then, as we can understand the subject, the theory of a balance of power is a mere chimera—a creation of the politician's brain—a phantasm, without definite form or tangible existence—a mere conjunction of syllables, forming words which convey sound without meaning. Yet these words have been echoed by the greatest orators and statesmen of England: they gingled successively from the lips of Bolingbroke, Chatham, Pitt, Burke, Fox, Sheridan, Grey, and Brougham;—ay, even whilst we were in the act of stripping the maritime nations of the Continent of their colonies, then regarded as the sole source of commercial greatness; whilst we stood sword in hand upon the neck of Spain, or planted our standard on the rock of Malta; and even when England usurped the dominion of the ocean, and attempted to extend the sphere of human despotism over another element, by insolently putting barriers upon the highway of nations—even then, the tongues of our orators resounded most loudly with the praises of the "balance of power!" There would be something peculiarly humiliating in connection with this subject, in beholding the greatest minds of successive ages, instead of exercising the faculty of thought, become the mere automata of authority, and retail, with less examination than the haberdasher bestows upon the length, breadth, and quality of his wares, the sentiments bequeathed from former generations of writers and speakers—but that, unhappily, the annals of philosophy and of past religions, afford too many examples of the triumph of mere imitativeness over the higher faculties of the human intellect.

We must not, however, pass over the "balance of power," without at least endeavouring to discover the meaning of a phrase which still enters into the preamble of an annual act of Parliament, for raising and maintaining a standing army of ninety thousand men. The theory, according to the historian Robertson, was first invented by the Machiavellian statesmen of Italy during the prosperous era of the Florentine (miscalled) republic; and it was imported into Western Europe in the early part of the sixteenth century, and became "fashionable," to use the very word of the historian of Charles V., along with many other modes borrowed, about the same time, from that commercial and civilized people. This explanation of its origin does not meet with the concurrence of some other writers; for it is singular, but still consistent with the ignis-fatuus character of the "balance of power," that scarcely two authors agree, either as to the nature or the precise period of invention of the system. Lord Brough-

am claims for the theory an origin as remote as the time of the
Athenians; and Hume describes Demosthenes to have been the
first advocate of the "balancing system"—very recommendatory,
remembering that ancient history is little else than a calendar
of savage wars! There can be little doubt, however, that the
idea, by whomsoever or at whatever epoch conceived, sprang
from that first instinct of our nature, fear, and originally meant
at least some scheme for preventing the dangerous growth of the
power of any particular state; *that power being always regarded,
be it well remembered, as solely the offspring of conquest and
aggrandizement:* notwithstanding, as we have had occasion to
show in a former page of this pamphlet, in the case of England
and the United States, that labour, improvements, and dis-
coveries, confer the greatest strength upon a people; and that,
by these alone, and not by the sword of the conqueror, can
nations, in modern and all future times, hope to rise to supreme power and grandeur. And it must be obvious that a system
professing to observe a "balance of power"—by which, says
Vattel, "no one potentate or state shall be able absolutely to
predominate;" or, according to Gentz, "to injure the independence or essential rights of another;" by which, says Brougham,
"a perpetual attention to foreign affairs is inculcated, and a
constant watchfulness over every nation is prescribed:"—it must
be obvious that such a "balancing system"—if it disregards those
swiftest strides towards power which are making by nations ex-
celling in mechanical and chemical science, industry, education,
morality, and freedom—must be altogether chimerical.

Lord Bacon, indeed, took a broader and more comprehensive
view of this question when he wrote, in his essay on empire
—*"First,* for their neighbours, there can no general rule be
given (the occasions are so variable) save one, which ever
holdeth; which is, that princes do keep due sentinel, that none
of their neighbours do overgrow so (by increase of territory, by
embracing of trade, by approaches, *or the like*), as they become
more able to annoy them than they were: and this is generally
the work of standing councils, to see and *to hinder it."* This
appears to us to be the only sound and correct view of such a
principle as is generally understood by the phrase, "the balance

of power." It involves, however, such a dereliction of justice, and utter absence of conscientiousness, that subsequent writers upon the subject have not dared to follow out the principle of hindering the growth of trade, and the like (which includes all advance in civilization); although, to treat it in any other manner than that in which it is handled by this "wisest, greatest, meanest of mankind," is to abandon the whole system to contempt, as unsound, insufficient, and illusory. As for the *rule* of Lord Bacon; were the great Enemy of mankind himself to summon a council, to devise a law of nations which should convert this fair earth, with all its capacity for life, enjoyment, and goodness, into one vast theatre of death and misery, more dismal than his own dark Pandemonium, the very words of the philosopher would compose that law! It would reduce us even below the level of the brute animals. *They* do not make war against their own instincts; but this "rule" would, if acted upon universally, plunge us into a war of annihilation with that instinct of progression which is the distinguishing nature of intellectual man. It would forbid all increase in knowledge, which, by the great writer's own authority, is power. It would interdict the growth of morality and freedom, which are power.

---

15. TWO ADDRESSES

Woodrow Wilson was the leading antagonist of balance-of-power politics in the twentieth century. In his address on the war aims of Germany and Austria delivered at a joint session of Congress in February, 1918 and his address at the Guildhall, London, in December, 1918, Wilson attacks the basic precepts of an international order based on a balance of power system.

For Wilson, balance of power meant an undemocratic world controlled by "selfish groups of autocratic powers." By his very definition such a world could never be free of war and it must be, therefore, buried forever on the battlefields of World War I. World peace could only be based on "universal principles of right and justice" guaranteed by a world organization of free and democratic states. The "unstable equilibrium of competitive interests," he held, must never again barter peoples and nations "as if they were mere chattels and pawns in a game, even the great game, now forever discredited, of the balance of power."

WOODROW WILSON

THE WAR AIMS OF GERMANY AND AUSTRIA*

On the eighth of January I had the honor of addressing you on the objects of the war as our people conceive them. The Prime Minister of Great Britain had spoken in similar terms on the fifth of January. To these addresses the German Chancellor replied on the twenty-fourth and Count Czernin, for Austria, on the same day. It is gratifying to have our desire so promptly realized that all exchanges of view on this great matter should be made in the hearing of all the world.

Count Czernin's reply, which is directed chiefly to my own address of the eighth of January, is uttered in a very friendly tone. He finds in my statement a sufficiently encouraging approach to the views of his own Government to justify him in believing that it furnishes a basis for a more detailed discussion of purposes by the two Governments. . . .

Count von Hertling's reply is, I must say, very vague and very confusing. It is full of equivocal phrases and leads it is not clear where. . . . But it is certainly in a very different tone from that of Count Czernin, and apparently of an opposite purpose. It confirms, I am sorry to say, rather than removes, the unfortunate impression made by what we had learned of the conferences at Brest-Litovsk. His discussion and acceptance of our general principles lead him to no practical conclusions. He refuses to apply them to the substantive items which must con-

---

* Delivered February 11, 1918, at a joint session of the Senate and the House of Representatives. From an official government publication. Reprinted in *The Public Papers of Woodrow Wilson*, ed. R. S. Baker and W. E. Dodd. New York: Harper and Brothers, 1927, Vol. I, pp. 178–184.

stitute the body of any final settlement. He is jealous of international action and of international counsel. He accepts, he says, the principle of public diplomacy, but he appears to insist that it be confined, at any rate in this case, to generalities and that the several particular questions of territory and sovereignty, the several questions upon whose settlement must depend the acceptance of peace by the twenty-three states now engaged in the war, must be discussed and settled, not in general council, but severally by the nations most immediately concerned by interest or neighborhood. He agrees that the seas should be free, but looks askance at any limitation to that freedom by international action in the interest of the common order. He would without reserve be glad to see economic barriers removed between nation and nation, for that could in no way impede the ambitions of the military party with whom he seems constrained to keep on terms. Neither does he raise objection to a limitation of armaments. That matter will be settled of itself, he thinks, by the economic conditions which must follow the war. But the German colonies, he demands, must be returned without debate. He will discuss with no one but the representatives of Russia what disposition shall be made of the peoples and the lands of the Baltic provinces; with no one but the Government of France the "conditions" under which French territory shall be evacuated; and only with Austria what shall be done with Poland. In the determination of all questions affecting the Balkan states he defers, as I understand him, to Austria and Turkey; and with regard to the agreements to be entered into concerning the non-Turkish peoples of the present Ottoman Empire, to the Turkish authorities themselves. After a settlement all around, effected in this fashion, by individual barter and concession, he would have no objection, if I correctly interpret his statement, to a league of nations which would undertake to hold the new balance of power steady against external disturbance.

It must be evident to everyone who understands what this war has wrought in the opinion and temper of the world that no general peace, no peace worth the infinite sacrifices of these years of tragical suffering, can possibly be arrived at in any such fashion. The method the German Chancellor proposes is the method of the Congress of Vienna. We cannot and will not return to that. What is at stake now is the peace of the world. What we are striving for is a new international order based upon broad and universal principles of right and justice,—no mere peace of shreds and patches. Is it possible that Count von Hertling does not see that, does not grasp it, is in fact living in his thought in a world dead and gone? Has he utterly forgotten the Reichstag Resolutions of the nineteenth of July, or does he deliberately ignore them? They spoke of the conditions of a general peace, not of national aggrandizement or of arrangements between state and state. The peace of the world depends upon the just settlement of each of the several problems to which I adverted in my recent address to the Congress. I, of course, do not mean that the peace of the world depends upon the acceptance of any particular set of suggestions as to the way in which those problems are to be dealt with. I mean only that those problems each and all affect the whole world; that unless they are dealt with in a spirit of unselfish and unbiased justice, with a view to the wishes, the natural connections, the racial aspirations, the security, and the peace of mind of the peoples involved, no permanent peace will have been attained. They cannot be discussed separately or in corners. None of them constitutes a private or separate interest from which the opinion of the world may be shut out. Whatever affects the peace affects mankind, and nothing settled by military force, if settled wrong, is settled at all. It will presently have to be reopened.

Is Count von Hertling not aware that he is speaking in the court of mankind, that all the awakened nations of the world now sit in judgment on what every public man, of whatever nation, may say on the issues of a conflict which has spread to every region of the world? The Reichstag Resolutions of July themselves frankly accepted the decisions of that court. There shall be no annexations, no contributions, no punitive damages. Peoples are not to be handed about from one sovereignty to another by an international conference or an understanding between rivals and antagonists. National aspirations must be respected; peoples may now be dominated and governed only by their own consent. "Self-determination" is not a mere phrase. It is an imperative principle of action, which statesmen will henceforth ignore at their peril. We cannot have general peace for the asking, or by the mere arrangements of a peace conference. It cannot be pieced together out of individual understandings between powerful states. All the parties to this war must join in the settlement of every issue anywhere involved in it; because what we are seeking is a peace that we can all unite to guarantee and maintain and every item of it must be submitted to the common judgment whether it be right and fair, an act of justice, rather than a bargain between sovereigns. . . .

This war had its roots in the disregard of the rights of small nations and of nationalities which lacked the union and the force to make good their claim to determine their own allegiances and their own forms of political life. Covenants must now be entered into which will render such things impossible for the future; and those covenants must be backed by the united force of all the nations that love justice and are willing to maintain it at any cost. . . .

Count Czernin seems to see the fundamental elements of peace with clear eyes and does not seek to obscure them. He sees that an independent Poland, made up of all the indisputably Polish peoples who lie contiguous to one another, is a matter of European concern and must of course be conceded; that Belgium must be evacuated and restored, no matter what sacrifices and concessions that may involve; and that national aspirations must be satisfied, even within his own Empire, in the common interest of Europe and mankind. If he is silent about questions which touch the interest and purpose of his allies more nearly than they touch those of Austria only, it must of course be because he feels constrained, I suppose, to defer to Germany and Turkey in the circumstances. . . .

After all, the test of whether it is possible for either government to go any further in this comparison of views is simple and obvious. The principles to be applied are these:

First, that each part of the final settlement must be based upon the essential justice of that particular case and upon such adjustments as are most likely to bring a peace that will be permanent;

Second, that peoples and provinces are not to be bartered

about from sovereignty to sovereignty as if they were mere chattels and pawns in a game, even the great game, now forever discredited, of the balance of power; but that

Third, every territorial settlement involved in this war must be made in the interest and for the benefit of the populations concerned, and not as a part of any mere adjustment or compromise of claims amongst rival states; and

Fourth, that all well-defined national aspiration shall be accorded the utmost satisfaction that can be accorded them without introducing new or perpetuating old elements of discord and antagonism that would be likely in time to break the peace of Europe and consequently of the world.

A general peace erected upon such foundations can be discussed. Until such a peace can be secured we have no choice but to go on. . . .

. . . Our resources are in part mobilized now, and we shall not pause until they are mobilized in their entirety. Our armies are rapidly going to the fighting front, and will go more and more rapidly. Our whole strength will be put into this war of emancipation,—emancipation from the threat and attempted mastery of selfish groups of autocratic rulers,—whatever the difficulties and present partial delays. We are indomitable in our power of independent action and can in no circumstances consent to live in a world governed by intrigue and force. We believe that our own desire for a new international order under which reason and justice and the common interests of mankind shall prevail is the desire of enlightened men everywhere. Without that new order the world will be without peace and human life will lack tolerable conditions of existence and development. Having set our hand to the task of achieving it, we shall not turn back. . . .

A League of Nations*

Mr. Lord Mayor: We have come upon times when ceremonies like this have a new significance, and it is that significance which

---

* Title supplied. Delivered December 28, 1918, in response to a welcoming address by the Lord Mayor of London at the Guildhall. From an official government publication. Reprinted in *The Public Papers of Woodrow Wilson,* ed. R. S. Baker and W. E. Dodd. New York: Harper and Brothers, 1927, Vol. I, pp. 178–184.

most impresses me as I stand here. The address which I have just heard is most generously and graciously conceived and the delightful accent of sincerity in it seems like a part of that voice of counsel which is now everywhere to be heard. . . .

I have not yet been to the actual battlefields, but I have been with many of the men who have fought the battles, and the other day I had the pleasure of being present at a session of the French Academy when they admitted Marshal Joffre to their membership. The sturdy, serene soldier stood and uttered, not the words of triumph, but the simple words of affection for his soldiers, and the conviction which he summed up, in a sentence which I will not try accurately to quote but reproduce in its spirit, was that France must always remember that the small and the weak could never live free in the world unless the strong and the great always put their power and strength in the service of right. That is the afterthought—the thought that something must be done now not only to make the just settlements, that of course, but to see that the settlements remained and were observed and that honor and justice prevailed in the world. And as I have conversed with the soldiers, I have been more and more aware that they fought for something that not all of them had defined, but which all of them recognized the moment you stated it to them. They fought to do away with an old order and to establish a new one, and the center and characteristic of the old order was that unstable thing which we used to call the "balance of power"—a thing in which the balance was determined by the sword which was thrown in the one side or the other; a balance which was determined by the unstable equilibrium of competitive interests; a balance which was maintained by jealous watchfulness and an antagonism of interests which though it was generally latent, was always deep-seated. The men who have fought in this war have been the men from free nations who were determined that that sort of thing should end now and forever.

It is very interesting to me to observe how from every quarter, from every sort of mind, from every concert of counsel, there comes the suggestion that there must now be, not a balance of power, not one powerful group of nations set off against another, but a single overwhelming, powerful group of nations who shall be the trustee of the peace of the world. . . . That is the most reassuring thing that has ever happened in the world. When this war began the thought of a League of Nations was indulgently considered as the interesting thought of closeted students. It was thought of as one of those things that it was right to characterize by a name which as a university man I have always resented; it was said to be academic, as if that in itself were a condemnation, something that men could think about but never get. Now we find the practical leading minds of the world determined to get it. No such sudden and potent union of purpose has ever been witnessed in the world before. . . . Those principles are clearly and definitely enough stated to make their application a matter which should afford no fundamental difficulty. And back of us is that imperative yearning of the world to have all disturbing questions quieted, to have all threats against peace silenced, to have just men everywhere come together for a common object. The peoples of the world want peace and they want it now, not merely by conquest of arms, but by agreement of mind. . . .

16. THE BOLSHEVIKI AND
WORLD PEACE *

In The Bolsheviki and World Peace, *Trotsky saw* World War
I *as part of the historical development of a world economy.*
    He agreed with Lenin's analysis of imperialism as the "highest stage of capitalism," and stated that "it is imperialism that has upset completely the European status quo, *maintained for*

---

* Leon Trotsky, *The Bolsheviki and World Peace.* New York: Boni and Liveright, 1918, pp. 20–37.

forty-five years." But if it was imperialism which had destroyed the European balance of power, it was the changes in the underlying economic forces which were destroying the capitalistic system itself. "The present war is at bottom," he said, "a revolt of the forces of production against the political form of nation and state." In other words, the nation-state was no longer viable as an "independent economic unit." For Trotsky, this meant the destruction of capitalism and the creation of a new socialist economic system.

LEON TROTSKY

The forces of production which capitalism has evolved have outgrown the limits of nation and state. The national state, the present political form, is too narrow for the exploitation of these productive forces. The natural tendency of our economic system, therefore, is to seek to break through the state boundaries. The whole globe, the land and the sea, the surface as well as the interior, has become one economic workshop, the different parts of which are inseparably connected with each other. This work was accomplished by capitalism. But in accomplishing it the capitalist states were led to struggle for the subjection of the world-embracing economic system to the profit interests of the bourgeoisie of each country. What the politics of imperialism has demonstrated more than anything else is that the old national state that was created in the revolutions and the wars of 1789–1815, 1848–1859, 1864–1866, and 1870 has outlived itself, and is now an intolerable hindrance to economic development.

The present War is at bottom a revolt of the forces of production against the political form of nation and state. It means the collapse of the national state as an independent economic unit.

The nation must continue to exist as a cultural, ideologic and psychological fact, but its economic foundation has been pulled from under its feet. All talk of the present bloody clash being a work of national defense is either hypocrisy or blindness. On the contrary, the real, objective significance of the War is the breakdown of the present national economic centres, and the substitution of a world economy in its stead. But the way the governments propose to solve this problem of imperialism is not through the intelligent, organized coöperation of all of humanity's producers, but through the exploitation of the world's economic system by the capitalist class of the victorious country; which country is by this War to be transformed from a Great Power into the World Power.

The War proclaims the downfall of the national state. Yet at the same time it proclaims the downfall of the capitalist system of economy. By means of the national state capitalism has revolutionized the whole economic system of the world. It has divided the whole earth among the oligarchies of the great powers, around which were grouped the satellites, the small nations, who lived off the rivalry between the great ones. The future development of world economy on the capitalistic basis means a ceaseless struggle for new and ever new fields of capitalist exploitation, which must be obtained from one and the same source, the earth. The economic rivalry under the banner of militarism is accompanied by robbery and destruction which violate the elementary principles of human economy. World production revolts not only against the confusion produced by national and state divisions but also against the capitalist economic organization, which has now turned into barbarous disorganization and chaos.

The War of 1914 is the most colossal breakdown in history of an economic system destroyed by its own inherent contradictions.

All the historical forces whose task it has been to guide the bourgeois society, to speak in its name and to exploit it, have declared their historical bankruptcy by the War. They defended capitalism as a system of human civilization, and the catastrophe born out of that system is primarily *their* catastrophe. The first wave of events raised the national governments and armies to unprecedented heights never attained before. For the moment the nations rallied around them. But the more terrible will be the crash of the governments when the people, deafened by the thunder of the cannon, realize the meaning of the events now taking place in all their truth and frightfulness.

The revolutionary reaction of the masses will be all the more powerful the more prodigious the cataclysm which history is now bringing upon them.

Capitalism has created the material conditions of a new Socialist economic system. Imperialism has led the capitalist nations into historic chaos. The War of 1914 shows the way out of this chaos by violently urging the proletariat on to the path of Revolution.

For the economically backward countries of Europe the War brings to the fore problems of a far earlier historic origin—problems of democracy and national unity. This is in a large measure the case with the peoples of Russia, Austria-Hungary and the Balkan Peninsula. But these historically belated questions, which were bequeathed to the present epoch as a heritage from the past, do not alter the fundamental character of the events. It is not the national aspirations of the Serbs, Poles, Roumanians or Finns that has mobilized twenty-five million soldiers and placed them in the battlefields, but the imperialistic interests of the bourgeoisie of the Great Powers. It is imperialism that has upset completely the European *status quo,* maintained for forty-five years, and raised again the old questions which the bourgeois revolution proved itself powerless to solve.

Yet in the present epoch it is quite impossible to treat these questions in and by themselves. They are utterly devoid of an independent character. The creation of normal relations of national life and economic development on the Balkan Peninsula is unthinkable if Czarism and Austria-Hungary are preserved. Czarism is now the indispensable military reservoir for the financial imperialism of France and the conservative colonial power of England. Austria-Hungary is the mainstay of Germany's imperialism. Issuing from the private family clashes between the national Servian terrorists and the Hapsburg political police, the War very quickly revealed its true fundamental character—a struggle of life and death between Germany and England. While the simpletons and hypocrites prate of the defense of national freedom and independence, the German-English War is really being waged for the freedom of the imperialistic exploitation of the peoples of India and Egypt on the one hand, and for the imperialistic division of the peoples of the earth on the other.

Germany began its capitalistic development on a national basis with the destruction of the continental hegemony of France in the year 1870–1871. Now that the development of German industry on a national foundation has transformed Germany into the first capitalistic power of the world, she finds herself colliding with the hegemony of England in her further course of development. The complete and unlimited domination of the European continent seems to Germany the indispensable prerequisite of the overthrow of her world enemy. The first thing, therefore, that imperialistic Germany writes in her programme is the creation of a Middle European League of Nations. Germany, Austria-Hungary, the Balkan Peninsula and Turkey, Holland, the Scandinavian countries, Switzerland, Italy, and, if possible, enfeebled France and Spain and Portugal, are to make one economic and military whole, a Great Germany under the hegemony of the present German state.

This programme, which has been thoroughly elaborated by the economists, political students, jurists and diplomats of German imperialism and translated into reality by its strategists, is the most striking proof and most eloquent expression of the fact that capitalism has expanded beyond the limits of the national state and feels intolerably cramped within its boundaries. The national Great Power must go and in its place must step the imperialistic World Power.

In these historical circumstances the working class, the proletariat, can have no interest in defending the outlived and antiquated national "fatherland," which has become the main obstacle to economic development. The task of the proletariat is to create a far more powerful fatherland, with far greater power of resistance—*the republican United States of Europe,* as the foundation of the United States of the World.

The only way in which the proletariat can meet the imperialistic perplexity of capitalism is by opposing to it as a practical programme of the day the Socialist organization of world economy.

War is the method by which capitalism, at the climax of its development, seeks to solve its insoluble contradictions. To this method the proletariat must oppose its *own* method, the method of the Social Revolution. . . .

In our war against Czarism, in which we have never known a

"national" truce, we have never looked for help from Hapsburg
or Hohenzollern militarism, and we are not looking for it now.
We have preserved a sufficiently clear revolutionary vision to
know that the idea of destroying Czarism was utterly repugnant
to German imperialism. Czarism has been its best ally on the
Eastern border. It is united to it by close ties of social structure
and historical aims. Yet even if it were otherwise, even if it
could be assumed that, in obedience to the logic of military
operations, it would deal a destructive blow to Czarism, in defiance of the logic of its own political interests—even in such a
highly improbable case we should refuse to regard the Hohenzol-
lerns as an ally by sympathy or even by identity of immediate
aims. The fate of the Russian Revolution is so inseparably
bound up with the fate of European Socialism, and we Russian
Socialists stand so firmly on the ground of internationalism, that
we cannot, we must not for a moment, entertain the idea of
purchasing the doubtful liberation of Russia by the certain
destruction of the liberty of Belgium and France, and—what is
more important still—thereby inoculating the German and Austrian proletariat with the virus of imperialism. . . .

The collapse of the Second International is a tragic fact, and it
were blindness or cowardice to close one's eyes to it. The position taken by the French and by the larger part of English
Socialism is as much a part of this breakdown as is the position
of the German and Austrian Social Democracy. If the present
work addresses itself chiefly to the German Social Democracy
it is only because the German party was the strongest, most
influential, and in principle the most basic member of the Socialist world. Its historic capitulation reveals most clearly the
causes of the downfall of the Second International.

At first glance it may appear that the social revolutionary
prospects of the future are wholly deceptive. The insolvency of
the old Socialist parties has become catastrophically apparent.
Why should we have faith in the future of the Socialist movement? Such skepticism, though natural, nevertheless leads to
quite an erroneous conclusion. It leaves out of account the good
will of history, just as we have often been too prone to ignore

its ill will, which has now so cruelly shown itself in the fate that has overcome the International.

The present War signalizes the collapse of the national states. The Socialist parties of the epoch now concluded were national parties. They had become ingrained in the national states with all the different branches of their organizations, with all their activities and with their psychology. In the face of the solemn declarations at their congresses they rose to the defense of the conservative state, when imperialism, grown big on the national soil, began to demolish the antiquated national barriers. And in their historic crash the national states have pulled down with them the national Socialist parties also.

It is not Socialism that has gone down, but its temporary historical external form. The revolutionary idea begins its life anew as it casts off its old rigid shell. This shell is made up of living human beings, of an entire generation of Socialists that has become fossilized in self-abnegating work of agitation and organization through a period of several decades of political reaction, and has fallen into the habits and views of national opportunism or possibilism. All efforts to save the Second International on the old basis, by personal diplomatic methods and mutual concessions, are quite hopeless. The old mole of history is now digging its passageways all too well and none has the power to stop him.

As the national states have become a hindrance to the development of the forces of production, so the old Socialist parties have become the main hindrance to the revolutionary movement of the working class. It was necessary that they should demonstrate to the full their extreme backwardness, that they should discredit their utterly inadequate and narrow methods, and bring the shame and horror of national discord upon the proletariat, in order that the working class might emancipate itself, through these fearful disillusionments, from the prejudices and slavish habits of the period of preparation, and become at last that which the voice of history is now calling it to be—the revolutionary class fighting for power. . . .

V

The Balance of Power
after World War II

After 1945, the structure of international politics was radically
changed by four interrelated events: the destruction of nearly all
the Continental European powers in war—especially Germany;
the sudden rise to preëminence of both America and Russia;
the development of thermonuclear weapons; and the revolutionary rising of non-Western nationalist movements against Western
imperial control.

Soviet pressure outwards, towards Central and Western Europe, and the Middle East, did not slacken after the Red Army
had moved into Eastern Europe during the war; nor did American power and influence repeat the practice of withdrawal
into isolation, as had been the case after World War I. Stalin's
Russia and its Communist Party apparatuses abroad chose to
exploit the postwar economic and social chaos of Europe;
American economic power sought to reestablish the European
economies. Within two years after Hitler's defeat, a cold war
began between America and Russia, whose central focal point
was Germany, but whose theater was, as William C. Bullitt
wrote, the "great globe itself."

In 1947, when the Soviet Union established the Cominform as
the Comintern's successor organization to rally Communist parties

around the U.S.S.R., Stalin's chief lieutenant, Andrei Zhdanov, gave theoretical form to the new configuration of world politics: the famous "two-camp" theory which saw the world split between socialist and capitalist orders. In Western countries, the idea of bipolarity came into common usage, to describe a new distribution of political and military power now polarized between two points: Washington and Moscow. Such a duopolistic distribution of political and military power was unique in the society of nations; the European balance system had been a multiple one, with normally four or five centers of relatively equal power, around which smaller states oscillated. In Europe, nearly all states which were free to choose quickly aligned themselves in a "Western" camp under American hegemonial leadership; while Eastern Europe, under de facto Soviet control, aligned itself with the Soviet Union in a complex net of military alliances.

Some Western leaders, as the late John Foster Dulles, regarded this bipolar condition as a global one, in which "free" nations were juxtaposed to "slave" nations; for Dulles, noncommitted or uncommitted nations objectively served the interests of the Soviet Union in the cold war. Yet most new nations of Asia and Africa saw little to be gained by aligning themselves with either side in this conflict. "Neutralism", exemplified by the strategies of the late Indian Prime Minister Nehru, sought rather to remain aloof from the conflict, to "opt out of" a bipolar situation, and, if possible, to mediate between the two power blocs.

In the realm of military power, bipolarity was most pronounced. None of the new non-Western nations possessed technological resources to develop modern weapons systems; few of the European powers could make the hard choice for guns instead of butter, and none of them had the economic or technological resources even to aspire to military parity with the "super-powers." Both America and the Soviet Union plunged ahead in the development of thermonuclear weapons systems in the 1950's, far outdistancing their only possible competitor, Britain. By 1960, their respective arsenals of atomic and hydrogen bombs had reached the state of "over-kill" capacity—each could annihilate the other if it wished to do so; and Winston

Churchill, commenting on this gloomy fact, coined the phrase, the "balance of terror."

What had lent strong cement to its cohesiveness, was the novel fact that bipolarity had strong universalist ideological overtones. The United States, a liberal "open society," based upon Lockean principles, confronted a system based upon Marxist doctrine. No such massive ideological polarization of politics in the society of nations had existed since the time of the religious wars, when Catholic and Protestant states and movements struggled for control of Europe. Classical balance politics had been either un-ideological, or had—as was the case in the 1930's—been informed by nationalist ideologies such as Fascism, and German racism.

Nonetheless, this configuration of bipolarized power was not to remain the dominant feature of world politics. For one thing, the mutual terror inspired by nuclear weapons cancelled out the effective political uses of these devices in all but the gravest circumstances; the Cuban missile crisis inspired both Russian and American leadership with an awareness of their common mortality. Nor could military power of the superpowers be brought to bear purposefully on important political developments outside Europe, especially in Africa and many parts of Asia. As Western Europe recovered its economic strength, its dependence on America no longer had economic overtones, and remained chiefly a military one. In the Communist bloc, China began to challenge Soviet ideological supremacy, and to undertake adventures in Southeast Asia which Soviet leaders could not regard as compatible with their own interests. Political polycentrism thus, in both "camps," came to underlie the continued fact of military bipolarity.

The following selections are presented here to show the emerging features of this new condition of bipolarity.

17. THE STALINIST ASSESSMENT*

*Andrei Zhdanov was a leading member of the Soviet Politburo
and Stalin's personal deputy to the founding conference of the
Communist Information Bureau (Cominform) in September
1947. His speech was the most comprehensive statement on Soviet policy since the end of the Second World War and the most
significant statement of the international communist position since
1928.*

*The major postwar development, declared Zhdanov, was the
division of the "international arena into two major camps; the
imperialist and antidemocratic camp, on the one hand, and the
antiimperialist and democratic camp, on the other." By setting
up a bipolar balance of power, Zhdanov is officially recognizing the demise of the old European balance of power and the
formation of a new power balance headed by the "imperialist"
United States and the "antiimperialist" Soviet Union. The
speech was, in effect, the Soviet declaration of a "cold war"
against the West.*

ANDREI ZHDANOV

I. THE POST-WAR WORLD SITUATION

The end of the Second World War brought with it big changes
in the world situation. The military defeat of the bloc of fascist
states, the character of the war as a war of liberation from
fascism, and the decisive role played by the Soviet Union in the
vanquishing of the fascist aggressors sharply altered the alignment of forces between the two systems—the Socialist and the
Capitalist—in favour of Socialism.

What is the essential nature of these changes? . . .

The war immensely enhanced the international significance
and prestige of the U. S. S. R. The U. S. S. R. was the leading

---

* Andrei Zhdanov, Address to the Communist Information Bureau,
September 1947, in *Strategy and Tactics of World Communism*, House
of Representatives' Document #619, 80th Congress, 2nd session, 1948,
pp. 212–220.

force and the guiding spirit in the military defeat of Germany and Japan. The progressive democratic forces of the whole world rallied around the Soviet Union. The socialist state successfully stood the strenuous test of the war and emerged victorious from the mortal struggle with a most powerful enemy. Instead of being enfeebled, the U. S. S. R. became stronger.

The capitalist world has also undergone a substantial change. Of the six so-called great imperialist powers (Germany, Japan, Great Britain, the U. S. A., France and Italy), three have been eliminated by military defeat (Germany, Italy and Japan). France has also been weakened and has lost its significance as a great power. As a result, only two great imperialist world powers remain—the United States and Great Britain. But the position of one of them, Great Britain, has been undermined. The war revealed that militarily and politically British imperialism was not so strong as it had been. In Europe, Britain was helpless against German aggression. In Asia, Britain, one of the biggest of the imperialist powers, was unable to retain hold of her colonial possessions without outside aid. . . .

World War II aggravated the crisis of the colonial system, as expressed in the rise of a powerful movement for national liberation in the colonies and dependencies. This has placed the rear of the capitalist system in jeopardy. The peoples of the colonies no longer wish to live in the old way. The ruling classes of the metropolitan countries can no longer govern the colonies on the old lines. Attempts to crush the national liberation movement by military force now increasingly encounter armed resistance on the part of the colonial peoples and lead to protracted colonial wars (Holland-Indonesia, France—Viet Nam).

The war—itself a product of the unevenness of capitalist development in the different countries—still further intensified this unevenness. Of all the capitalist powers, only one—the United States—emerged from the war not only unweakened, but even considerably stronger economically and militarily. The war greatly enriched the American capitalists. The American people on the other hand, did not experience the privations that accompany war, the hardship of occupation, or aerial bombardment; and since America entered the war practically in its concluding stage, when the issue was already decided, her human casualties were relatively small. For the U. S. A., the war was primarily and chiefly a spur to extensive industrial development and to a substantial increase of exports (principally to Europe). . . .

The purpose of this new, frankly expansionist course is to establish the world supremacy of American imperialism. With a view to consolidating America's monopoly position in the markets gained as a result of the disappearance of her two biggest competitors, Germany and Japan, and the weakening of her capitalist partners, Great Britain and France, the new course of United States policy envisages a broad program of military, economic and political measures, designed to establish United States political and economic domination in all countries marked out for American expansion, to reduce these countries to the status of satellites of the United States, and to set up regimes within them which would eliminate all obstacles on the part of the labour and democratic movement to the exploitation of these countries by American capital. The United States is now endeavouring to extend this new line of policy not only to its enemies in the war and to neutral countries, but in an increasing degree to its wartime allies. . . .

But America's aspirations to world supremacy encounter an obstacle in the U. S. S. R., the stronghold of anti-imperialist and anti-fascist policy, and its growing international influence, in the new democracies, which have escaped from the control of Britain and American imperialism, and in the workers of all countries, including America itself, who do not want a new war for the supremacy of their oppressors. Accordingly, the new expansionist and reactionary policy of the United States envisages a struggle against the U. S. S. R., against the labour movement in all countries, including the United States, and against the emancipationist, anti-imperialist forces in all countries.

Alarmed by the achievements of Socialism in the U. S. S. R., by the achievements of the new democracies, and by the postwar growth of the labour and democratic movement in all countries, the American reactionaries are disposed to take upon themselves the mission of "saviours" of the capitalist system from Communism.

The frank expansionist program of the United States is therefore highly reminiscent of the reckless program, which failed so ignominiously, of the fascist aggressors, who, as we know, also made a bid for world supremacy.

Just as the Hitlerites, when they were making their preparations for piratical aggression, adopted the camouflage of anti-Communism in order to make it possible to oppress and enslave all peoples and primarily and chiefly their own people, America's present-day ruling circles mask their expansionist policy, and even their offensive against the vital interests of their weaker imperialist rival, Great Britain, by fictious considerations of defence against Communism. The feverish piling up of armaments, the construction of new military bases and the creation of bridge-heads for the American armed forces in all parts of the world is justified on the false and pharisaical grounds of "defense" against an imaginary threat of war on the part of the U. S. S. R. With the help of intimidation, bribery and chicanery, American diplomacy finds it easy to extort from other capitalist countries, and primarily from Great Britain, consent to the legitimization of America's superior position in Europe and Asia—in the Western Zones of Germany, in Austria, Italy, Greece, Turkey, Egypt, Iran, Afghanistan, China, Japan and so forth. . . .

II. THE NEW POST-WAR ALIGNMENT OF POLITICAL FORCES AND THE FORMATION OF TWO CAMPS: THE IMPERIALIST AND ANTI-DEMOCRATIC CAMP, AND THE ANTI-IMPERIALIST AND DEMOCRATIC ONE

The fundamental changes caused by the war on the international scene and in the position of individual countries has entirely changed the political landscape of the world. A new alignment of political forces has arisen. The more the war recedes into the past, the more distinct become two major trends in post-war international policy, corresponding to the division of the political forces operating on the international arena into two major camps; the imperialist and anti-democratic camp, on the one hand, and the anti-imperialist and democratic camp, on the other. The principal driving force of the imperialist camp is the U. S. A. Allied with it are Great Britain and France. The existence of the Attlee-Bevin Labour Government in Britain and the Ramadier Socialist Government in France does not hinder these countries from playing the part of satellites of the United States and following the lead of its imperialist policy on all major questions. The imperialist camp is also supported by colony-owning countries, such as Belgium and Holland, by countries with reactionary anti-democratic regimes, such as Turkey and Greece, and by countries politically and economically dependent on the United States, such as the Near-Eastern and South-American countries and China.

The cardinal purpose of the imperialist camp is to strengthen imperialism, to hatch a new imperialist war, to combat Socialism and democracy, and to support reactionary and anti-democratic pro-fascist regimes and movements everywhere.

In the pursuit of these ends the imperialist camp is prepared to rely on reactionary and anti-democratic forces in all countries, and to support its former adversaries in the war against its wartime allies.

The anti-fascist forces comprise the second camp. This camp is based in the U. S. S. R. and the new democracies. It also includes countries that have broken with imperialism and have firmly set foot on the path of democratic development, such as Rumania, Hungary and Finland. Indonesia and Viet Nam are associated with it; it has the sympathy of India, Egypt and Syria. The anti-imperialist camp is backed by the labour and democratic movement and by the fraternal Communist parties in all countries, by the fighters for national liberation in the colonies and dependencies, by all progressive and democratic forces in every country. The purpose of this camp is to resist the threat of new wars and imperialist expansion, to strengthen democracy and to extirpate the vestiges of fascism.

The end of the Second World War confronted all the freedom-loving nations with the cardinal task of securing a lasting democratic peace sealing victory over fascism. In the accomplishment of this fundamental task of the post-war period the Soviet Union and its foreign policy are playing a leading role. This follows from the very nature of the Soviet Socialist state, to which motives of aggression and exploitation are utterly alien, and which is interested in creating the most favourable conditions for the building of a Communist society. One of these conditions is external peace. As embodiment of a new and superior social system, the Soviet Union reflects in its foreign policy the aspirations of progressive mankind, which desires lasting peace and has nothing to gain from a new war hatched by capitalism. The Soviet Union is a staunch [defender] of the liberty and independence of all nations, and a foe of national and racial oppression and colonial exploitation in any shape or form. The change in the general alignment of forces between the capitalist world and the Socialist world brought about by the war has still further enhanced the significance of the foreign policy of the Soviet state and enlarged the scope of its activity on the international arena.

All the forces of the anti-imperialist and anti-fascist camp are united in the effort to secure a just and democratic peace. It is this united effort that has brought about the strengthened friendly cooperation between the U.S.S.R. and democratic countries on all questions of foreign policy. These countries, and in the first place the new democracies—Yugoslavia, Poland, Czechoslovakia and Albania, which played a big part in the war of liberation from fascism, as well as Bulgaria, Rumania, Hungary and to some extent Finland, which have joined the anti-fascist front—have proved themselves in the post-war period staunch defenders of peace, democracy and their own liberty and independence against all attempts on the part of the United States and Great Britain to turn them back in their course and to bring them again under the imperialist yoke.

The successes and the growing international prestige of the democratic camp were not to the liking of the imperialists. Even while World War II was still on, reactionary forces in Great Britain and the United States became increasingly active, striving to prevent concerted action by the Allied powers, to protract the war, to bleed the U. S. S. R., and to save the fascist aggressors from utter defeat. The sabotage of the Second Front by the Anglo-Saxon imperialists, headed by Churchill, was a clear reflection of this tendency, which was in point of fact a continuation of the Munich policy in the new and changed conditions. But while the war was still in progress British and American reactionary circles did not venture to come out openly against the Soviet Union and the democratic countries, realizing that they had the undivided sympathy of the masses all over the world. But in the concluding months of the war the situation began to change. The British and American imperialists already manifested their unwillingness to respect the legitimate interests of the Soviet Union and the democratic countries at the Potsdam tripartite conference, in July 1945. . . .

Soviet foreign policy proceeds from the fact of the co-existence for a long period of the two systems—capitalism and socialism. From this it follows that co-operation between the U. S. S. R. and countries with other systems is possible, provided that the principle of reciprocity is observed and that obligations once assumed are honoured. Everyone knows that the U. S. S. R. has always honoured the obligations it has assumed. The Soviet Union has demonstrated its will and desire for co-operation.

Britain and America are pursuing the very opposite policy in the United Nations. They are doing everything they can to renounce their commitments and to secure a free hand for the prosecution of a new policy, a policy which envisages not co-operation among the nations, but the hounding of one against the other, violation of the rights and interests of democratic nations, and the isolation of the U. S. S. R.

Soviet policy follows the line of maintaining loyal, good-neighbour relations with all states that display the desire for co-operation. As to the countries that are its genuine friends and allies, the Soviet Union has always behaved, and will always behave, as their true friend and ally. Soviet foreign policy envisages a further extension of friendly aid by the Soviet Union to these countries.

Soviet foreign policy, defending the cause of peace, discountenances a policy of vengeance towards the vanquished countries.

It is known that the U. S. S. R. is in favour of a united, peace-loving, demilitarized and democratic Germany. Comrade Stalin formulated the Soviet policy towards Germany when he said: "In short, the policy of the Soviet Union on the German question reduces itself to the demilitarization and democratization of Germany. The demilitarization and democratization of Ger-

many is one of the most important guarantees of the establishment of a solid and lasting peace". However, this policy of the
Soviet Union towards Germany is being encountered by frantic
opposition from the imperialist circles in the United States and
Great Britain.

The meeting of the Council of Foreign Ministers in Moscow
in March and April 1947 demonstrated that the United States,
Great Britain and France are prepared not only to prevent the
democratic reconstruction and demilitarization of Germany, but
even to liquidate her as an integral state, to dismember her,
and to settle the question of peace separately.

Today this policy is being conducted under new conditions,
now that America has abandoned the old course of Roosevelt
and is passing to a new policy, a policy of preparing for new
military adventures. . . .

---

18. KHRUSHCHEV AND THE BALANCE
OF WORLD POWER *

*In this masterly analysis of Khrushchev's thought on interna-
tional affairs, Joseph Whelan argues that for the Soviet leader
the balance of world power has decisively and irrevocably shifted
in the communist world's favor.*

*Viewing the world through the prism of Marxist-Leninist
ideology, Khrushchev sees the "correlation of world forces" since
the end of World War II as having progressively favored the
power position of the Soviet Union at the expense of the United
States and its allies. This correlation of ideological, political,
economic and military forces has doomed the West and "under
present conditions", states Khrushchev, "the balance of forces*

---

* Joseph G. Whelan, *Khrushchev and the Balance of World Power*,
Senate document #66, 87th Congress, 1st Session, July 27, 1961. Footnotes omitted.

*has changed considerably to the advantage of socialism." Due
to this change in the balance of power, Khrushchev began at the
Twentieth Congress of the Communist Party of the Soviet Union in 1956 to revise some of the basic tenets of Leninist-
Stalinist dogma especially in regard to "capitalist encirclement"
and the "inevitability of war." Thus, the inevitable triumph of
communism will be the result of ideological and economic competition between the two systems and not the result of a cataclysmic nuclear war.*

JOSEPH G. WHELAN

Nikita Khrushchev views international politics through the prism
of Marxism-Leninism. His image of the world is far different
from ours. To try to understand the dimensions of this image and
the underlying perspective he brings to the conduct of Soviet
diplomacy presents a formidable problem. Yet, there are certain
indicators in traditional Soviet theory and thought that provide a
tool for analysis. One such indicator is the concept of the
"correlation of world forces."

Fundamental to Khrushchev's view of international politics
is a sober calculation of what he calls the "correlation of world
forces." Distilled of its Marxist-Leninist content, this simply means
that Khrushchev makes first of all an appraisal of total Soviet
political, economic, and military strength in relation to that of his
principal adversaries, and then a comparative assessment of the
general distribution of power between world communism and
world capitalism. On the basis of this appraisal he lays down the
main lines of Soviet foreign policy. This is not a new principle
in Soviet foreign policy; it was originally formulated by Lenin,
and Stalin's adherence gave in the force of historical tradition
and immutable doctrinal authority. It remains a basic operational
concept in Soviet ideology and is the first and most important
determinant in Soviet foreign policy planning.

How Khrushchev views the "correlation of world forces" today
has the greatest relevance, since his position of uncontested authority in Soviet decision-making lends to his judgment great
weight in the formulation of Soviet foreign policy. There can be
no doubt that Khrushchev believes the "correlation of world

forces" has now shifted decisively to the Soviet's favor. For the
past three years he has stressed this change in doctrine. In an
interview with Averell Harriman in June, 1959, he stated categorically that the West must face the central "fact" that the
balance of world power has now shifted to the Communist
camp. . . .

I

To understand the significance of recent claims by Khrushchev
that the balance of world forces now favors the Soviet Union, it
is necessary to grasp three essential aspects of the historic Soviet
outlook upon the world. (1) Until the emergence of the new
neutralist states of Asia and Africa, the Soviets conceived the
world as being divided into two hostile, conflicting camps—the
Socialist, that is to say, the Communist camp, and the capitalist
camp. One of the basic tenets of Soviet theory is the belief that
these two camps are contending for world predominance. (2)
Inherent in traditional Soviet doctrine is the further belief that
both systems are antithetical and that in the final analysis, perhaps after a series of wars among the capitalist states or between
the capitalist and Communist states, communism will triumph.
(3) Bolshevik success in Russia in 1917 partially transformed
the essential character of the class war described by Marx into
an alignment of opposite national forces: the nations representing world capitalism against the Socialist Motherland, Communist
Russia. From this inequitable equation of power evolved the
idea of "capitalist encirclement." During the interwar period when
the Soviet Union was emerging from difficult years of war, revolution, and internal stress, Soviet theorists stressed this concept of
"capitalist encirclement," a fundamental tenet in Soviet doctrine,
important to us particularly because it provides an index for
measuring Soviet attitudes toward the relative balance of world
forces.

During the years following the revolution, according to Soviet
belief, the balance of world forces was preponderantly weighted
in favor of the capitalist, non-Communist world. Western capitalism was powerful and strong, although, according to Marxist-
Leninist predictions, inner contradictions would eventually bring
about its collapse. An essential factor adding to its strength, but

only momentarily, was its far-flung colonial empires. By contrast, Soviet power was for a time practically at its nadir. This was the era when "capitalist encirclement" was most challenging and unchallengeable. As Stalin warned when speaking at the Eighteenth Party Congress: "Never * * * forget we are surrounded by a capitalist world."

World War II, however, radically changed the power relationships in the world, and in the postwar era Soviet leaders were quick to appreciate this change. Western colonial empires, long the focus of Soviet attack as the most vulnerable area of capitalism, declined under the impact of war and the rising national liberation movements. Western power diminished proportionately as new states emerged on the international scene. The United States became the center of Western power, while the Soviet Union, immensely strengthened by its postwar gains, assumed a leading role as a great world power. For a time the Soviets continued to cite the doctrine of the divided world, as they are likely to do as long as two "camps" exist in the same world. Now they, however, stressed particularly the strength of what they termed the "Socialist camp," under the leadership of the Soviet Union, in opposition to the so-called "imperialist camp" led by the United States. Andrei Zhdanov, a prominent Soviet leader early in the postwar era, defined this new alignment of political forces in an address before the first meeting of the Cominform in 1947, and, equally important, assured his listeners that the growing power of the Communist bloc "still further enhanced the significance of the foreign policy of the Soviet state and enlarged the scope of its activity on the international arena."

On the eve of the Nineteenth Party Congress in October 1952 Stalin restated Soviet theory on this general question in his economic thesis. Acknowledging the concept of the divided world, Stalin stressed the inevitability of war among the capitalist states and established a unique role for the Soviet Union which, guided by a "peaceful" policy, would be immune from active engagement. War among the capitalist states was still inevitable, because of the familiar "contradictions" between capitalist countries. But war between the capitalist camp and the "camp of peace" was unlikely since in such a future war, the "very existence of capitalism" would inescapably be brought into question and thus capitalists would seek to avoid such a war. . . .

When Khrushchev came to power, he reversed both ideas. In addressing the Twentieth Party Congress in 1956, he made a distinction between the conflicting forces of capitalism and socialism. He took special note of the neutralist states emerging from the former colonial areas, referring to them collectively as a "zone of peace," and included them as part of the "socialist bloc" in his equation of power. Khrushchev noted with satisfaction the enlargement of the "socialist camp," owing to the accretion of Soviet military and economic power, the creation of a large and powerful Communist bloc in Europe and Asia, and the emergence of new neutralist states. Speaking in general terms of the growing preponderance of Soviet strength in the world balance of forces, Khrushchev asserted that the "international camp of socialism is exerting ever-growing influence on the course of world events."

But Khrushchev did not believe that war was a "fatalistic inevitability." Here is another measurable indicator of Khrushchev's thinking on the changing equation of world power. The preponderance of Soviet power, augmented by the new Communist bloc of states and the so-called "zone of peace" of neutralist states, affected the distribution of power sufficiently to enable the "socialist camp" to prevent aggression. Prior to World War I and II the "world proletariat" and the "socialist camp," respectively, had failed to forestall war, owing to the inequitable equation of forces; but now the ratio of world power has changed "radically." The "world camp of socialism," possessing manpower, material means, and moral forces, has become a "mighty force" capable of preventing "the imperialists from unleashing war and, if they try to start it, to give a smashing rebuff to the aggressors and frustrate their adventurist plans." Khrushchev did not invalidate the basic Lenin thesis that so long as capitalism exists the economic base remains for producing wars; he only asserted that Soviet power had become so overwhelming that the "camp of capitalism" would be deterred from provoking war. This concept of denying the "fatalistic inevitability" of war has become a central theme in Khrushchev's world view since the Twentieth Party Congress.

On the question of "capitalist encirclement," Khrushchev has drastically changed Soviet doctrine. . . .

At the Twenty-first Party Congress Khrushchev was even more emphatic in reasserting the change in the doctrine of "capitalist encirclement." Addressing the Congress on January 27, 1959, Khrushchev explained the nature of "hostile capitalist encirclement" of the earlier period, elaborated upon the growing Soviet strength and stated categorically: "The situation in the world has fundamentally changed. Capitalist encirclement of our country no longer exists."

Since then, Khrushchev seems to have dropped this expression from his political lexicon, presumably because in his mind it no longer has relevance to reality. Thus, his political statements are now based on the idea that "capitalist encirclement" has ended, not only as an implied assumption but as an incontestable fact. Now he stresses the doctrine of denying the "fatalistic inevitability" of war, which is inferentially a declaration of Soviet military preponderance, and boldy asserts that the "correlation of world forces" favors the Soviet Union. This serves the propaganda purpose of placing the Soviet Union in the role of a peacemaker, while the previous thesis claiming the inevitability of war was used against the Soviet Union to expose its warlike intent. More significantly, it now connotes that the Soviet Union and its associates are so powerful that whether or not the capitalist world recognizes the inevitability of its demise, it still will not now dare to risk war. It suggests further this interpretation of Khrushchev's "peaceful coexistence" line: Traditional Marxist-Leninist doctrine asserts that Western capitalism needs arms production to survive. In this age of instantaneous massive destruction the West must recognize that all-out thermonuclear war is suicidal and thus must engage the Soviet Union in "peaceful competition." Therefore, once the West reduces its armaments, the "inner contradictions" latent in the capitalist system will assert themselves, and as a consequence capitalism will decline. . . .

To sum up, therefore, Khrushchev's outlook on world affairs and the broad intellectual structure within which he conceives Soviet foreign policy are conditioned by a belief, (1) that the era of "capitalist encirclement" has come to an end; (2) that

Soviet supremacy is undeniable; and (3) that the balance of forces in the world has now shifted decisively, and thus irrevocably, in favor of the "socialist camp."

II

Essential to an analysis of Khrushchev's thought in foreign policy is a determination of what he means by the "correlation of forces." This is a general, all-inclusive term used in a distributional sense. It implies the establishment of an orderly connection between various "forces" which together determine the relative strength or weakness of a state or a grouping of states. In Khrushchev's mind these "forces" fall into such categories as ideological and political, economic, and military. And he stated in a speech in Moscow on October 20, 1960, upon returning from his visit to the United Nations General Assembly in New York, "it would be wrong to gage the demarcation and balance of forces of socialism and peace and of imperialism by applying the parliamentary yardstick"—an allusion, presumably, to the prestige issue debated in the American presidential campaign. The number of states on each side did not determine the balance. "Many factors," he said, "must be taken into account in assessing the balance of forces: the economic and military potential, population, and many other factors of a material and moral nature." Calculations are made within each category for the capitalist and then the Communist world and a comparison of the grand totals would seem to provide a measure of the power differential. Inescapably, highly subjective judgments color the process of calculation, but no doubt some solid, concrete factors enter the estimate.

Whatever the precise process of calculation, there is no denying that Khrushchev believes the balance of ideological and political forces are now in Moscow's favor. Permeating his views on Communism's future is a strong conviction that the forces of Communism are rapidly encompassing the world and that world capitalism with equal speed is approaching its demise. "All the world will come to Communism. History does not ask whether you want it or not"—this is the essence of Khrushchev's conceptions of Communism's inevitable victory. Personal preferences do not enter into the matter. The inexorable laws of history have doomed capitalism and no act of individual will can change them. . . .

. . . Success of the Soviet political-economic offensive in the Middle East, Southeast Asia, and Latin America and the expanding strength of the world Communist movement to a membership of 33,000,000 in 1957 cannot help but influence Khrushchev's thinking and condition his world outlook. In all probability the sum total of these successes adds to his predictions the force of certainty.

III

Expectations of economic primacy in the immediate future have had an enormous impact on Khrushchev's thought. With extraordinary self-assurance he has often asserted that the steady growth of the Soviet economy has contributed substantially to tipping the world balance in favor of Communism. . . .

It is self-evident that Khrushchev is profoundly influenced by the increasing economic growth of the Communist world. Only recently he boasted to Americans that the Communist bloc produces one-third of the world's industrial output. In Khrushchev's mind economic power is political power: both are indissolubly wedded in a marriage of historical necessity. To Khrushchev, the growth of the Soviet economy, (*a*) demonstrates to the world the asserted superiority of the Soviet system, (*b*) increases Soviet capability to use trade and aid to influence the political destinies of other countries, and (*c*) enormously enlarges Soviet military power. Calculations of the world balance of economic forces, therefore, play an extremely important part in determining Khrushchev's world outlook.

IV

Yet it is equally certain that the balance of military power is the decisive factor in Khrushchev's assessment of the "correlation of world forces." For the past two years he has consistently asserted the claim that the balance of military power, in addition to the general balance of forces, has shifted to the Soviet advantage. Launching sputniks demonstrated Soviet intercontinental rocket capability and Soviet progress generally in military technology which Khrushchev interpreted as evidence that a "serious change has occurred in the balance of forces between the countries of socialism and capitalism in favor of the socialist nations." . . .

Khrushchev's belief in the military supremacy of the Soviet Union and its capacity to destroy any aggressor—another important facet of his thought—fortifies his convictions of the shifting balance thesis. He does not doubt that the "mighty camp of democracy and socialism," that is, the Communist bloc, could give a "worthy rebuff to the lovers of military adventures," meaning the United States and its allies. "Should the imperialists unleash a new, third world war," he told the 1954 Congress of the Czechoslovak Communist Party, "they will choke on it and it will end in a catastrophe for the capitalist world." At Kabul, Afghanistan, in March, 1960, he stated categorically that it was "generally known that militarily the Soviet Union is the world's most powerful state." And a month later in Baku he warned the West: "Our might is invincible." . . .

V

To sum up, Khrushchev's thinking in foreign affairs is determined first and foremost by an estimate of the correlation of ideological and political, economic, and military forces ranged within the "socialist" and capitalist "camps." Khrushchev now estimates that the balance favors the Communist bloc. He has "full confidence" based on a "thorough analysis of the balance of forces" that this is the "reality" of international life today. "Not only I myself but all my friends who have made a realistic assessment of the international situation think so," were his words to a Calcutta audience in March 1960. For Khrushchev this change is the "decisive" factor of our time. His thesis has now become the central political line for the Soviet Union and all world Communists. As such, it has taken on the shape of immutable, unchallengeable doctrine, since Khrushchev and his theorists have asserted the change to be "decisive." The moral and political choice for world Communists is now simply whether to be a believer or an apostate. In fact, Khrushchev has endowed his shifting balance thesis with the full authority of "moral" righteousness and the absolute certainty of reason. "Every sober-minded person today," he told a Hungarian audience in Decem-

ber 1959, realized this change. "Both strength and justice are on
our side," he said. Justice coincides with strength in the Soviet
case because despite the "tilting of the balance of forces" the
Soviets do not alter their "peace-loving policy." "We do not
propose unacceptable alternatives to our partners," he concluded,
"but, on the contrary, continue our policy of justice and reason."

Khrushchev's total image of the world as he sees it and his
belief in the correctness and righteousness of his shifting balance
thesis are the most critically relevant facts in world affairs today.
It is a truism that images of the mind find their way into reality.
The image in Khrushchev's mind in this particular instance is
the favorable "correlation of world forces." To him, this *is* reality
and as such *is* the basis for all decision making in the Soviet
state. It provides the general conceptual framework for determining broad foreign policy lines. It is the most essential element in
the entire Soviet foreign policy process. The concept is mechanistic in that it assumes a manipulative view of politics but philo-
sophically assumes the inevitable triumph of Communism. The
calculation of forces in the political realm as in the military
determines the permissible limits of advance and retreat. If the
"correlation of forces" is favorable, one must advance, not as a
particular preference but as a doctrinal necessity. In this sense
the balance concept is a convenient device for determining the
equation of power in various eras until the enemy is destroyed.
. . .

---

19. SELECTED STATEMENTS ON INDIA'S
FOREIGN POLICY *

*In the following selections from his foreign policy addresses,
Nehru describes and defends India's policy of nonalignment. The*

---

* From various issues of *India*. Several are statements or speeches made
in the Lower House of the Indian Parliament (Lok Sabha, "House of the
People.")

advent of nuclear weapons has made war "unthinkable," states Nehru, and there exists, therefore, "a certain balance—it may be a very unstable balance, but it is still some kind of balance— when any kind of major aggression is likely to lead to a world war." With the "world divided into two great camps—the communist and the noncommunist" only India's policy of nonalignment, and the growing bloc of Afro-Asian nations following in India's path, offer some "hope for the world" that its future will not be "wholly disposed of by one mighty armed group or the other."

JAWAHARLAL NEHRU

CORRECT PERSPECTIVE*

I am a little afraid that this House in its enthusiasm might perhaps imagine that we are doing more than we are really doing. I am referring particularly to the international sphere because some hon. Members in their speeches seemed to make out that India was playing a very important role, almost a dominating role, in regard to some world problems. Let us have a more correct perspective.

I believe that we have helped, occasionally, in regard to the solution of some problems, and in the relaxation or lessening of tension. We might take due credit for that, but let us not go beyond that. After all a country's capacity to influence events is determined by various factors. You will find that India is lacking in most of those factors. If we have been successful in some measure, the success has been due not obviously to any kind of military strength or financial power, but because we took a correct view of events. If I may say so in all modesty, we understood them more correctly than others, because we were more in tune with the spirit of the age. We do not have the strength to threaten anybody; nor do we want to. . . .

One hears frequently about pacts and military alliances in Europe, in the Middle East, in South-East Asia and elsewhere. There are in the world today two mighty powers, the United

---

* Speech in Lok Sabha during debate on the President's Address, February 25, 1955.

States of America and the Soviet Union. There are some other great powers also, the United Kingdom and one or two others, who are also big in varying degree. I can understand, although I would not approve, military alliances between great powers. That would have some meaning. But I do not understand military pacts and alliances between a huge giant of a power and a little pigmy of a country. It has no meaning in a military sense to me. In this nuclear age the only countries that count, from the point of view of nuclear war, are those great countries which are, unfortunately, in a position to use these bombs. But to attach small countries to themselves in alliance really means—and I say so with all respect to those countries—that they are becoming very much dependent on these countries. Such associates do not add to their defensive power, for they have little or no military value. Perhaps such alliances have some psychological value. I wish to refrain from saying anything which might militate against others. But in this nuclear age, to think of war itself is insanity. Any person who has given thought to it—many generals, in England, France, the U.S.A. and the Soviet Union have done so —would realize that war today is unthinkable, because a war is fought to achieve certain results, not to bring ruin on oneself. War, today, will bring ruin to every country involved, not only one. All the great countries appear to be clear about it and are absolutely certain that there is no country in the world which wants war. To talk about warmongers and the rest is completely wrong. There may be some individuals who might want war, but no country wants it. If that is so, what is the value of this policy of military alliances and armaments? It does not logically follow from the first assumption. The development of the thermo-nuclear bomb has changed the whole picture of fighting today. What might have been good a few years ago is no longer good.

The fact that one country has a few more bombs than the other is of no great relevance. The point is that even the country that has less has reached the saturation point, that is, it has enough to cause infinite damage to the other country. There is no real defence against nuclear weapons; you can at best damage or ruin the other country. When you have arrived at the saturation point, you have arrived at the stage of mutual extermination.

Then the only way out is to prevent war, to avoid it. There is
no other way. All talk of reduction of armaments, good as it is,
does not help much. That is the first point we should remember.

Secondly, we must consider what use alliances and pacts really
have in this age of nuclear warfare. As I said earlier, they
do not help in a military sense, though they may psychologically.
I am not asking these countries to disband their armies or their
air forces. The only effect of these pacts and alliances, it appears
to me, is to hold a kind of threat. These threats are being thrown
about by both the power blocs. But even this business of threatening through military pacts has become obsolete in this nuclear
age. You cannot threaten a big power which has nuclear weapons,
for it is not likely to be frightened. You can at best threaten
small countries.

As things are today, we have reached a certain balance—it
may be a very unstable balance, but it is still some kind of
balance—when any kind of major aggression is likely to lead to
a world war. That itself is a restraining factor. Whether aggression takes place in a small country or a big one, it tends to upset
the unstable balance in the world and is, therefore, likely to
lead to war. It is because of this that in the Geneva Conference
there was so much argument about the Indo-China States. Either
of the major parties was afraid that if any of these States linked
up with or was coerced into joining one group, it would be to the
disadvantage of the other. For instance, suppose countries like
Laos and Cambodia were overwhelmed and drawn into the
sphere of China, the countries on the other side would naturally
be frightened. On the other hand, if Laos and Cambodia became
hostile to China and could be used as bases for an attack on
China, naturally China would object to it very strongly. What is
the way out of the difficulty? Either you have war to decide
who is stronger, or you place Laos, Cambodia and all the Indo-
China States more or less outside the spheres of influence, outside
the alignments, and outside the military pacts of the two groups,
so that both could feel, at least to some extent, secure in the
knowledge that these Indo-China States were not going to be
used against them. There is no other way out. So at Geneva
they wisely decided, more or less, though not in clear language,

that the Indo-China States should keep out of military pacts or alliances on either side, or, in other words, remain neutralized.

If you extend the argument, you will see that the only way to avoid conflicts is to accept things more or less as they are. No doubt, many things require to be changed, but you must not think of changing them by war. War does not do what you want to do; it does something much worse. Further, by enlarging the area of peace, that is, of countries which are not aligned to this group or that, but which are friendly to both, you reduce the chance of war.

As the House knows, the policy adopted by India and followed consistently during the last few years has been appreciated by many countries. Some other countries of Asia, not because of us, but because of their own reasons, have followed a similar policy. Even countries which have not followed it have begun to appreciate our policy. We are following it because we are convinced that it is the right policy. We would follow it even if there was no other country in the world that followed it. It is not a question, as some hon. Members seem to imagine, of balancing the considerations and sitting on the fence. Ours is a positive policy and we follow it with conviction and faith. . . .

The world seems to be divided into two mighty camps, the communist and the anti-communist, and either party cannot understand how anyone can be foolish enough not to line up with itself. That just shows how little understanding these people have of the mind of Asia. Talking of India only, and not of all Asia, we have fairly clear ideas about our political and economic structure. We function in this country under a Constitution which may be described as a parliamentary democracy. It has not been imposed upon us. We propose to continue with it. We do not intend changing it. We intend to function on the economic plane, too, in our own way. With all respect to some hon. Members opposite, we have no intention to turn communists. At the same time, we have no intention of being dragooned in any other direction. Putting it simply, we mean no ill to anybody. Every country has a right to choose its own path and go along it. We have chosen our path and we propose to go along it, and to vary it as and when we choose, not at somebody's dictate or pressure; and we are not afraid of any other country imposing its will upon us by military methods or any other methods. The only way for us is to build up our own strength, which we intend doing. Meanwhile we want to be friendly with other countries. Our thinking and our approach do not fit in with this great crusade of communism or crusade of anticommunism. . . .

"NEUTRALS"*

As I have said repeatedly, I do not like the word "neutral" as being applied to India. I do not even like India's policy being referred to as "positive neutrality" as is done in some countries. Without doubt, we are unaligned; we are uncommitted to military blocs; but the important fact is that we are committed to various policies, various urges, various objectives, and various principles; very much so. When proposals have been made that we should form some kind of a bloc of "neutral" countries, I have not taken very kindly to them. While I do not like the system of blocs as such, we meet and discuss, have some measure of common thinking, sometimes common action, and we cooperate.

Till three or four years ago, the great and powerful countries, and the leaders of these big armed blocs, used to speak rather slightly of the "neutrals" who, according to them, had no moral basis, and, therefore, sat perched up on a hedge, as it were, not daring to come down this way or that way. That attitude has now changed a great deal. It has changed into one of considerable respect for these countries which are unaligned, and a realization has come that the position and the policy to which they adhere are certainly good for them. And now, with a large group of independent countries from Africa also more or less joining this unaligned group—not a formal group—it has made a big difference. Whether it is in the United Nations or elsewhere, this major fact is emerging, namely, that the world cannot wholly be disposed of by one mighty armed group or the other, even though they play a great part in its affairs; the

---

* From speech in Lok Sabha, November 22, 1960. Title supplied.

others have a say also, and sometimes, an important say. This development is taking place because, in spite of the terrible importance of nuclear bombs and the like, human beings and their ideas and their urges count. These provide the hope for the world. . . .

POWER VACUUM THEORY*

. . . [There] is one approach that troubles me, and that is the idea of thinking that areas in Asia, for instance in West Asia, are vacuums which have to be filled by somebody stepping in from outside. That, I feel, is a dangerous approach. It is an unreal approach to say that every country which has insufficient armaments is a vacuum. At that rate, if you think in terms of armament, there are only two countries which have an adequate supply of hydrogen bombs, the United States of America and the Soviet Union. You may say all other countries are vacuums, because they do not have hydrogen bombs, which would be an absurd thing to say. What is the test then? Military power? Two countries stand out above all others. There are two or three or four other countries which are powerful military nations, and even great powers. Outside of these five or six, are all the smaller and militarily weaker countries vacuums? What is the test of this vacuum idea, which is a dangerous idea, especially for Asia and African countries? It seems to me really to lead to the conclusion that where circumstances compel an imperialist power to withdraw, necessarily you must presume that it has left a vacuum. If so, how is that vacuum to be filled? Surely if somebody else comes in, it is a repetition of the old story, perhaps in a different form. It can only be filled by the people of that country growing and developing themselves economically, politically and otherwise.

There is another difficulty when an outside power wants to fill such a vacuum, if I may use the word. When there is conflict in the world between two countries which have their areas of influence, as soon as one country tries to fill a vacuum, the other

---

* From speech during debate on Foreign Affairs in Lok Sabha, March 25, 1957.

group suspects its intentions and tries to extend its own area of influence there or elsewhere. You thus get back into this tug-of-war of trying to capture as areas of influence various parts of the world which are not strong enough to stand by themselves.

No "THIRD FORCE"*

. . . What the Third Force means I have been wholly unable to understand. I think any idea or advocacy of a Third Force has absolutely no relation to reality. It would be a wrong step, amounting to ourselves coming into the arena of power politics. Possibly this so-called Third Force will try sometimes to join this group and sometimes the other, and on occasions keep apart.

How is force measured today? By armed strength, nuclear strength, ballistic strength, monetary strength—call it what you like. India has none of these; nor has any country which is likely to be a member of the so-called Third Force any pretensions to armed might or financial power. I do not know what exactly this collection of countries together would do, apart from the fact that they will not collect together.

So let us give up these rather fanciful ideas. We have to deal with a situation in which there are two giant powers with enormous military might. But they are also afraid of each other's might, afraid that the other party might get a certain lead. Sometimes one is a little ahead, sometimes the other. It really matters very little now who has the lead because both have passed that mark which gives them enough power to destroy. If they have passed the mark, it does not really make too much difference whether the world is destroyed completely once or twice over. If you are dead you are dead. It is no good trying to make you "deader."

AGAINST A "THIRD FORCE"†

Sometimes it is suggested that the small countries of the world should band themselves together. If that implies what has been

* From reply to debate on Foreign Affairs in Lok Sabha, December 17, 1957.

† From reply to debate on Foreign Affairs in Lok Sabha, August 20, 1958. Title supplied.

called a Third Force, it is a contradiction in terms, because numbers do not create a force. They may create moral pressures, but not a force. It will not make the slightest difference to the great military powers of today if the militarily weak countries band themselves together. If it takes the shape of banding together, even the ability to exert moral pressure goes into the background, and the physical side comes up.

Of course, it is right that countries of a like way of thinking should come close together, should confer together, should jointly function in the United Nations or elsewhere. That exactly has been the policy of India. We do not presume to call ourselves leaders; and we dislike being called the leaders of Asia. We have tried to work together with other countries on the basis of comradeship and we have done so without breaking our friendly ties with other countries. But it would be a wrong approach to gather together a number of like countries which, like us, are militarily weak, and raise our voice in hostility to the great powers. We have, therefore, opposed the idea of a Third Force. The moment we talk in these terms, we adopt to some extent the cold war approach and language of hostility. . . .

20. ADDRESS TO THE
AMERICAN PUBLIC *

On October 22, 1962 President John F. Kennedy in a national television and radio address notified the American people that the Soviet Union was in the process of placing in Cuba a large number of ballistic missiles capable of carrying nuclear war-

---

* John F. Kennedy, *Television Address to the Nation*, October 22, 1962, U. S. Department of State, *Bulletin*, Vol. XLVII, No. 1220, November 12, 1962, pp. 715–720.

heads. This clandestine attempt to put nuclear weapons in the Western Hemisphere, argues President Kennedy, is an attempt by the Soviet Union to upset in its own favor the existing nuclear balance of terror. Previous to this very dangerous maneuver "both the Soviet Union and the United States," states Kennedy, "have deployed strategic nuclear weapons with great care, never upsetting the precarious status quo which insured that these weapons would not be used in the absence of some vital challenge."

JOHN F. KENNEDY

Good evening, my fellow citizens. This Government, as promised, has maintained the closest surveillance of the Soviet military build-up on the island of Cuba. Within the past week unmistakable evidence has established the fact that a series of offensive missile sites is now in preparation on that imprisoned island. The purposes of these bases can be none other than to provide a nuclear strike capability against the Western Hemisphere.

Upon receiving the first preliminary hard information of this nature last Tuesday morning (October 16) at 9:00 A.M., I directed that our surveillance be stepped up. And having now confirmed and completed our evaluation of the evidence and our decision on a course of action, this Government feels obliged to report this new crisis to you in fullest detail.

The characteristics of these new missile sites indicate two distinct types of installations. Several of them include medium-range ballistic missiles capable of carrying a nuclear warhead for a distance of more than 1,000 nautical miles. Each of these missiles, in short, is capable of striking Washington, D.C., the Panama Canal, Cape Canaveral, Mexico City, or any other city in the southeastern part of the United States, in Central America, or in the Caribbean area.

Additional sites not yet completed appear to be designed for intermediate-range ballistic missiles capable of traveling more than twice as far—and thus capable of striking most of the major cities in the Western Hemisphere, ranging as far north as Hudson Bay, Canada, and as far south as Lima, Peru. In addition, jet bombers, capable of carrying nuclear weapons, are now being uncrated and assembled in Cuba, while the necessary air bases are being prepared.

This urgent transformation of Cuba into an important strategic base—by the presence of these large, long-range, and clearly offensive weapons of sudden mass destruction—constitutes an explicit threat to the peace and security of all the Americas, in flagrant and deliberate defiance of the Rio Pact of 1947, the traditions of this nation and Hemisphere, the Joint Resolution of the 87th Congress, the Charter of the United Nations, and my own public warnings to the Soviets on September 4 and 13.

This action also contradicts the repeated assurances of Soviet spokesmen, both publicly and privately delivered, that the arms build-up in Cuba would retain its original defensive character and that the Soviet Union had no need or desire to station strategic missiles on the territory of any other nation.

The size of this undertaking makes clear that it has been planned for some months. Yet only last month, after I had made clear the distinction between any introduction of ground-to-ground missiles and the existence of defensive antiaircraft missiles, the Soviet Government publicly stated on September 11 that, and I quote, "The armaments and military equipment sent to Cuba are designed exclusively for defensive purposes," and, and I quote the Soviet Government, "There is no need for the Soviet Government to shift its weapons for a retaliatory blow to any other country, for instance Cuba," and that, and I quote the Government, "The Soviet Union has so powerful rockets to carry these nuclear warheads that there is no need to search for sites for them beyond the boundaries of the Soviet Union." That statement was false.

Only last Thursday, as evidence of this rapid offensive build-up was already in my hand, Soviet Foreign Minister Gromyko told me in my office that he was instructed to make it clear once again, as he said his Government had already done, that Soviet assistance to Cuba, and I quote, "pursued solely the purpose of contributing to the defense capabilities of Cuba," that, and I quote him, "training by Soviet specialists of Cuban nationals in handling defensive armaments was by no means offensive," and that "if it were otherwise," Mr. Gromyko went on, "the Soviet Government would never become involved in rendering such assistance." That statement also was false.

Neither the United States of America nor the world community of nations can tolerate deliberate deception and offensive threats on the part of any nation, large or small. We no longer live in a world where only the actual firing of weapons represents a sufficient challenge to a nation's security to constitute maximum peril. Nuclear weapons are so destructive and ballistic missiles are so swift that any substantially increased possibility of their use or any sudden change in their deployment may well be regarded as a definite threat to peace.

For many years both the Soviet Union and the United States, recognizing this fact, have deployed strategic nuclear weapons with great care, never upsetting the precarious status quo which insured that these weapons would not be used in the absence of some vital challenge. Our own strategic missiles have never been transferred to the territory of any other nation under a cloak of secrecy and deception; and our history, unlike that of the Soviets since the end of World War II, demonstrates that we have no desire to dominate or conquer any other nation or impose our system upon its people. Nevertheless, American citizens have become adjusted to living daily on the bull's eye of Soviet missiles located inside the U.S.S.R. or in submarines.

In that sense missiles in Cuba add to an already clear and present danger—although it should be noted the nations of Latin America have never previously been subjected to a potential nuclear threat.

But this secret, swift, and extraordinary build-up of Communist missiles—in an area well known to have a special and historical relationship to the United States and the nations of the Western Hemisphere, in violation of Soviet assurances, and in defiance of American and hemispheric policy—this sudden, clandestine decision to station strategic weapons for the first time outside of Soviet soil—is a deliberately provocative and unjustified change in the status quo which cannot be accepted by this country if our courage and our commitments are ever to be trusted again by either friend or foe.

The 1930's taught us a clear lesson: Aggressive conduct, if

allowed to grow unchecked and unchallenged, ultimately leads to war. This nation is opposed to war. We are also true to our word. Our unswerving objective, therefore, must be to prevent the use of these missiles against this or any other country and to secure their withdrawal or elimination from the Western Hemisphere.

Our policy has been one of patience and restraint, as befits a peaceful and powerful nation, which leads a worldwide alliance. We have been determined not to be diverted from our central concerns by mere irritants and fanatics. But now further action is required—and it is underway; and these actions may only be the beginning. We will not prematurely or unnecessarily risk the costs of worldwide nuclear war in which even the fruits of victory would be ashes in our mouth—but neither will we shrink from that risk at any time it must be faced.

Acting, therefore, in the defense of our own security and of the entire Western Hemisphere, and under the authority entrusted to me by the Constitution as endorsed by the resolution of the Congress, I have directed that the following initial steps be taken immediately:

First: To halt this offensive build-up, a strict quarantine on all offensive military equipment under shipment to Cuba is being initiated. All ships of any kind bound for Cuba from whatever nation or port will, if found to contain cargoes of offensive weapons, be turned back. This quarantine will be extended, if needed, to other types of cargo and carriers. We are not at this time, however, denying the necessities of life as the Soviets attempted to do in their Berlin blockade of 1948.

Second: I have directed the continued and increased close surveillance of Cuba and its military build-up. The Foreign Ministers of the Organization of American States in their communiqué of October 3 rejected secrecy on such matters in this Hemisphere. Should these offensive military preparations continue, thus increasing the threat to the Hemisphere, further action will be justified. I have directed the Armed Forces to prepare for any eventualities; and I trust that in the interest of both the Cuban people and the Soviet technicians at the sites, the hazards to all concerned of continuing this threat will be recognized.

Third: It shall be the policy of this nation to regard any

nuclear missile launched from Cuba against any nation in the
Western Hemisphere as an attack by the Soviet Union on the
United States, requiring a full retaliatory response upon the
Soviet Union.

Fourth: As a necessary military precaution I have reinforced
our base at Guantanamo, evacuated today the dependents of
our personnel there, and ordered additional military units to be
on a standby alert basis.

Fifth: We are calling tonight for an immediate meeting of the
Organ of Consultation, under the Organization of American
States, to consider this threat to hemispheric security and to
invoke articles six and eight of the Rio Treaty in support of all
necessary action. The United Nations Charter allows for re-
gional security arrangements—and the nations of this Hemisphere
decided long ago against the military presence of outside powers.
Our other allies around the world have also been alerted.

Sixth: Under the Charter of the United Nations, we are asking
tonight that an emergency meeting of the Security Council be
convoked without delay to take action against this latest Soviet
threat to world peace. Our resolution will call for the prompt
dismantling and withdrawal of all offensive weapons in Cuba,
under the supervision of United Nations observers, before the
quarantine can be lifted.

Seventh and finally: I call upon Chairman Khrushchev to halt
and eliminate this clandestine, reckless, and provocative threat to
world peace and to stable relations between our two nations. I
call upon him further to abandon this course of world domination and to join in an historic effort to end the perilous arms
race and transform the history of man. He has an opportunity
now to move the world back from the abyss of destruction—by
returning to his Government's own words that it had no need to
station missiles outside its own territory, and withdrawing these
weapons from Cuba—by refraining from any action which will
widen or deepen the present crisis—and then by participating
in a search for peaceful and permanent solutions.

This nation is prepared to present its case against the Soviet
threat to peace, and our own proposals for a peaceful world,
at any time and in any forum in the Organization of American

States, in the United Nations, or in any other meeting that could be useful—without limiting our freedom of action.

We have in the past made strenuous efforts to limit the spread of nuclear weapons. We have proposed the elimination of all arms and military bases in a fair and effective disarmament treaty. We are prepared to discuss new proposals for the removal of tensions on both sides—including the possibilities of a genuinely independent Cuba, free to determine its own destiny. We have no wish to war with the Soviet Union, for we are a peaceful people who desire to live in peace with all other peoples.

But it is difficult to settle or even discuss these problems in an atmosphere of intimidation. That is why this latest Soviet threat —or any other threat which is made either independently or in response to our actions this week—must and will be met with determination. Any hostile move anywhere in the world against the safety and freedom of peoples to whom we are committed —including in particular the brave people of West Berlin—will be met by whatever action is needed.

Finally, I want to say a few words to the captive people of Cuba, to whom this speech is being directly carried by special radio facilities. I speak to you as a friend, as one who knows of your deep attachment to your fatherland, as one who shares your aspirations for liberty and justice for all. And I have watched and the American people have watched with deep sorrow how your nationalist revolution was betrayed and how your fatherland fell under foreign domination. Now your leaders are no longer Cuban leaders inspired by Cuban ideals. They are puppets and agents of an international conspiracy which has turned Cuba against your friends and neighbors in the Americas—and turned it into the first Latin American country to become a target for nuclear war, the first Latin American country to have these weapons on its soil.

These new weapons are not in your interest. They contribute nothing to your peace and well being. They can only undermine it. But this country has no wish to cause you to suffer or to impose any system upon you. We know that your lives and land are being used as pawns by those why deny you freedom.

Many times in the past Cuban people have risen to throw out

tyrants who destroyed their liberty. And I have no doubt that most Cubans today look forward to the time when they will be truly free—free from foreign domination, free to choose their own leaders, free to select their own system, free to own their own land, free to speak and write and worship without fear or degradation. And then shall Cuba be welcomed back to the society of free nations and to the associations of this Hemisphere.

My fellow citizens, let no one doubt that this is a difficult and dangerous effort on which we have set out. No one can foresee precisely what course it will take or what costs or casualties will be incurred. Many months of sacrifice and self-discipline lie ahead —months in which both our patience and our will will be tested, months in which many threats and denunciations will keep us aware of our dangers. But the greatest danger of all would be to do nothing.

The path we have chosen for the present is full of hazards, as all paths are; but it is the one most consistent with our character and courage as a nation and our commitments around the world. The cost of freedom is always high—but Americans have always paid it. And one path we shall never choose, and that is the path of surrender or submission.

Our goal is not the victory of might but the vindication of right —not peace at the expense of freedom, but both peace and freedom, here in this Hemisphere and, we hope, around the world. God willing, that goal will be achieved.

---

21. THE BALANCE OF POWER AND THE
BALANCE OF TERROR

The "balance of terror," a phrase first employed by Sir Winston Churchill, came into circulation when the Soviet Union, in the early 1950's, developed a thermonuclear capability and, after

1956, acquired intercontinental missiles capable of delivering nuclear bombs to the Americas. Because of its ring of air bases around the Soviet Union, the United States had possessed corresponding strategic capability even in the late 1940's. Symmetry in destructive capability led some now to speak of a "balance" in nuclear weaponry between America and Russia.

Classical concepts of the balance of power, as Professor Snyder's essay shows, had been far more embracing in the types of power which made up "national power." This new supposed equilibrium was a bipolar balance between "nationbusters." How stable it might prove, no one could say; yet certainly it introduced a new reason for prudence in the behavior of the superpowers towards each other. Could rational men devise means to make this relationship less unstable, or—optimistically—more stable? During the late 1950's, critical voices in the Western world pointed out reasons why, despite an apparent balance of terror weapons, an aggressor might be rationally tempted to strike a preventive blow, to remove an adversary's ability to strike back. Other critics of the notion of terror equilibrium could point out that defense policies, such as those in the early Eisenhower administration, concentrating on such strategic-force development, might neglect "conventional" power of less magnitude, and be at a disadvantage in employing military power in situations where nuclear power was clearly unsuited, or too risky to employ.

Professor Snyder, a student of military strategy and politics, here seeks to show the links and relationships between older conceptions of balance of power, and the new balance of unconventional weaponry in the atomic age. His paper appears in print for the first time in Balance of Power.

GLENN H. SNYDER

It is now rather widely believed that the balance of power has been overtaken by technology; that nuclear weapons and missiles have brought the balancing process to a halt and substituted a new and quite different regulator—that of nuclear deterrence.* This article will challenge this view. The balance of

---

* For an early statement of this view, see Arthur Lee Burns, "From Balance to Deterrence," *World Politics*, Vol. IX (1957), pp. 494–529.

power theory is still generally valid and still a useful model of at least certain important aspects of contemporary world politics. The new military technology has not terminated but only modified the balance of power process. It has superimposed a new system of equilibrium (the phrase "balance of terror" will serve) upon the old system which was based on nonnuclear capabilities. The two systems operate according to different tendencies and principles and can be separated analytically, but in practice they are inextricably mixed in a new balance of power in which elements of the old coexist with the new. I will attempt to compare the two subprocesses at certain salient points and then describe the nature of their interaction in an integrated process.

THE BALANCE OF TERROR

There are naïve and sophisticated versions of the "balance of terror" or the nuclear strategic balance. The naïve view, the image held by relatively uninformed laymen, is simply that both sides are deterred from using nuclear weapons against the other by the fear of devastating retaliation. In this image, the targets of the nuclear strikes are cities. To initiate nuclear war would be to commit national suicide; hence a "balance" or "stalemate" exists.

The sophisticated version focuses on "counterforce" rather than "countervalue" (city) targeting. One or both sides could eliminate or drastically reduce the other side's retaliatory capacity by directing the first strike at the opponent's nuclear striking forces rather than at his cities. There are circumstances, theoretically at least, in which thermonuclear war initiated in this manner would be a rational act. According to this version, a "balance of terror" exists when neither side can, by executing a counterforce first-strike, reduce the opponent's retaliation to "acceptable" proportions. Or, to use the jargon of the trade, neither side has a "full first-strike capability," or (what amounts to virtually the same thing) both sides possess at least a "minimum strike-back capability"—i.e. a residual capacity which after suffering the attrition of the attacker's first blow, could still inflict intolerable damage on the attacker's cities, population and economic assets in a retaliatory blow.

But the "sophisticated" version, as here defined, is not sophisticated enough. What, for example, is the criterion for defining the degree of retaliation that is "acceptable"? What purpose does the victim serve by retaliation against the attacker's cities, other than revenge? What motivates the attacker to strike in the first place; what purpose of political goal is served by a counterforce first strike? Eliminating or reducing the victim's capacity to retaliate is not a purpose but a precaution. How is the war terminated after the initial strike and reprisal? What then determines the terms of settlement? What constitutes "victory" or "defeat"?

To make use of the sophisticated version for our purposes, it is necessary to return part way to the naïve image. I shall assert, somewhat heretically, that the *ultimate* function of nuclear weapons (especially the "strategic" variety) is either to destroy the enemy's cities and conventional war potential, or to support a threat to do so for purposes of blackmail or deterrence. To make this clear it is convenient to start with a model of the balance of terror in its "pure" form. Assume two states, A and B armed only with nuclear strategic missiles. Assume that both states are expansionist—i.e., that they both would like to subjugate all or part of the other if they could do so at acceptable cost.

In this model, the only means of subjugation is by nuclear blackmail. Blackmail, of course, cannot succeed as long as the opponent can make a "deterrent" counterthreat of devastating retaliation. But A, for example, may be able to blackmail B successfully if it can meet two requirements. First, it must be able to disarm B by a counterforce "first strike" or at least destroy enough of B's forces to restrict its retaliation to "acceptable" proportions. The criterion of "acceptability" is the amount of retaliatory damage to A which is just equivalent to the value which A places on B's capitulation to its demands. The demand may be for B's total capitulation or for some lesser concession. Secondly, A must maintain in reserve a force sufficient to blackmail B into conceding by the threat of "countervalue" or population destruction. Roughly, the necessary size of this force is measured by the value which A thinks B places on the things he is being asked to concede. If A fires all its forces in attempting to disarm B, it dissipates its blackmail or bargaining power and cannot achieve its political goal.

If (A or B, or both) can meet both of these requirements the balance of terror is in disequilibrium. If both sides fall short of one or both requirements, an attack by either side is either futile or too costly and the balance of terror is in a state of equilibrium.

Note that A's initial counterforce strike is merely preliminary, undertaken only to put itself in a position to blackmail B. Counterforce strikes do not contribute *directly* to "winning the war," as is suggested in some of the current literature; they contribute only indirectly by improving the attacker's relative bargaining power—i.e., his power to coerce the victim by the threat to strike cities. And they contribute to this end *with high confidence* only if they are sufficient to reduce the victim's retaliatory capacity to below A's "acceptable" level. If B is left with residual forces higher than this level, he may be able to resist A's postattack blackmail.

In the "real world," of course, A will have conventional forces; a combination of counterforce and countervalue strikes against B may so prostrate B as to make physical conquest possible and blackmail unnecessary. But such conquest would be the result of A's preponderance in the conventional balance after the nuclear exchange, and therefore falls under the heading of "interaction" between the two balances, which is discussed below.

DIFFERENCES BETWEEN THE CONVENTIONAL BALANCE AND THE NUCLEAR BALANCE

To compare and then integrate the two balancing systems, the first questions to be asked are: What is the nature of the "power" being balanced? What is the nature of "equilibrium" in each case? In traditional theory of (conventional) balance of power, the kind of power involved was the physical capability to take or hold territory. Equilibrium was said to obtain when military capabilities and war potential on each side were roughly equal, so that neither side had the capacity to defeat the other in war and by so doing to change the territorial status quo. The preceding discussion shows that this is not the case in the nuclear "balance of terror." Nuclear weapons cannot, when employed, in and of themselves, take or hold territory. Physical conquest during or after a nuclear exchange requires the intervention of conventional forces. In the "pure" balance of terror, the political status quo can be changed only by political coercion—that is, by a process of blackmail supported by the threat of severe punishment. The status quo is preserved by "deterrence" supported by a similar threat. Thus the power that is balanced in the balance of terror is essentially "political power" rather than physical capabilities; capabilities enter in only as the threatened sanction supporting the political demand; not as an instrument for the direct physical achievement of political goals as is usually the case in the traditional or conventional balance of power.

The balance of terror is more subjective in nature than the old balance of power. Whether "equilibrium" exists depends at least as much on factors "within the minds" of the opponents as upon an objective comparison of military capabilities. Subjectivity is obvious in the fact that equilibrium is defined in terms of "acceptability" of damage for both sides; what is acceptable depends on the values attached to the political stakes. Thus, in contrast to the old balance of power, in which the state of the equilibrium could be objectively—if roughly—determined by the uninvolved observer, such an observer can only intuitively guess at equilibrium in the balance of terror, since it depends principally on whether the gains to be made or losses to be avoided by striking first are less than the costs to be incurred—all as subjectively valued in the minds of the decision-makers.

The balance of terror is subjective in still another sense. The participants themselves, while presumably they can judge what is unacceptable damage for themselves, cannot be certain what is unacceptable for the opponent. Thus the determination of whether equilibrium exists is ultimately reduced to a guessing game about the opponent's values and intentions. There is therefore vast scope for disagreement or asymmetrical perceptions about the state of the balance and about the degree of political, military or technological change which would throw it "out of balance." For example, the balance may actually be in equilibrium, but one side may fear the other side *may* possess a full first-strike capability. Then the latter may achieve its political aims by bluff, whether these aims are of a deterrent or blackmail nature. In the obverse case—when the balance is in disequilibrium because one side can be provoked to strike first, but its opponent doesn't perceive this—the outcome could be war by "miscalculation."

Subjective considerations determine the "location" or "boundaries" of equilibrium within the spectrum of possible force ratios, but a comparison of relative capabilities is obviously still necessary for estimating whether equilibrium actually exists at any given time.

However, in sharp contrast to the traditional balance of power, the notion of quantitative equality between striking forces is totally irrelevant as a criterion for "balance." Equilibrium can exist when one side's offensive forces are far inferior to the other's, provide the inferior side's forces are relatively invulnerable to a counterforce strike and provided the forces surviving such a strike can penetrate the attacker's air defenses in sufficient numbers to inflict unacceptable damage. Or equilibrium might require having more striking forces than the opponent if one's own forces are highly vulnerable, and the enemy has a very good air defense and civil defense system. The essential criterion for equilibrium is a mutual capacity to inflict intolerable damage in retaliation, and this depends on a variety of technological factors in addition to numbers of delivery vehicles.

A corollary of this distinction is that, while a balance of conventional power can be said to exist only within a rather narrow range of relative capabilities on either side of strict equality, a balance of terror can exist within a wide range of force ratios. To illustrate: assuming relatively invulnerable offensive forces and rather impotent air-missile defense systems on both sides, side A, with 100 missiles, might be in a state of equilibrium against side B with 500 missiles; equilibrium might still obtain if side A were to increase its force to 1,000 missiles. In other words, even a ten-fold increase by one side might not overturn the balance. The "range of equilibrium" would be the difference between the forces which A needs for a "minimum strike-back capability" and the forces it needs for a "full first-strike capability." This consideration has important implications for the *stability* of the balance of terror, to be discussed below.

Another important contrast between the two systems lies in the relative weight given to the functions of *deterrence* and *defense*. Both were functions of the prenuclear balance (and still are in today's conventional balance of power); but deterrence was secondary in the sense that it was an incidental consequence of an obvious capacity to defend territory successfully. It was also secondary in the sense that the primary purpose of balancing techniques—armaments, alliances, etc.—was to be ready to frustrate an expansionist state rather than to influence the intentions of that state. If deterrence failed, defensive war was considered to be a normal technique of the balancing process, a continuation of the process by violent means.

By contrast, the balance of terror centers heavily on the function of deterrence. Deterrence is achieved by the threat of devastating punishment or damage, not as a simple by-product of a capacity to defend territory or otherwise to frustrate the aggressor's aims. If deterrence fails, the system will have broken down completely; nuclear war cannot be considered a normal "technique" for adjusting or restoring the balance. This does not mean that it is not useful or wise to take measures in advance of war to mitigate the dreadful consequences of nuclear war, or even to "win the war" in some sense. In particular, it may be desirable (as the United States has done) to develop a "surplus" of offensive striking forces far beyond the amount needed for a deterrent equilibrium, in order to be able to destroy a maximum amount of the attacker's postattack residual forces, while holding in reserve a powerful force for bargaining purposes. Such additional forces do not essentially disturb the equilibrium, unless they create a degree of preponderance which begins to approach a full first-strike capability.

INTERACTIONS IN THE "MIXED" BALANCE OF POWER

Nuclear and conventional balancing processes do not operate independently; they impinge on each other in various ways. The contemporary balancing process, in an overall sense, is a mixture of the two. Generally speaking, the entire system is in overall "balance" when either of two conditions exist. One is when each of the two subprocesses is "out of balance" but in different directions—i.e., when one side preponderates in one component and the other side in the other. The other condition is when both conventional and nuclear balances are separately in equilibrium. If one is in balance and the other is not, the entire system is in a state of disequilibrium, at least with respect to any particular political issue. This is also the case when both processes are unbalanced in favor of one side.

To illuminate these somewhat cryptic remarks, let us turn away from our abstract model to the world of reality. We see a world of two nuclear powers (the Soviet Union, and the United States-Great Britain as a unit) which also have conventional forces; we also see two incipient nuclear powers and many nonnuclear powers. All possess conventional forces; some of them enjoy the protection of one or the other of the nuclear great powers.

That the latter enjoy the protection of the nuclear great powers means that the political function of nuclear weapons has been extended from strictly bilateral deterrence and blackmail between nuclear powers to that of deterring aggression against other (nonnuclear) countries. This function may require the nuclear protector to create an actual or apparent nuclear disequilibrium in his favor to make credible a determination to strike first if provoked by an attack on his allies. Short of this, or concurrent with it, he can threaten the *limited* use of nuclear weapons in either a "tactical" or "strategic" manner.

The best example of interaction is the balance of power in Europe. Here, the Soviets preponderate in the conventional balance (although not so greatly as we thought a few years ago); while the United States, as West Europe's protector, remains superior in nuclear forces. Yet it is doubtful whether the United States superiority, while quantitatively great, really constitutes a "full first-strike capability." If it did in its maximum sense— i.e., if we could completely eliminate the Soviet nuclear forces in a first strike—it would be possible, theoretically at least, to dispense with conventional forces in Western Europe. Total and obvious strategic nuclear disequilibrium would remove any need to even partially balance the Soviets at the conventional level. Conversely, if it were true that the United States obviously lacked a first-strike capability (meaning that we were clearly not willing to strike first in any circumstances), then this might reinstate the conventional balancing process in Europe in its full prenuclear dimensions—i.e., it might well stimulate a build-up of conventional forces sufficient to hold successfully against a Red Army invasion.

That this has not occurred, is due in part to the uncertainty of Soviet leadership as to whether equilibrium exists or whether the United States nuclear preponderance really amounts to disequilibrium. In other words, the Soviets may suspect that the United States has a full first-strike capability which could be activated if sufficiently provoked. Or they may believe that we are irrational enough to strike even when our force does not meet the objective requirements of such a capability. For in the case of deterrence (or blackmail) it is what the opponent thinks or fears that counts, and the United States nuclear superiority is great enough that the Soviet leadership no doubt fears some probability of a United States first strike in particularly tense or provocative circumstances. Considering the very great damage they would suffer if we did strike, a quite low probability in their calculations may be sufficient to deter.

Any remaining doubts which the Russians might have about our implicit threat of a strategic first strike are offset by the presence of tactical nuclear weapons in the hands of the NATO forces on the "central front" in West Germany. The American resolve in NATO to use these weapons if necessary to stop a Soviet invasion has been firmly declared and implemented by the rather thorough incorporation of their use into NATO's military plans and organization. It is no doubt highly credible to the Soviets that these weapons would be used if necessary and considering their own apparent belief that a tactical nuclear war in Europe could not remind limited, our tactical nuclear posture constitutes, in effect, a very credible threat of all-out nuclear war. Even if they were to assume that the *strategic* nuclear balance by itself was in a state of equilibrium, the tactical nuclear weapons would make it a rather unstable equilibrium. This instability is a potent deterrent of Soviet conventional provocations and reduces the need for balancing at the conventional level.

The function of the conventional NATO forces on the central front—apart from turning back small and medium-scale incursions—is further to enhance the credibility of nuclear deterrence by forcing the Soviets to undertake a major attack provocative enough to exceed the United States "threshold of nuclear response." Thus the overall balance of power in Western Europe is a function of three factors: the U. S. first-strike capability at the strategic level; the tactical nuclear threat; and the defense and deterrent effects of conventional forces. Each probably would be inadequate by itself, but the three together have created a mixed conventional-nuclear equilibrium which effectively deters Soviet aggression. The primary function of the tactical nuclear weapons is to form a "bridge" between a nonexistent conventional balance and a *possibly* extant strategic nuclear equilibrium. In other words, they assure the Soviets, in case they might otherwise have doubts, that a combined tactical-strategical nuclear imbalance in favor of the United States does exist.

We may turn the point around and note that during the period of the United States nuclear monopoly (strategic nuclear disequilibrium in our favor) we were deterred from capitalizing on this imbalance at least partly by the obvious Soviet superiority in the conventional balance which potentially enabled them to resist our nuclear pressure by credibly threatening to overrun Western Europe. An overall equilibrium obtained precisely because of a sharp disequilibrium in opposite directions in each of the two subcomponents.

Whereas in Europe conventional forces serve as auxiliary to the nuclear deterrent, in Asia the reverse is probably true. The obvious disequilibrium in the strategic nuclear balance between the United States and Communist China serves to deter the Chinese from openly committing their own conventional forces in internal wars (e.g. South Vietnam) and thus tends to create a conventional balance of power in Southeast Asia which might not otherwise exist. Alternatively, should the Chinese become involved with the United States in an overt conventional conflict, they probably would be deterred from committing enough forces to defeat the United States forces in fear of a United States nuclear response. Nuclear disequilibrium favoring the United States tends to limit our Communist opponents in Asia to a commitment of conventional forces which the U. S. and our allies can deal with successfully at the conventional level. In short, nuclear disequilibrium tends to promote conventional equilibrium or operational conventional preponderance for the United States.

When nuclear deterrence is extended to the protection of allies, the element of mutual assessment of *intentions* becomes critically important, much more so than in simple bilateral deterrence where the "credibility" of retaliation can more or less be taken for granted. In such "extended deterrence," the deterring side tries to create the impression that the balance of terror is out of balance in its favor or could be thrown into disequilibrium by sufficient provocation. He attempts to establish the "credibility" of his threat to strike first "all-out" or to initiate limited nuclear action. Estimates of relative capability are not irrelevant, but because of the essential subjectivity and hence uncertainty (in the opponent's mind) about what actually constitutes a "first-strike capability" for the deterrer, or about his willingness to run the risk of escalation, capability comparisons tend to be overshadowed by appraisals of the deterrer's apparent "resolve," "nerve," irrationality, gambling propensities and other subjective factors that bear upon his intentions. Paradoxically, it would seem that intent-perception has become more crucial in today's balance of power than in the prenuclear balance, even though (or perhaps, *because*) the physical capabilities have become many orders of magnitude more destructive.

Appraisals of intent not only are now more important, but important in a different way than in the old balance of power. In the latter, the relevant intentions were largely political in nature, centering on the question of *which* countries were likely to fight on either the offensive or the defensive side. It could reasonably be assumed that the countries which did participate in a war would do so to the full extent of their capabilities, but there was often considerable uncertainty about who would participate. With the emergence of bipolarity, the uncertainty about alliance partners drastically declined, but nuclear technology introduced a new form of intent-perception and a new form of uncertainty—that concerning what types of military capability the opponent was likely to use and what degree of violence he was willing to risk or accept.

One might say that this new kind of uncertainty has replaced the former uncertainty about alliance partners as a major source of stability in the balance of power. Or, to put it slightly differently, the implicit or explicit threat to "raise the ante" in order to avoid defeat has taken the place of the threat to recruit additional states to the defending alliance. Such a threat is more or less analogous to the practice of "holding the ring" in the old balance—when a state promised to be neutral if its ally were attacked by one country, but to come to its aid if it were attacked by two or more powers. In short, technology has to some extent provided a substitute for the political flexibility and stability which was lost to the balancing process when it shifted to a bipolar structure after World War II.

STABILITY

A careful distinction should be made between "equilibrium" and "stability" in both the conventional balance of power and the nuclear balance. The two terms often are erroneously used interchangeably. Equilibria in both balances can have varying degrees of stability; and it is even possible to have disequilibrium with relatively high stability, if the dominant side is not aggressively inclined and this fact is recognized by other members of the system.

In the traditional balance of power theory, the idea of stability usually referred generally to a supposed perpetual tendency of the system to maintain itself at or near a state of equilibrium.

Deviations from equilibrium generated "feedback" forces which moved the balance back in the direction of equilibrium. Within this general notion, stability had at least three subdimensions which, so far as I know, were never precisely delineated. These were: the tendency or lack of tendency toward an arms race, tendencies either to stimulate or inhibit war, and the tendency of the process to preserve the independence of the major actors. Theorists tended to emphasize the third dimension; in fact, armament and warfare often were treated not as types of instability but as *methods* for preserving stability in the third sense, along with alliances and other techniques.

By contrast, the dimension of stability which receives most attention in the balance of terror, and by extension, in the contemporary balancing process as a whole, is the propensity of the system to produce war, the obvious reason being the possibility of *nuclear* war, the horrifying nature of which seems to outweigh all other considerations. How stable is the contemporary balance of power in this sense?

The basic criterion of stability in the balance of terror is the "distance" which both sides are from possessing a full first-strike capability. If neither side has forces which even approach this capacity—i.e., if both have a very strong "strike-back" capability—the balance of terror is very stable. If one or both are very close to having a first-strike capability, or actually do have it, the balance can be very unstable. It might be only moderately unstable if only one side possessed such a capability if that side were benevolent; but if both sides had it, fears of a first strike by the other, and consequent incentives to preempt, would be strong, even despite intrinsic benevolence on both sides.

Stability can be defined alternatively as the degree of economic, technological, or politicomilitary "shock" which the system can sustain without creating for one side or the other a capability and willingness to strike first. Economic shock (or degree of instability) refers to the amount of resource expenditure required for one or the other to acquire the *quantity* of forces required for a successful first strike—assuming a given technology, if neither side has the economic resources to produce such a capability, the balance is stable in this sense. Technological instability refers to magnitude of the technological breakthrough (e.g., the degree of efficiency of an antimissile defense) which would create a sufficient first strike force for either side. Politicomilitary instability means the extent of "provocation" by either side which would touch off a first strike by the other. The word "provocation" includes a wide variety of contingencies: being "backed into a corner" in a confrontation of threats and counterthreats, becoming involved in a limited conventional war which one is in danger of losing, suffering a limited nuclear strike by the opponent, becoming involved in an escalating nuclear war, and many others. Any of these events may drastically increase the potential cost and risk of *not* striking first and thereby potentially create a state of disequilibrium in the strategic nuclear balance. As noted earlier, whether equilibrium exists depends on the context of events; the "acceptability" of damage is calculated not only against the gains to be made by striking first but also against the *losses to be avoided,* in any particular set of circumstances.

Although these three criteria of stability-instability interact, it is my judgment that the balance of terror is currently most stable in the "economic" or resource sense, somewhat less stable technologically, and least stable according to the "politicomilitary" criterion. The apparently firm United States commitment to use nuclear weapons in the defense of Western Europe, if necessary, indicates that there are types of Soviet provocation at the lower levels of violence which could touch off a United States strategic first strike, or more likely, a tactical nuclear response, from which the war could escalate. It is hoped, of course, that the Soviets' recognition of the U. S. commitment will deter the provocation; that instability in this dimension will preserve a stable equilibrium in the overall balance of power. However, the risks of Soviet miscalculation and subsequent escalation which this commitment creates should not be underestimated and probably are the most serious potential sources of instability in the contemporary balance.

The point is often made in the strategic literature that the greater the stability of the "strategic" balance of terror, the lower the stability of the overall balance at its lower levels of violence. The reasoning is that if neither side has a "full first-strike capability," and both know it, they will be less inhibited about initiating conventional war, and about the limited use of nuclear weapons, than if the strategic balance were unstable. Thus firm stability in the strategic nuclear balance tends to destabilize the conventional balance and also to activate the lesser nuclear "links" between the latter and the former. But one *could* argue precisely the opposite—that the greater likelihood of gradual escalation due to a stable strategic equilibrium tends to deter both conventional provocation and tactical nuclear strikes—thus stabilizing the overall balance. The first hypothesis probably is dominant, but it must be heavily qualified by the second, since nations probably fear the possibility of escalation "all the way" nearly as much as they fear the possibility of an "all-out" first strike.

There is another stability hypothesis which is just the reverse —although not contradictory to—the one just described: a stable conventional equilibrium tends to increase the stability of the nuclear component of the balance. When both sides can defend themselves successfully at the conventional level, conventional aggression is likely to be deterred, and if it is not, there is little pressure on the defender to resort to nuclear action. But this one also has its obverse: it is sometimes argued that when the *status quo* side attempts to create a conventional equilibrium, the credibility of its nuclear threats is undermined since it might thereby indicate an unwillingness to initiate nuclear war by seeking to create an alternative to it. The potential aggressor might be then more willing to attack when he believes (perhaps mistakenly) that he has achieved a margin of conventional superiority. The first hypothesis tends to stress the effect of conventional balance in reducing the probability of escalation if war occurs; the second stresses the increased chances of the outbreak of war due to the apparently lower risk incurred by starting it.

When a great nuclear power places smaller nonnuclear countries under its nuclear protection (as a substitute for creation of a conventional equilibrium), one effect may be to reduce the sta-

bility of the strategic nuclear balance in the sense of stimulating
an arms race. Nuclear deterrence of attacks on "third parties"
theoretically requires a strategic nuclear capability approaching
first strike dimensions. Forces of this size may raise fears of an
aggressive surprise first strike in the opponent's mind and therefore place psychological pressure on him to increase his nuclear
force in order to strengthen his deterrence, perhaps to strengthen
his chances of winning the war should his fears materialize, and,
at the extreme, to develop a first-strike force himself to be in a
position to preempt. This type of instability would be much
weaker if the great nuclear powers were to limit themselves to
bilateral mutual deterrence.

The nature of the "balance of power" process in a world of
many nuclear powers is a challenging speculative problem which
can only be touched upon here in connection with the question
of stability. It is rather remarkable that the balance of terror
is generally believed to be most stable when it is bipolar and
least stable when it is multipolar, whereas the exact reverse was
said to be true in the traditional theory of the balance of power.
In the latter, bipolarity was said to be unstable because of the
absence of a strong unattached power center (a "holder of the
balance"), or several centers, which could be recruited to block
one of the "poles" which had developed marginal preponderance of capabilities and apparently aggressive intentions. A multiplicity of power centers would provide such balancing material
and create uncertainty for an incipient aggressor as to the amount
of power which would oppose his designs. A bipolar balance of
terror is said to be relatively stable because only two power
centers have the capacity to initiate nuclear war and because
they are likely to be cautious in conflict situations which involve
the danger of nuclear war. The major powers in the contemporary bipolar balance are said to be relatively "responsible"
powers.

Many specific arguments have been advanced in support of
the hypothesis that nuclear diffusion would greatly increase instability, but two in particular are probably the most influential.
One is the "statistical argument": the notion that the more
countries that have nuclear weapons, the more likely it is

that some of these weapons will be fired, accidentally or otherwise, and the firing of nuclear weapons anywhere in the world may trigger a global holocaust. The other is the "irresponsibility argument": the idea that some of the countries which may acquire nuclear power will lack the caution and restraint which seems to characterize the nuclear great powers; they may threaten or use their nuclear weapons recklessly, perhaps because of domestic instability or simply a lack of concern for, or lack of comprehension of, the broader consequences of their actions.

The point is raised merely to note the striking difference between the two sets of stability hypotheses, not to analyze either, which would be far beyond the scope of this paper.

IN LIEU OF CONCLUSION

International relations theory and military-strategic analysis have been ignoring each other for too long. This essay has attempted to introduce a measure of integration, focusing on an idea which is common to both fields—that of equilibrium. Balance of power theory cannot embrace all phenomena of international politics, not even all military phenomena. Yet it has enjoyed a rather high degree of historical validation, as political theories go, and deserves to be rehabilitated, refined and renovated.

Ancient ideas die hard; the notion that military preponderance means superior strength and that this means superior political power is so deeply ingrained that it continues to be believed and acted upon by both sides even though, in the strategic nuclear balance, it has little objective or logical basis. Further research would surely uncover many additional deviations which would serve to qualify and thus to enrich the logical analysis presented here.

VI

The Status Quo and
the Balance

22. THE IDEA OF THE STATUS QUO

PAUL SEABURY

The idea of the status quo belongs among those conceptions of politics which give precedence to form over motion, to order over justice, to stability over change. Thus, it is commonly regarded as a telltale shibboleth for a conservative theory of politics. Liberals and progressives, as do radicals, assign priority to motion, process, and movement over form; conservatives assert the priority of order and the status quo over movement. To them, motion and movement, if given priority over form, threaten form either with destruction or transformation; to them, also, process and movement are nihilistic, if not contained and regulated within a system of order.

For such reasons, we often distinguish between parties of order—those which stress form, permanence and continuity over motion and change—and parties of movement, which stress movement over form, action and spontaneity over rules. The former are deemed static; the latter, dynamic. Dynamic con-

202

servatism, Senator Goldwater to the contrary, is a peculiar contradiction in terms.

But this simple distinction between conservatives and liberals, radicals and reactionaries, makes little sense in many concrete situations today. Form and order, which the conservative may wish to preserve, may contain and nourish certain forces working to radically transform the nature of society and politics (a point made, with considerable effect, by Karl Marx). Thus, form and order may be objectively "radical" in consequences. The political order that a reactionary may wish to see restored may require radical surgical measures if it is to be obtained at all.

Conversely, liberals and radicals normally justify themselves by painting attractive future utopias, ultimately no less static than the reactionary, nostalgic dream-things of a Ruskin. Both conservative realists and Marxists, during the nineteenth century, exposed the lack of realism of "perfectibilians" like Robert Owen, who believed that by reason and suasion rational men might reconstruct society. In this instance, conservatives were persuaded of the absurdity of such an enterprise, since it defied the imperfect nature of man; the Marxist, since such utopianism defied the technologically determined nature of the historical process.

Perhaps what chiefly distinguishes such forces of movement from those of order is the priority which these forces assign to future justice over present order: the alleged greater felicity and excellence of men's future lives within some order not yet born, or some order to be reestablished. What gives edge to the radical in this contest is the open-endedness of the future, in which men may escape the limitations of the past in a profusion of possibilities, in which they may choose among possibilities and thus assert their freedom. What causes us to listen to both the conservative and the reactionary is their warning: among limitless possibilities, justice and freedom are only two. The past supplies tangible merchandise; the future is a grab-bag.

Motion and change, as opposed to order, rarely serve as their own justification to the liberal or radical, unless through them more perfect order can be obtained. There are, of course, important exceptions to this rule. When Nazism tyrannized Europe, important elements in its ideological appeal exalted action, struggle, and violence as ends in themselves. Violence and struggle not only were deemed natural to man's milieu and character, but also were deemed conditions of behavior whereby heroic men bore witness to their intrinsic greatness. The nihilism latent in this special attitude is today widely acknowledged, and its consequences too well seen in Maidanek, Dachau, and Auschwitz to arouse enthusiasm except in pathological European minds, or among those who have forgotten or have never known. Fortunately, our Marxist adversaries in the cold war are inclined to regard conflict and violence not as ends in themselves but rather as means by which "objective" historical forces and their servants attain a future condition in which conflict would have no proper, meaningful place.

These reflections on the status quo are introduction to a problem: What is the relevance of conservatism and liberalism, reactionary and radical philosophies, to the realm of world politics within which we live and which we fearfully experience?

I

The idea of the status quo is made ambiguous by two meanings simultaneously present within it. One refers to a preexisting order of things, which might be reestablished, but which in any event serves as referent-point for change: the *status quo ante,* which was, or has been. The other refers to a supposed present condition of order which is either to be maintained or transformed: the "existing order of things." Often the two are commingled; so that the "existing order of things" becomes identified with "the past."

Within an individual political community, the status quo usually is associated with specific social institutions, political elites, and constitutional arrangements which make up the existing "social structure" and seek to keep it together. They comprise, let us say, the "traditional order." In transitional societies, such established forces supposedly work against those forces making for change or for revolution.

In the totality of the society of nations, however, the idea of the status quo attaches to some existing or preexistent order of things *among* states and political communities. It differs from the order of things within an individual political community, in that it may describe territorial and power relationships among discrete political entities, regardless of their internal natures and political forms.

To take an instance: the European statesmen, convened in Vienna in 1815 after the Napoleonic wars, met to establish peace, a status quo, an international order. Some of them, notably Metternich, wished to reestablish conservative regimes in Europe, resembling those which had existed before the Revolution, Napoleon, and French imperialism had destroyed and violently reshaped it. Yet conservative and liberal alike—Metternich and Castlereagh—sought above all to establish an agreed-upon European balance of power. In concert, liberal and conservative finally achieved a mutually agreeable territorial structure for the European continent; they sought to legitimize it and thus endow it with permanence. The outlines of order which they drew up persisted for a very long time afterwards. They came to be accepted by most Europeans as quite normal. In this order, justice took the back seat. This was to be the constitution of Europe for nearly a century.

The chief participants in the Vienna Congress stressed two considerations, incorporating rather than transcending special, separate, national interests: first, to establish a pattern of order embracing the entire European continent, coextensive with the society of nations as then known; second, to confirm the existence of this order in interlocking systems of treaties and conventions, which would then become the heart of European public international law and, as such, the referent point of all major strategies of Powers in their subsequent relationships. The second consideration was this: that such an international order was not independent of internal conditions within states. To Metternich in particular, there was a conjoining of the idea of legitimacy within individual polities with the idea of legitimacy for the system as a whole. It is impossible to dissociate the figure of Metternich from the very idea of the status quo in both senses. To him, legitimacy, order, authority, were as necessary to international order as they were to the internal order of the Austrian empire itself. He personifies classically the conservative statesman for whom there was no essential contradiction between the existing order among states and the existing order within his own; to him, they were mutually interdependent.

To Metternich, we may contrast Woodrow Wilson as statesman. Wilson's aim was not to restore the Europe which "had been," but rather to establish Europe upon wholly new principles and institutions. To him, justice took precedence over restored legitimacy in the establishment of order; only a "just peace" would be a durable one. Justice required a sharp break with important continuities of recent history. (Interestingly enough, the logic of Wilson's principles, and of his statecraft at Paris, contributed a century after Vienna to the final, irremediable liquidation of Metternich's own multinational empire.)

Despite the profound philosophical differences between these two men, their thought is conjoined upon one point: that order be established. Wilson's concern for justice was linked to and involved in his concern to establish order. Sanction for Wilson's new status quo, however, was to be derived from popular consent; Metternich's, from traditional political authorities. Wilson may thus be seen not as nemesis of European conservatism but rather as its surrogate and replacement: a new order, a new status quo, required intrinsic ethical justification to endure.

Peacemakers, who assemble new patterns of international order after major international wars, derive concepts of postwar order from three general sources: territorial and politico-economic configurations which preceded war; existing distribution of influence and power which fortunes of war bring about; and, new patterns of relationships which it is their intent to impose by covenant upon the amorphous aftermath of war. Thus, the statesman who builds postwar orders must try to be at once historian, political realist, and artist. The historian sees form as arising out of facts of history, even when history seems buried in the rubble. The realist sees it arising out of transient contemporary power realities. The artist finds form in new patterns which might be imposed by fiat upon a chaotic face of things. The statesman ideally unites in himself the past, present and future shapes of things.

The intellectual defect of Wilson in Paris lay not in his sudden utopianism but in his insufficient comprehension of the European past and in his failure to perceive in time the nature of European power across the conference table from him, which was arrayed against his simple blueprint of a "just settlement" and his institutional proposals for a durable postwar order. Clemenceau, Wilson's adversary, had the opposite defect: a canny opportunist, realist and historian, he held "justice" in contempt and disregarded the "future."

The distinctive mark of the statesmen of any age or time is this: the act of establishment and creation in which they engage elicits a special political quality from them. Each of these statesmen conceived his task to be the establishment of a new order of things holding promise of permanence. What distinguishes statesman from politician, then, is not necessarily higher intelligence or loftier motives but an awareness of a unique undertaking—that of building institutions according to political designs. This quality redeems even a Machiavellian.

II

In a certain sense today, the idea of the status quo and order among nations and other political communities hardly seems germane to the inchoate totality of the society of nations. Among the reasons is that the idea of order is most clearly visible within, not between, political communities. Another reason is that virtually no human beings alive today have known and experienced an era in which an international order existed and was taken for granted.

Since the time of the Greek philosophers, systems of political thought have usually conceived of man as a political animal within some finite state or community. Politics pertained to a set of triangular relations of power and ethics between man and state, society and state, man and society. A fourth relationship was that between man-society-state and the political environment

—composed of other such finite orders and of orders in the process of dissolution or of becoming. This relationship constituted a special realm of activity called "foreign affairs." Within preexisting order, conservatism and liberalism obtained their significance as ways of looking at politics. The chief concern within this fourth dimension of politics, however, was the survival of man-society-state within an often dangerous environment whose nature could not be subject to policy except in most limited fashion. War and diplomacy, imperialism and "peaceful coexistence"—in fact, all foreign strategies of states could be seen as measures by which the welfare of the state as a whole might be advanced or endangered. We quickly see that the merits of such policies were primarily to be judged by values arising within these special individual entities and not by transcendent considerations pertaining to the structure and ordering of the whole universe of politics or the so-called society of nations.

A tension thus arises between a theory of conservatism pertaining to the inner condition of a state or polity; and one claiming to transcend this special order, pertaining thus to the international system of states. Trying to maintain an existing status quo within an individual polity, statesmen might rationally embark upon foreign policies whose effects might disturb or destroy an existing equilibrium of things in the society of nations as a whole—or would even prevent such an equilibrium from being established. Conversely, liberal statesmen concerned with attaining certain improvements at home might embark upon foreign policies designed to attain a comprehensive static order *among* states—for instance, with the object that domestic improvements might more easily take place within such a relatively placid context of broader order. Even revolutionary leaders have done so: Stalin, for instance, between 1934 and 1939 not only pursued prudent foreign policies but even sought to strengthen the League of Nations and its principles of collective security, to shore up the European status quo against the flood tide of Nazi expansionism and Japanese imperialism. Thus arose the seeming incongruity of Soviet Russia's policies during this time: abroad, the genial Litvinov, a Wilson in wolf's clothing, speaking of the need for collective measures to preserve the peace and security of Europe; at home, Stalin, police terror, forced collectivization, and brutal extinction of countless peasants.

In rare instances, as with Metternich and Churchill, there appears the ideal fusion between the conservative wish to maintain a domestic status quo and the conservative wish to maintain or establish an international status quo. In his statecraft, Metternich never was so imprudent as to forget his concern for this overarching settlement of peace; his concern (that stable, antiliberal regimes in Central Europe flourish and survive) entailed his reciprocal acknowledgment of the larger context of order which contained within it these subsidiary orders. In a later time, Churchill also sought to fuse his domestic and foreign strategies, to attain a stable order both in Britain and Europe. Elements of this fusion can be found even in Wilson.

A further difficulty, however, in speaking of the idea of the status quo in world politics as opposed to that within a finite political community, is this: How could a theory of conservatism build an overarching order over such multifarious political systems? How could this order, in any event, be endowed with a philosophic sanction compatible with its own domestic principles? How could a conservative admit that a revolutionary polity might be necessary to international order, without abandoning his deepest instincts and convictions? Burke easily comes to mind in this instance. We regard him today as a singularly farsighted political prophet because of his Jeremiads against the French regicides and his predictions of the course which the Revolution would take in Europe as a whole. Yet we may also note that Burke could not possibly imagine a future condition of Europe in which a new Republican France, stained with royal blood, might some day occupy a normal role. This future actuality to him was an impossibility.

In practice, of course, conservative statesmen and revolutionaries made compromises with reality when faced with dilemmas in concrete circumstances. But such compromises, by political figures heavily weighted with ideological convictions, are at best provisional. Presumably, when Stalin betrayed revolution in Spain, in 1938, for fear of endangering his valuable relation with the liberal-conservative regimes of the West, he did so provisionally: revolution could wait; Soviet security came first.

III

Certain political theorists—including Locke and Hobbes—were led by this contrast between the civil society at home and the society of nations to conclude that, whereas a state of peace might exist within the bounds of an individual polity, in the international realm there lay a state of nature—in Hobbes' familiar words, a "war of all against all." Yet it has always been clear that this dramatic contrast between civil order and an international state of nature quite imperfectly described the condition before and since the nineteenth century. In our own era, the intensity of conflict between the Communist world and the West springs in large measure from everyone's refusal to accept such arbitrary distinctions between civil and international realms. The ideological features of this conflict reject such distinctions.

The Hobbesian state of nature, applied to the international realm, can also be deemed too doctrinaire and rigid to apply to circumstances in which the very state of the nation itself is provisional: when influential men are not sure which of the possible entities are to be deemed political communities. The communal affinities working to establish cohesion within Western Europe and the North Atlantic area, for instance, cannot be explained away as "merely" acts of separate national entities joining together in temporary connivances to protect themselves from a passing external danger. In our time, the significant affinities among Western nations find more expression in large groupings of states joined by common consent in enlarged common enterprises than they do in forced groupings of territorial entities organized by imperialist force. The Western democracies, since 1947, have built far more stable communal relationships among themselves, without *force majeure,* than the totalitarian states have been able to accomplish among themselves.

Nor was the idea of international politics as a war of all against all to be found reflected in normal relations among European powers in the age of their supremacy. Until 1914, in fact, it was possible to discern within the European heartland of world politics a public law grounded in international conventions, acts, understandings, and diplomatic forms. This law of nations served as chief referent-point for statesmen when they spoke of the idea of European peace; it fortified the European status quo. Europe's legitimacy, in the eyes of its member states, lay in mutual acceptance of the existing territorial distribution of power, of the legitimacy of existing states, regimes, and nations; and of the accepted condition of certain sensitive zones (such as Belgium) as neutralized from Great Power influence. This public law had grown out of the basic foundation stones of the Vienna treaties of 1815 and of subsidiary international acts which the European community of states diplomatically fashioned later. This covenant enabled Europe to live with itself, without major war, for a century. It was far more than merely a particular balance or distribution of power among states; it was a constitutional order. Even at the outset of World War I, we remember, it was not the aim of any Power to radically reconstitute or to destroy it, or to destroy any major nation within it.[1] Ironically, the war of 1914 was provoked, not by any Great Power's intention to "smash" other components of the European order, but rather by Austria's abrupt unilateral attempt to preserve her own part of it by ultimative force.[2]

---

[1] Except, possibly, in the case of Serbia and the Austro-Hungarian Empire; here, of course, we find the origins of the war, and something which strikes us as typically "modern."

[2] A special tragic aspect of that war, then, lay in this: that the belligerents employed "total war" for limited goals. At the war's outset all belligerents assumed it would be brief, and that limited political and territorial changes would ensue from it. None assumed—until much later in the war—that radical internal changes in the conditions of states should be included among war aims. By way of contrast, the belligerents of World War II fought to reconstitute the map and power structure of Europe radically, and to radically alter the internal regimes of states. The more cataclysmic military operations became, the easier it was for civil authorities to act without civil restraints.

IV

One symptom of our present international crisis is that today no such overriding constituent order of world politics exists, even as a standard of injustice for men to assail. The last consummated attempt to establish such comprehensive ordering of the society of nations was made in Paris in 1919—over forty years ago. Whatever its merits, the Versailles Treaty was the last act of the Great Powers to establish jointly a comprehensive juridical, political and territorial order in the society of nations, one which was ratified and accepted in the form of a covenant by smaller powers as well.

It is also symptomatic of our present crisis that no one today seriously believes that any future similar act of international reestablishment, of such scope, can possibly occur. Grandiose acts of summitry seem absurd as methods of ordering the new boundless complexities of world politics. We recall that such constituent acts took place after major war, when force had registered important political changes which diplomacy could not otherwise have effected. Such constituent acts took place in an atmosphere of exhaustion and relief. Such war and force now appear to be out of the question.

For these reasons, the idea of the status quo today is virtually meaningless, as a description of conditions in the totality of the society of nations. The Treaties of Vienna and Versailles designated and outlined the constitutional orders of Europe. In the interwar years, 1919–1939, the customary distinction between "status quo" and "revisionist" powers was between those which accepted the constitutional order of things and those which denied its legitimacy or sought to alter it.

Since 1945, however, there is no standard by which fundamental disagreement might be measured among the powers; the reordering of Central and Eastern Europe, of the Pacific and East Asia, became matters of conflict, not between status quo and revisionist states, but among revisionist states, each with widely differing conceptions about what future conditions should be. Order now depends upon power, force, and influence rather than upon consensus among major powers. After 1945, the chief impulses to political changes in the international community, primarily aimed at new structures and systems of things. Thus, international consensus today is missing. The understandings upon which the idea of a status quo must necessarily depend cannot be comprehended when they rest not upon authority, legitimacy, and consent, but upon constantly changing equations of power. Now, we speak of year-to-year "order" between East and West as arising exclusively from "balance," "nuclear stalemate," and equations of influence. "Order" arises from power relationships; hence, its content is provisional and dependent upon power. But power does not legitimize conditions.

V

Certain disconcerting aspects of Marxist-Leninist doctrine may be juxtaposed to traditional Western attitudes toward the status quo. They have not discernibly changed since the coming of the Bolshevik Revolution—regardless of the ways in which, from time to time, Soviet behavior might seem to contradict them. Yet they are so fundamental to Marxist-Leninist thought that it is difficult to imagine how the edifices of Communist states could stand, today, without their support. These ideas, seem so profoundly disruptive—as postulates of political and social reality and history—that their articulation by Soviet and Communist authorities constitutes an incitement to all of the noncommunist world. What makes it especially difficult to imagine a future stable relationship between the West and the Communist world is that, even if Soviet leadership were cynically to disavow these disruptive views in private, it could not publicly do so without seriously endangering its authority. Without them, the Communist leadership would have no grounds upon which to justify its monopoly of government over the Russian people or over peoples in other Communist states.

If the stability of power relationships in the Communist world depends not merely upon force and its satisfaction of popular material wants, but also upon authority, we should realize that this authority, paradoxically, is grounded upon a conception of politics-as-movement which rules out any fixed and enduring constitutional relations among men and nations; this in turn means that the necessary contractual basis of a new order or status quo among states—namely, legitimacy and legality, makes no sense in a Marxist scheme of things. Only transient commitments and promises can have meaning for Soviet Marxists in the international community. Accordingly, international stability is not merely imperiled, but becomes impossible unless grounded in force; yet order so grounded, to come full circle, can have no legitimacy and is only provisional.

Stripped of Marxist vocabulary, the basic point is this: Political order and human solidarity exist in history only within forces, movements, and processes. The idea of order as a permanent system within which such actions are contained, limited, and regulated is therefore meaningless. Order, in this view, does not arise out of constituent acts which establish constitutional orders and the institutions embodied in them. All such arrangements are provisional and contingent. Temporal artifacts of men and movements (their existence) depend upon the command of forces which transcend and give life to them.

To speak, then, as Marxist-Leninist, of an "existing order of things", a status quo, is either to speak of something absurdly incongruous with belief and doctrine; or else to speak of the kaleidoscopic relationship among dynamic movements and forces, varying greatly in vigor and pace, through space and time. Men's political thoughts and actions, hence, have meaning only in reference to these; not to persistent, possibly durable, historical communities; nor, for that matter, to any locus of loyalty which may lie outside the "factualness" of immediate politics and the processes of historical change (or which, like Christianity, may claim to transcend them).

By ironic twist, then, order, solidarity, and cohesion among men is to be seen and discovered only within force, counterforce, and revolutionary processes.

If movement alone incorporates order, then the Communist world must see the status quo as a description of processes of change. Walter Lippmann, interviewing Khrushchev in 1959, was startled afresh by this attitude. As he later described it:

In his (Khrushchev's) mind, the social and economic revolution now in progress in Russia, China and elsewhere in Africa and Asia *is* the status quo, and he wants us to recognize it as such. . . .

Whereas we think of the *status quo* as the situation as it exists at the moment, he thinks of it as the process of revolutionary change which is in progress.[3]

VI

Thus it is that the drift and pressure of events, the speed of change, constitute in themselves the indices of Marxist "order." And here we see what appears to be the heart of the intellectual difficulty which divides the Western, and notably, the American world from the Communist: the temperamental distinction which separates the styles as well as the purposes of traditional Western diplomacy from those of the Communist world. A characteristic of Western diplomacy has been that although many of its practitioners regarded both diplomacy and statesmanship skeptically as the difficult arts of coping with kaleidoscopic reality, still they saw in diplomacy a supreme contractual purpose: establishing and negotiating order through commitments, agreements and promises. The task, which gave diplomacy its highest reputation, was not service to the nation or the state but the search for agreement, the attempt to pull order out of conflict —an effort which incidentally could best be made within contexts of established procedures and institutions. To impose order upon recalcitrant facts and seemingly anarchic processes required in the realm of international relations the making of covenants; covenants, in turn, made it possible for future action and change to be guided and made predictable. A nation's style and reputation could in part be measured by its attitude, through time, toward covenants with others. The nation's willingness and the ability to make promises could be seen as a signal index of its "civilized" behavior.

Nietzsche pointed out that the distinguishing feature of human life, setting man apart from animals, was the ability to make promises; so also we might say that the distinguishing feature of a civilized state was its capacity to make and fullfill covenants. Only then could humane life, with its requirements of reasonable predictibility, be fulfilled in the international arena.

---

[3] Walter Lippmann, *The Communist World and Ours,* p. 13. Boston: Little, Brown and Company, 1959.

The Nazis, too, flouted contractual obligations, despising them as scraps of paper. But this special disregard for international obligations arose from a nihilistic contempt for law itself, a criminal lack of concern for any obligation which blocked their will to power. With Marxist-Leninists, the matter was quite different: an overriding philosophical doctrine simply transcended covenants. The highest purpose to which the contracting power of traditional Western states has been put was to establish frameworks of order within which action might henceforward regularly occur and have reasonably clear meaning. The otherwise random and often conflicting activities of states thus could acquire regularity and reasonable predictability. But what meaning could any basic international contract have, for Marxist-Leninists, with respect to the broader order of things among nations, since they necessarily undertook such a contract in foreknowledge and conviction that "processes" in any event must sweep away all provisional forms and institutions? If "justice" lay only within processes, then the "justice" intrinsic to any specific covenant was provisional.[4]

VII

Our Cold War frustrations arise not just because of fearsome dangers of thermonuclear war but more because there is so much talk (often seemingly absurd and beside the point) about reaching some new international status quo, which men might take for granted as normal and tolerable, if not just. Western diplomacy and statesmanship, unable to plan and act in anticipation of some "victory" which "war" might bring, thus must seek either to maintain or fashion political orders within the noncommunist world or else to devise patchwork, provisional, *ad hoc* arrangements with the Communist states as a means of diminishing

---

[4] In Western international law, a tension has always existed between two principles governing the obligations of states in contractual agreements: the doctrine of *pacta sunt servanda*—treaties are to be observed; and the doctrine of *rebus sic stantibus*—treaties are to be observed only so long as the original circumstances attending their birth remained substantially unchanged. Yet the making of promises becomes impossible if one or all contracting powers believe in advance that the fundamental conditions are bound to change.

dangers of upward-spiralling conflicts which no one really wants. This form and style of diplomacy was bound to be frustrating: If what one could at most hope for from it was provisional agreement, what most frequently was obtained was nothing at all. The bargaining process could be corrupted into a device for creating suspicion or conflict among one's adversaries; or as means of propagandizing the other's publics with proposals which one did not take seriously oneself but which one's opponent was sure to reject.

Underneath rhetoric and polemic, the signs of genuine desire for temporary agreement and *détente* might sometimes be found. Yet an equilibrium expressed in agreement arising only from the momentary distribution of power and influence, not from the intrinsic merits of particular solutions or from a wish to see them as permanent, could hardly be regarded as the stuff out of which new systems of order could be composed. Of all the specific *modi vivendi* achieved by diplomacy between the two blocs since the beginning of the Cold War, only one may stand as exception to this general rule: the Austrian State Treaty of 1955, which established Austria's position within the postwar European state system and set limits upon its foreign policy. This alone was regarded as legitimate and possibly durable, both by Austrians and by most of Austria's neighbors.

Elsewhere, in Germany, Korea, the Formosa Straits, Indo-China, no one could be really satisfied with the provisional character of understandings brought about between hostile antagonists, often because of their mutual fear of major war. In such locales, whole nations could be divided; frontiers wrenched along arbitrary parallels; populations arbitrarily transferred; irredentism shared by the severed parts of a once-united political community, each of which, like the halves of a severed earthworm, sought to recover the identity it had been once a part of. So at any given moment in time there was no sense pretending that the substance of armistices constituted "justice"—only that force and fear argued in favor of drawing a line here, not there; establishing this kind of regime, not that.

Mutual fear of war might breed provisional settlements; but these could pile on top of each other like compost heaps and

breed their own conflagrations. One might sometimes hope that
out of such provisional understandings and agreements "time"
might create "normalcy" and men take them for granted. But
this was to assume that the power relationships between blocs
would remain roughly as they had been, and thus permit the
provisional, even the intolerable provisional, to become acceptable some day.

VIII

If deadlock, equally unpleasant to all, becomes surrogate for a
status quo as basis for peace, then interbloc statesmanship becomes primarily the art of preventing things from getting out of
hand. It becomes the art also of building strength and order and
community *within,* but not between, the opposing camps. Understandings and regularities of behavior *between* camps are provisional, contingent upon degrees of strength and order *within*
camps. If the existing state of affairs includes elements which
are intolerable or unjust, men must endure it when they see the
impossible price to be paid for rectifying it by force. As most
Central Europeans today know, it could be suicidal to place
justice on a higher plane than the survival of societies, as
inspiration to political action. In the twentieth century, a Byron
may end up as a war criminal, not for his motives but for the
likely consequences of his actions.

Thus, an ethic of responsibility subtly replaces an ethic of
ultimate ends; prudent men recoil from the "pure in heart" even
as they may be embarrassed by the presence of purity. Justice
must work often at great disadvantages, with and within injustice,
rather than conspire to destroy it as an enemy. In the interest
of survival, freedom acquires a vested interest in the order which
tyranny maintains if only because the political events within the
totalitarian world could easily lead to extremely dangerous consequences. There is danger in the belief that whole social
systems, or their governments, cannot live together. Westerners,
as Cordell Hull said in 1944, had in the 1930's a "careless toler-
ance of evil institutions." So may we. But a thermonuclear ethic
would seem to require the opposite: a careful intolerance of
evil institutions, which does not lead men to deceive themselves